This book belongs to

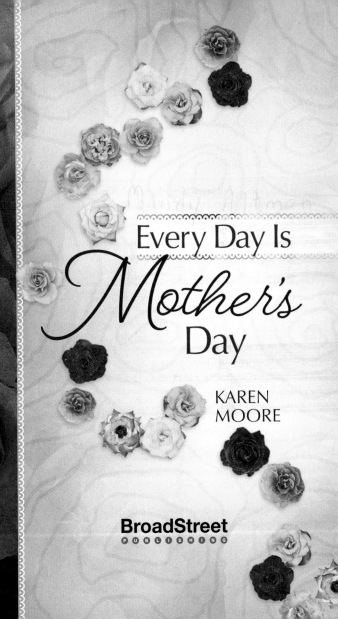

Every Day Is
Mother's
Day

KAREN
MOORE

BroadStreet
PUBLISHING

BroadStreet Publishing Group, LLC
Savage, Minnesota, USA
Broadstreetpublishing.com

Every Day Is Mother's Day

978-1-4245-5831-5 (faux)
978-1-4245-5110-1 (e-book)

Cover and interior design by Chris Garborg at garborgdesign.com
Typesetting by Kjell Garborg at garborgdesign.com

Printed in China
19 20 21 22 23   5 4 3 2 1

Being a mother means that your heart is no longer yours; it wanders wherever your children go.

AUTHOR UNKNOWN

Dedication

For every mom and every woman who has been like a mom to others, this book celebrates you. It recognizes your strength, your influence, and the beauty you alone bring to the lives of children. It honors the commitment you've made to God and to your family to always do your best. Officially, Mother's Day comes but once a year, but for you, the gratitude, love, and praise never end. For you, *Every Day Is Mother's Day!* May God bless you abundantly for the generous love you always share with your friends and family.

Karen Moore

The Gift of Motherhood

Motherhood: All love begins and ends there.

ROBERT BROWNING

For some of us, motherhood just seemed to happen; for others, it was hoped for and prayed for. For all of us, it is a role to be cherished. In fact, it's the role of a lifetime where we learn many things about ourselves. We begin to understand the difference between what's important and what's necessary, and when to talk and when to listen. We learn to trust our instincts and to love in ways we never thought imaginable. Motherhood gives us a life purpose like nothing else can, and love makes everything possible.

As the New Year begins, may love carry you through each day, may faith sustain your heart and soul, and may hope stay ever before you.

This is how we know that we love the children of God:
by loving God and carrying out his commands.

1 JOHN 5:2

Mom's Prayer

Dear Lord, thank you for the gift of motherhood. Thank you for all you do to help me be a strong and loving mother. Thank you for watching over my children. I pray for your continued guidance each day. Amen.

Finding the Possible

Some days you're a champion of possibility. You're a shining example for your family, and everything runs smoothly. You feel protected and blessed. You embrace the hope that God has placed in your heart for everything you need to do.

On other days, though, hope flies out the window. Nothing seems to go right. Your work is too demanding, the kids can't get along to save their lives, and God seems to have moved far from your neighborhood.

When that happens, seek God's face and start again. Let this be the day that you see the amazing things God planned for you and those you love. May hope prevail, and may love surround you. Trust with all your heart that everything is possible.

But Jesus looked at them and said to them, "With men this is impossible, but with God all things are possible."

MATTHEW 19:26 NKJV

Mom's Prayer

Dear Lord, sometimes I lose sight of what is possible. I'm uncertain of my decisions and wonder about the things I do as a mom. Help me to always see your grace in the faces of my children. Let me always be a possibility thinker. Amen.

Mothers Are Mothers Forever

You may be brand new at this parenting thing. Perhaps you have tiny tots or freckle-faced children who need your patient guidance all through the day. Maybe your kids are teenagers who don't seem to invite your direction much, but you love them and they love you. Or perhaps your children are fully grown adults and your parenting duties are not as obvious.

Though the job may change through the years, one thing never changes: once a mom, always a mom. You're a mother forever, and your heart will always be connected to the ones you raised with such love and joy.

The same thing is true for God. Once your Father, He's always your Father. You never outgrow His love. May you feel His presence today, ready to guide your heart and mind in all you do. You're His child forever too!

And I heard a loud voice from the throne, saying, "Now God's presence is with people, and he will live with them, and they will be his people. God himself will be with them and will be their God."

REVELATION 21:3 NCV

Mom's Prayer

Lord, thank you for being my Father forever. Help my children know how important they are to me and to you. They will always be part of my life. I thank you for the gifts they bring to my days. Amen.

Can't Fool Mom!

You can fool all of the people some of the time, and some of the people all of the time, but you can't fool Mom!

AUTHOR UNKNOWN

Do you remember when you were a kid and you thought to yourself, *Oh boy, I can't tell this to Mom*? You did your best to cover your tracks and probably never knew whether Mom had figured out your secret or not. Well, the "eyes in the back of her head" thing…it was true! Mom knew most everything you did, and now that you're a mom, you understand how that happens.

You're not easily fooled, and your Father in heaven isn't either. He knows you so well that there's nothing you have to avoid telling Him. After all, He already knows! He's just waiting for you to come and talk with Him about it. If anything today takes away from your work or your ability to move forward, have a chat with the One who sees you and loves you always. After all, He can't be fooled!

You have searched me, LORD, and you know me.

PSALM 139:1

Mom's Prayer

Lord, I may be a mom, but I still have to confess the things that are going on in my life because I know I can't fool you. I ask that you would be near me today and forgive the little things I do that are causing my spirit to drag and my heart to suffer. Help me to be the woman and the mom you want me to be. Amen.

The Fix-It Mom

When children are little, they go to Mom with every problem, fully trusting and believing she can fix it. As a mom, you can fix the wheel that fell off the red wagon or a doll's messy hair, and you can fix dinner or a torn sleeve. But sometimes you need help. Sometimes you need to take the things that are broken and give them to someone else to fix.

That's where your heavenly Father comes in. He is always ready to help you when you lay your burdens at the foot of the cross. He is ready to help no matter what kind of fix is needed.

Give God thanks today for walking beside you in all that you do. Trust Him to help you anytime you simply can't fix it yourself.

She must be known for her good works—works such as raising her children, welcoming strangers, washing the feet of God's people, helping those in trouble, and giving her life to do all kinds of good deeds.

1 TIMOTHY 5:10 NCV

Mom's Prayer

Lord, I try to help my children in any way I can and to fix the things that bring stress into other people's lives. Thank you that I can always come to you, knowing that you will help me and others, and thank you for working to make things right again. Amen.

Super Mom

Moms really are the heroes of the family. They somehow manage to get everyone out the door on time in the morning. They make sure lunches are packed, homework is done, after-school plans are set, and dinner is figured out for each evening. They do all that, and then many moms get themselves out the door to go to a job of their own or to volunteer. Some moms walk into their home offices as well. How do they do it? What amazing time managers they are. Somehow they can be in six places at once…or so it seems.

When you aren't feeling quite up to superhero status as a mom, check in with your true hero, the One who sustains your life, your energy, and all that you do each day. He'll quicken your spirit and give you a place to rest. You can relax and put everything on your to-do list in His capable hands.

You're a super mom every day of the week!

She sets about her work vigorously;
her arms are strong for her tasks.

PROVERBS 31:17

Mom's Prayer

Lord, there are days when I can scarcely remember where the hours went. I know I was busy and that things I accomplished were good, but somehow they all become a blur. Help me to set my sights on you to keep things clear. Help me to know when to do one more thing and when to simply rest. Amen.

Ask Mom

There's something uncanny about Mom. When you lose something, she almost always knows where to find it. When you start to tell her something, she already has a good idea what you're going to say. When you need help, she's ready to lend a hand. It seems that anytime things are a bit confusing, the best course of action is to simply ask Mom.

It's amazing how often you get it right as a mom. You know when to offer good advice and when to listen quietly. However, you don't always have the answers or know the best course of action. That's when you can heave a sigh of relief that you have an awesome Father who waits for you to ask for His help.

Whatever you want to ask Him, He's there 24/7. You'll never get a busy signal or be out of cell phone range. You can even call Him just to say thank you.

And whatever you ask in My name, that I will do, that the Father may be glorified in the Son.

JOHN 14:13 NKJV

Mom's Prayer

Lord, I sometimes forget that I can come to you in the same way my children come to me, knowing you'll do your best to answer me just as I do my best to answer them. I'm grateful for the wisdom and insight you share with me. Thank you for trusting me to guide my family. Amen.

What's Cooking?

Mom cooks up everything with love.

ANONYMOUS

Whether you're one of the world's best cooks or simply the woman who helps put food on the table, everyone is nourished best by Mom's love. Perhaps your chocolate chip cookies keep everyone running to the kitchen no matter how old the "kids" might be. When you're a mom, you're always cooking up something special, and no matter how it turns out, it can still win a blue ribbon if you do it with love.

The good news is that no matter what you're cooking—whether it's charred on the bottom or crispy on the top—you can ask God to bless it. He'll do His part to make sure your family has everything they need. Ask God to help you cook up the best love recipes that were ever created.

So whether you eat or drink, or whatever you do, do it all for the glory of God.

1 CORINTHIANS 10:31 NLT

Mom's Prayer

Lord, I like to cook and it's great when my family appreciates my efforts. I'm so thankful for all the ways you provide for our well-being. Even so, remind me to cook up a little more time with you, so that I can be well fed by your presence and your Word. Amen.

Mom's Heart

All that I am or ever hope to be, I owe to my angel Mother.

ABRAHAM LINCOLN

Before you become a mother, it's easy to think of all the idyllic ways you might behave. When the first tiny infant is placed in your arms, though, all that idealism goes right out the window. Now there's a tiny human being who looks to you for everything and trusts you to take care of every need. It's a big job—an important job—and it takes a lot of heart.

A mom's heart grows bigger over time. Learning to care for and love a child is an awesome experience. Could that love be the same kind of tenderness God feels toward His children? Could that love be why God keeps on forgiving, trying to communicate, and loving us no matter what we do?

Thank God for giving you a heart like His when it comes to your children. May your heart keep getting bigger so it can take in His love as well.

And may the Lord make your love for one another and for all people grow and overflow, just as our love for you overflows.

1 THESSALONIANS 3:12 NLT

Mom's Prayer

Lord, I pray that my heart will always expand and grow so that I can be filled with your love and share that love with my children. I ask that you would teach me in every possible way how to love them and you with all my heart. Amen.

Mom on a Mission

Today's the day! You're ready. You've made up your mind that you're going to accomplish every task on your list and nothing will stop you. You take a deep breath, look at item number one, and you're off. Yes, the cupboards have needed cleaning for some time. Whew! You've done it, and now for the next item, cleaning the oven. Ugh. Why does it have to get all grimy like that? No matter. You're on a mission.

As you go through the day, cleaning, creating dinner plans, picking up the kids from various activities, and working on the agenda for the meeting at work, you can get exhausted. Your mission mind-set is great and really works to keep you moving toward your goals, but here's a suggestion. What if you started your mission with prayer? What if before you even spent a moment taking cans out of a cupboard, you simply prayed and gave the day, the mission, and your life to God?

God wants to be part of your mission. You just have to ask Him to be there.

Devote yourselves to prayer, being watchful and thankful.

COLOSSIANS 4:2

Mom's Prayer

Lord, I dive into my list of activities without giving much thought to you. Forgive me when I don't stop to pray, and remind me that you are part of everything I do and that you can bless my missions only when I ask you to be with me. Amen.

Mom Is Cool!

You may not think of yourself as a cool mom. After all, you're the organizer of family activities, the cook and bottle washer, the mender of torn papers, and the one who takes the dog to the vet. What about that is cool? The answer is…everything!

Everything about your life is cool because God put you right where you are for such a time as this. He knew you were good at organizing a calendar, a house, and the shoes in your closet, and so the things you do please Him. That's cool. You get the kids where they need to go, make dinner, and smile through it all, so your kids think you're cool too.

As you go about doing all the little things for the hundredth time, remind yourself that there are many people in your life who think you're cool. Let that idea bless you and make you smile.

There, in the presence of the LORD your God, you and your families shall eat and shall rejoice in everything you have put your hand to, because the LORD your God has blessed you.

DEUTERONOMY 12:7

Mom's Prayer

Lord, it's a little hard to imagine anyone thinking I'm cool, but I like the idea. Help me to rest in your hands today and trust that you have blessed my life according to your will and purpose. Amen.

Momisms

Moms say the most amazing things! You probably remember a few things your mom said. She may have told you that "burnt toast is good for your digestion" or that "there are lots of poor children who would love to eat your peas." At the time, you thought all those things were true, and so you ate the burnt toast and the peas without a word.

Many of the adages attributed to moms came out of the wisdom of others like Benjamin Franklin or even from misquoted Bible texts. The wonder of those bits of wisdom is that they stuck with you and you've shared them with your kids.

Today, think about your favorite phrases from God's Word. See if you can impact the ones you love with a few of those. You never know, they might just carry those words around for the rest of their lives. After all, you're the "apple" of God's eye.

Keep me as the apple of Your eye;
Hide me under the shadow of Your wings.

PSALM 17:8 NKJV

Mom's Prayer

Lord, I often repeat the little phrases my mother said to me. I guess they really do stick in my mind. Today, let me help your Word stick in the minds of people I love. Amen.

Blessings for Mom

You're pretty good at counting your blessings. After all, you often say how blessed you are to have kids, a home, and a family. You have a grateful heart, and you're a warm and loving example to others.

But there are times when it's a little harder to get that sense of feeling blessed. Maybe all the kids are home from school with the flu, or your teenagers aren't getting along and there's a lot of door slamming. Perhaps your dog got out of the yard and you had to drop everything to get him back home. Maybe it was a "throw up your hands" kind of day. You start wondering what you did to deserve all this.

Ah, there it is, the blessing! You've done so many things right that God gave you the gift of a real family. You may have wanted a TV family where all the problems get worked out by the end of the episode, but the fact is you and your family have to work things out together, one crisis at a time, one blessing after another.

Thank God for your many blessings today, and while you're busy tossing up your hands in frustration, grab on to His hand until you find your peace again.

"May the LORD bless you and keep you.
May the LORD show you his kindness and have mercy on you.
May the LORD watch over you and give you peace."

NUMBERS 6:24–26 NCV

Mom's Prayer

Lord, some days I feel like I endure my blessings rather than rejoice in them. Help me to trust you for the peace I need and to be grateful for the too-numerous-to-count blessings in my life. Amen.

Mom, CEO

Moms have a lot of titles because they provide the family with an array of services. One minute they act as gourmet chef, another minute they're chief chauffeur, and another minute they're Little League coach. In fact, it seems there are few things that moms can't do. No wonder they are the CEO of the family—the Chief Everything Officer.

It's certain that you have a fair amount of say about what goes on under your roof. That kind of power is both gratifying and humbling. It's gratifying because God has entrusted you with the most precious people He knows, His children. It's humbling because He believes in you and knows you can do it well.

Go ahead, hang up a shingle in your home office, because you've taken on a big job and you do it so well. *Mom, CEO* indeed!

"His master replied, 'Well done, good and faithful servant! You have been faithful with a few things; I will put you in charge of many things. Come and share your master's happiness!"

MATTHEW 25:21

Mom's Prayer

Lord, you've put a lot of responsibility in my hands and I thank you for trusting me so much. I ask that you would walk beside me and give me wisdom in the things I do so that I please you and bring joy and peace to my family. Amen.

Mom 101

When you got into your mom role, you probably didn't get a lot of training. There are few Mom 101 classes going on in the world. Depending on when and where you grew up, you may have taken a home economics class in eighth grade. Or maybe you babysat as a teenager. Even so, the knowledge you gained hardly prepared you for the many faces of being a mom.

Fortunately, God provides you with a pretty clear road map. He invites you to read up on how to live in the world and then pass that on to your children. He offers you a shoulder to cry on and a place to go when you've simply run out of fuel or ideas.

When you need help, don't try to find a mom book in the bookstore. Instead, go back to the Book you probably already have on your shelf, the one with great wisdom and good advice. Start there and you'll always be ahead of the class.

All Scripture is inspired by God and is useful for teaching, for showing people what is wrong in their lives, for correcting faults, and for teaching how to live right.

2 TIMOTHY 3:16 NCV

Mom's Prayer

Father, you know how often I need another lesson from your Book. Help me to stay strong in you and to trust that you will guide me in all grace and truth so that I can be a good mom. Amen.

Mom's Love Notes

Moms are good at love notes. Sometimes their love notes show up in a lunch box or in a shirt pocket. Sometimes they leave a gentle thought on a pillow, offering encouragement and support. Other times, their love notes come in the form of freshly baked cookies or a favorite meal. Moms know that the little things make a difference.

The good news is that God knows how to send love notes too. His love notes come in the form of a friend who calls just when you need to hear her voice, or a perfect Scripture that floats through your mind and reminds you of the best way to look at a situation.

Today, see if there's a love note you could share with your children, no matter how old they might be. After all, you never outgrow your need for a little extra love.

But God's strong foundation continues to stand. These words are written on the seal: "The Lord knows those who belong to him."

2 TIMOTHY 2:19 NCV

Mom's Prayer

Lord, I know you do endless things to help support and encourage me as a mom. Sometimes I'm simply moving too fast to pay attention. Help me to slow down enough to appreciate your little notes of love. Amen.

Mama Love

Moms are called by many sweet names, from Mother and Mama, to Noni and Mommy. You may identify with these names in different ways, feeling connected to being Mommy when you have little children and being Mom as your kids grow up. One thing is for sure, there's nothing quite like the love of a mama for her family. It's a love that can be seen in nature and in the ways God loves each of us.

Many names exist for God as well, and sometimes we use one over the other because of what we're feeling in our relationship with Him. He can be Father, Abba, Daddy, or Creator and Redeemer. His list goes on and on.

No matter how you choose to address moms—or to address God—every way you choose is a name that stands for love.

And God said to Moses, "I AM WHO I AM." And He said, "Thus you shall say to the children of Israel, 'I AM has sent me to you.'"

EXODUS 3:14 NKJV

Mom's Prayer

Lord, when I feel close to you, I often address you as Father. When I step back, I tend to see you as my Father up in heaven. Help me to remember that no matter what name I use, you always think of me with love. Amen.

Aw, Mom!

At times, moms can seem perfectly unreasonable, at least to a kid. After all, moms have the authority to put the kibosh on the best-made plans. They can practically ruin a kid's life with one little word: "No!" At that point, the sagging-shouldered, gloomy-faced kid is sure to say something like, "Aw, Mom!" Of course, as a kid, you aren't allowed to say much else without being considered rude.

So what about you? What happens when you've made great plans and are excited about something that would simply mean the world to you? Maybe you want a job promotion, or a house by the river, or any number of things, and God says, "No." What do you do? Sag your shoulders perhaps? Or put on a gloomy face? Maybe you even say, "Aw, God!"

Today, as you guide the people around you, be sure to look at all sides of any request put before you and imagine how your Father in heaven might answer. No matter what else, answer with love.

"I thought, 'Those who are older should speak,
for wisdom comes with age.'"

JOB 32:7 NLT

Mom's Prayer

Lord, help me to remember to listen with my heart anytime I'm
in a position of authority as the one who can say yes or no.
Help me to make decisions that are fair and prompted by
good reason and wisdom. Amen.

Monday Mom

Where does the time go? Every Friday you heave a sigh of relief and think that maybe this weekend you'll get far enough past the cooking, cleaning, and extracurricular activities that you'll have a little time for yourself—to read a good book, soak in the tub, or get your nails done. Yes, those Friday thoughts always feel a bit like a dream, because somehow Monday comes swiftly and you start all over again.

Perhaps it will make being a Monday mom a bit easier if you give yourself a break right now. In fact, plan a few-minutes break each day of the week. Close your eyes for five minutes and say a little gratitude prayer for everything you've already done and all the things you're just starting. Ask God to give you a sense of peace and to refresh your heart and mind. No matter what day of the week it is, you'll feel better.

No, your beauty should come from within you—the beauty of a gentle and quiet spirit that will never be destroyed and is very precious to God.

1 PETER 3:4 NCV

Mom's Prayer

Father, I thank you for Mondays and all the days you give me to learn more about being a good mom. Bless the people I love, and help me through my quiet times to feel blessed by Mondays and all days! Amen.

Mom's Workout

Many moms don't have time to join a health club or go to a gym. They have to exercise as they can, taking walks with a baby stroller in front of them, jogging with a six-year-old riding a bike close behind, or getting up earlier than anyone else simply to have time to take a few deep breaths. Moms continually stretch and bend to make everything come together.

God works with us that way too. He reaches down and hopes we'll grab on to His hand so He can lift us up and energize our spirits. He bends over backward to try to understand the foolish choices we make and then washes away our bruises and bumps every time we come running back to Him. Yes, He is always helping us work out just what it means to live in His love.

Today, whether you're pumping some iron or doing the ironing, remember that your Father in heaven is there to keep you steady and strong.

Therefore, my dear friends, as you have always obeyed—not only in my presence, but now much more in my absence—continue to work out your salvation with fear and trembling.

PHILIPPIANS 2:12

Mom's Prayer

Lord, I need to exercise more, but somehow I don't seem to accomplish that. I pray that you will help me to stay healthy and strong. Guide me to work out my body, my soul, and my mind according to your will and purpose. Amen.

Mom's Voice

There's something special about Mom's voice. It's the voice that soothes you when you don't feel well. It's the one that assures you when your confidence is at an all-time low. It's the voice that always reminds you how much you're loved and how special and unique you are.

Sometimes you can hear God's voice too. It's the one that beckons you to pray when your heart is downcast and you're no longer sure of your direction. It's the voice that offers assurance that you're loved wherever you are. And it's the one that bids you to come and reason things out together.

Today, as you reflect on the voice you share with your family—or on your own mom's voice—take a few moments to stop everything and see if you can hear the loving voice of your heavenly Father. His voice can make all the difference in your day.

He says, "Be still, and know that I am God;
I will be exalted among the nations,
I will be exalted in the earth."

PSALM 46:10

Mom's Prayer

Lord, help me to let go of the noises that surround me. Quiet my heart to seek your voice. Today I will wait with eagerness to hear your loving voice. Amen.

Mom Is So Funny!

Do you ever stop to think about your own mom's sense of humor, or perhaps wonder if your kids can recognize your sense of humor? Laughter is good medicine and can play a great part in making a home feel warm and happy. You contribute to family fun anytime you allow the things that are truly funny to bring out the girl in you.

Do you think God laughs? Surely He has a good sense of humor. Look at all the amazing combinations He put together to design the creatures in the ocean and on land—even you and me. Look for ways that might make you sense God's laughter today. It will do your heart good.

Then our mouth was filled with laughter,
and our tongue with shouts of joy;
then they said among the nations,
"The LORD has done great things for them."

PSALM 126:2 ESV

Mom's Prayer

Lord, I do need to laugh more. Help me to step outside myself, my worries, and the other things that weigh me down so I can simply laugh a little. I pray you'll be laughing with me today. Amen.

Mom Is so Smart!

Moms are smart. They have to be because they have an incredible load on their shoulders and only twenty-four hours in a day. They need to keep a lot of plates spinning in the air—and then set the table with them, wash them, and start all over again. It's simply the gift, the blessing, and, yes, the job of being a mom.

Still, keep in mind that as a mom, you don't have to totally depend on your own brilliance. You aren't alone in keeping all those plates in the air. Your Creator, whose brilliance is beyond measure, is always willing to guide you, give practical assistance, and teach you a little more of what you need to know to do your work well. He wants you to succeed and so He's with you in all the details. Check in with Him anytime you're not so sure you can figure everything out yourself.

The mind of a person with understanding gets knowledge;
the wise person listens to learn more.

PROVERBS 18:15 NCV

Mom's Prayer

Father, I do believe you've provided me with adequate abilities
to think things through and do things well. I don't have all the
answers, and I often need your help. Grant me wisdom for all
I do today. Amen.

Mom's Beautiful Hands

Have you ever thought about all the things you do with your hands each day? You create, you cook, you clean, and you give amazing hugs and a few high fives. You work at a computer keyboard, you make lists, and you help others. Your hands are beautiful! God has put a lot of responsibility in your hands, and He knows you do an awesome job with all He has given you.

The blessing of it all is that you too are in good hands. You're in God's beautiful hands all the time. He holds you close when you need comfort and assurance. He opens doors when you need to move forward. He hugs you to His heart to remind you how precious you are, and He gives you an extra hand when you have too many burdens to bear. You're in the best hands possible.

Today, every time you do something with your hands, think of the One who holds you forever in His tender grasp.

So I reflected on all this and concluded that the righteous and the wise and what they do are in God's hands.

ECCLESIASTES 9:1

Mom's Prayer

Lord, I am so busy that sometimes I forget to ask if you can lend me a hand. I pray now that you will tug on my sleeve or nudge me a little more often when I need to seek more of you. Amen.

What's Up with Mom?

Even moms have off days. They get discouraged, find no reason to smile, or can't figure out which way is up. They feel like the clouds are hanging over their heads and the storms of life have pushed them a little too far. When this happens, family members are often unsure how they should respond.

Some moms feel guilty when they allow life to get to them. They think they should be above all that, able to keep coping and keep hoping and keep everyone else feeling good. Those are good thoughts, but they aren't practical. Moms are people too.

So when your family is wondering, *What's up with Mom?* suggest that they say a prayer for you and give you some time to spend in prayer by yourself. Your heavenly Father will bring you comfort, peace, and a sense of calm that will override the chaos. After all, when they ask, *What's up with Mom?* you want them to add something like, *She's always so happy.*

Peace I leave with you, My peace I give to you; not as the world gives do I give to you. Let not your heart be troubled, neither let it be afraid.

JOHN 14:27 NKJV

Mom's Prayer

Father, I do have down days, just like everybody else. The problem is I try to put on a happy face and keep going, but sometimes I just can't do it. I thank you for being there to lift my spirits and help me smile again. Amen.

When Mom Prays

Moms who pray have a bit of an edge over moms who don't. The reason is not simply that they have a source of hope and comfort, though that's certainly part of it; the real reason is that prayer time allows them to stop, take a breath, read the Word, and rest in God's grace and peace. There's no other comfort quite like that.

Today, as you work through all the things on your generous list of chores, make sure you've given yourself a time or two for some prayer. You don't have to stop and say a long, drawn-out prayer. You can do shower prayers, car-driving prayers, cleaning-the-house prayers, or making-dinner prayers. You can also do nothing prayers—that is, when you do nothing but sit quietly and wait on the Lord. Those prayers are the best of all.

Listen for God's voice, and feel His comfort and His blessing on your life today.

Rejoice always, pray without ceasing, in everything give thanks; for this is the will of God in Christ Jesus for you.

1 THESSALONIANS 5:16–18 NKJV

Mom's Prayer

Lord, I am so grateful that I can come to you early in the morning or late at night. I'm grateful that I know whenever I take the time to talk with you, you're always ready and willing to listen. Amen.

Mom Hears and Mom Listens

Moms are queens of multitasking. They do the laundry while cleaning the house and putting another tray of cookies in the oven. They work in home offices, fill out school forms, and make a grocery menu. They've even perfected the ability to respond to questions without breaking their pace or changing direction. Ultimately, they do a lot in a short amount of time.

Moms can also stop any task, no matter how pressing it may be, and listen when something important comes up. How do they listen? They listen heart first, considering all sides of a question and all the logical pieces and then giving an answer straight from the heart.

When, as a mom, you need someone to listen, you can go to God. God always hears and always knows everything that's going on. He listens whenever you seek Him. He draws you near and helps you find a solution. He listens to your heart.

Hear what's going on in your household, but be willing to listen when someone calls your name. After all, that's God's example. He always listens when you call His name.

"They will call on my name and I will answer them;
I will say, 'They are my people,'
and they will say, 'The Lord is our God.'"

ZECHARIAH 13:9

Mom's Prayer

Lord, I can nod in agreement to a conversation that doesn't really include me, but I don't truly listen unless I'm invited to share my thoughts. Help me to listen with love anytime that kind of invitation comes my way. Amen.

Mom Wins

Moms take care of their jobs, their kids, and their personal lives with as much energy as they can muster. So how does a mom win when it comes to her home and family?

Mom wins every time someone in the family says, "I love you." Mom wins whenever she receives an unexpected helping hand. Mom wins when she gets to soak in the tub and have some time to herself. Mom wins when she can be herself and share her love with the people around her.

As a mom and a woman managing many duties inside and outside the house, you need wins. You need to feel victorious. Perhaps the best ways to win are to thank God for the little things that make your day special and to hand over all the complex issues to Him. Then, settle back, slip into bed, and rest. Close your eyes, because with Him, you win every day.

But he said to me, "My grace is sufficient for you, for my power is made perfect in weakness." Therefore I will boast all the more gladly about my weaknesses, so that Christ's power may rest on me.

2 CORINTHIANS 12:9

Mom's Prayer

Lord, there are many days when I don't feel victorious. Help me to stay close to you and keep coaching me so I can win at the best job you ever gave me—being a mom. Amen.

Thank God There's Mom!

It's often said that God couldn't be everywhere so He created mothers. Certainly God appreciates the work that moms do to raise happy, healthy children. He trusts them with the most precious things He ever created—His children.

Moms are generally selfless, which means they do all they can to take care of the needs of others before they take care of themselves. Some days, they wish they had a mom to help them in the same ways they help their children.

As a mom, you're the thread that runs through everything your family does and the glue that holds them together. You are the one who makes them say, even if only to themselves, "Thank God there's Mom!" They wouldn't know what to do without you.

Today, ask God to bless your family in every possible way. Thank Him for giving you the opportunity to make a difference in the lives of each person who depends on your care and keeping.

Oh, give thanks to the LORD, for He is good!
For His mercy endures forever.

PSALM 106:1 NKJV

Mom's Prayer

Lord, I'm pleased that my family thinks I'm so special and important in their lives. I thank you for my own mother who helped me become the person I am. Thank you for being the One who truly guides my steps each day. Amen.

Mom's List

Many moms are list makers. There are so many things to take care of that it's much easier if they consult the list on the refrigerator door or their cell phone to keep them moving ahead and getting things done. They keep track of where everyone in the house is and when they're coming home again, and they keep supplies coming into the house and make sure the bills are paid. Some moms have a list for nearly everything.

If you're a list maker, be sure you also have time with God on your list. Make certain that you note what Scripture you read today and what blessings from God you feel. If you have a list of things that seem too difficult to accomplish, then hand that list over to God, because He doesn't expect you to carry your burdens all by yourself. Lean in and stay close. It will make tomorrow's list a bit lighter.

Give all your worries to him, because he cares about you.

1 PETER 5:7 NCV

Mom's Prayer

Father in heaven, I do my best to keep organized. Help me to always start my list with you, with quality time to pray, meditate on your Word, and offer up my concerns for others. Always be at the top of my list. Amen.

Where's Mom?

Have you ever noticed that when the stars finally align and you take a day off, that when you come home, things are never going as smoothly as you hoped? Instead, chaos has reigned. There are muddy footprints everywhere, the dog seems to have shed on every inch of the sofa, and all the dishes from breakfast are still in the sink. It feels like everyone at home took the day off too. Of course, what no one really thought about is what happens when Mom returns. When "Where's Mom?" turns into "Here's Mom," everybody scrambles.

The same thing can happen between us and God. When we think God is watching, we clean up our act, but when we aren't paying attention, we let things slide. Even for us, it may be that "Where's God?" turns into "Here's God" at any given moment. Our task is to always be prepared.

It's good to take a day off as long as we know how to keep things in order.

"When the Son of Man returns, it will be like it was in Noah's day. In those days before the flood, the people were enjoying banquets and parties and weddings right up to the time Noah entered his boat. People didn't realize what was going to happen until the flood came and swept them all away."

MATTHEW 24:37–39 NLT

Mom's Prayer

Lord, when I go out for the day, it makes me feel put out when my family doesn't take care of things while I'm away. Help me to remember that feeling so I take care of things about my faith. When you come back, I don't want to have to apologize for making such a mess. Amen.

February

Help, I'm a Mom!

Do you ever wonder how a nice girl like you got into the family you're in? Do you wonder who the kids are that live in your house? After all, they seem to have totally different ideas about how the world works or what the rules of the house ought to be. Safe to say there are situations that might find you crying out, "Help! I'm a mom!"

When that happens, step outside and go for a walk, no matter how cold it is. Think your own thoughts and try to feel more at ease. Call your best friend and beg for a coffee chat complete with a cream puff somewhere nearby.

Of course, the best help of all is to shout out to God, because He already knows what's going on. He'd probably tell you that His children have been difficult to manage for centuries. Today, if you're struggling with any part of the whole mom thing, just stop whatever you're doing, find a place where you can breathe more easily, and talk to your heavenly Father. He'll listen and understand.

Now this is the confidence that we have in Him, that if we ask anything according to His will, He hears us. And if we know that He hears us, whatever we ask, we know that we have the petitions that we have asked of Him.

1 JOHN 5:14–15 NKJV

Mom's Prayer

Lord, sometimes I can't figure out what my children really need.
Please grant me your wisdom for better days ahead. Amen.

Mom's Closet

When you were a little girl, did you ever sort through your mom's clothes and find the prettiest blouses, or go through her jewelry to play dress-up? Did you try to walk in her high heels or search through her old purses? It was fun to pretend you were a grown-up.

Now that you're the mom, you may have little girls who like to go through your closet. As an adult, you know that growing up may come with cute high heels, but it also brings a lot of responsibility. You may feel like your closet is a mess, and you might wish someone else could walk in your shoes for a while.

You can't go back in time, but remember that you're still your heavenly Father's little girl. When you don't feel quite strong enough to carry the load, simply close your eyes. Imagine God is near you and that He wants to keep you safe and take care of all your needs.

But it is good for me to draw near to God;
I have put my trust in the Lord GOD,
That I may declare all Your works.

PSALM 73:28 NKJV

Mom's Prayer

Lord, help me to remember that safe kind of feeling today, trusting that you are with me and my family, watching over all we do. Keep us always in your care. Amen.

Mom, the Storyteller

Your mom probably read storybooks to you when you were a child. Perhaps she read them so much that you both had them memorized. When that happened, you could even play a game where you could make up a different ending or be the hero of the tale.

Jesus was a great storyteller too. He told stories in the form of parables, and He drew on ordinary life to make His point. He always wanted to connect His listeners in a way that they could understand what the story was about.

As a mom, you're creating a story in the life of your children. You're helping to write new chapters in their lives that will be told and retold for years to come. You may have some old stories that are ready for a new ending because now you have a different life perspective and are able to spin new tales. Keep weaving those stories.

His disciples came and asked him, "Why do you use parables when you talk to the people?" He replied, "You are permitted to understand the secrets of the Kingdom of Heaven, but others are not. To those who listen to my teaching, more understanding will be given, and they will have an abundance of knowledge."

MATTHEW 13: 10–12 NLT

Mom's Prayer

Lord, I know we learn a lot of things in life through good stories. I also know that you did your best to teach others through parables. Help me to create warm and positive stories for my family. Amen.

When Mom Speaks

We like to believe that when Mom speaks, everybody listens. It's a nice thought, but not necessarily a true one. If Mom speaks loudly, some listen. If Mom speaks softly, others listen even more. However, it's safe to say that much of the time, Mom's not sure anyone hears her voice. She may even talk to herself just to be sure someone is listening.

If your household is so busy that communication is at an all-time low, it may be time to stop everything. Stop the noise. Stop trying to talk to people who are not standing still. Instead, gather the ones who most need to hear your voice, and when they are very close to you, talk softly. Set a time to talk with each one.

If that doesn't work, take all the things you want to talk about to God. Ask Him to prepare the hearts of your family members so you can have a meaningful conversation with them. Ask Him to show you when to try to share your heart with the people you love.

Hear my voice in accordance with your love;
preserve my life, Lord, according to your laws.

PSALM 119:149

Mom's Prayer

Dear Lord, sometimes I feel like I talk to catch up with my own family. Help us all to be more intentional about sharing what happens in our day with each other. Amen.

Mom Doesn't Drive a Tractor

Of course, Mom could drive a tractor, but the idea here is that moms cannot and do not do everything. Some moms bake great cookies, and some moms find it best to avoid the kitchen. Some moms can trim your hair, and some moms should stay away from the scissors. Some moms are movers and shakers, and some moms are quiet good-deed doers. The fact is that moms are skilled in lots of ways.

As a mom, you may sometimes wish you had skills other than the ones you've been blessed to share with your family. You may look at moms around you and wonder if you should be striving to do more of what they do.

When those thoughts creep into your mind, take a good look at what you do already. You may be surprised to realize the many amazing gifts you bring to your household. There's no mom competition going on. The only ones to please are those in your family and the One who put each family member in your care. When in doubt, ask God to help you see the gifts He's given you.

It's your day to be simply wonderful you.

I also saw something else here on earth: The fastest runner does not always win the race, the strongest soldier does not always win the battle, the wisest does not always have food, the smartest does not always become wealthy, and the talented one does not always receive praise.

ECCLESIASTES 9:11 NCV

Mom's Prayer

Lord, I thank you for teaching me what it means to love and what it means to do good deeds for others. Bless me with the kind of energy and desire to grow according to the work you alone would have me do. Amen.

Moms Laugh

Do you have memories of hearing your mother laugh out loud? Maybe she was laughing so hard that tears rolled down her cheeks and everyone around her was laughing too. It was a moment that made everybody feel good. How about you? Do you laugh out loud and give your children the pleasure of hearing you simply give in to the joy of the moment? If not, or if you haven't done that in a long time, it may be time to put laughter back on your to-do list.

If you've lost your sense of humor, imagine what it must have been like for Abraham and Sarah when God announced to them at ages well past ninety years that they would conceive and have a child. Of course, we might not think that was very funny if we were quite that mature, and yet it only helps us see that God can do anything. He can change our lives at any given moment, and He can cause us to laugh out loud at the good things He does.

Today, look for those moments when a little laughter will be just the right medicine for you.

And Sarah said, "God has made me laugh, and all who hear will laugh with me."

GENESIS 21:6 NKJV

Mom's Prayer

Lord, I have to tell you that if I had been in Sarah's shoes at ninety years old, the very thought of having a child would surely have made me laugh. We are so finite in our thinking. Remind me that you can change everything and that those changes can cause me to laugh in joy and awe. Amen.

Mom...Butcher, Baker, Candlestick Maker

Moms do so many things that it may not be a stretch to imagine that they could also do the tasks of the ones mentioned in an old nursery rhyme. They may not clean the fish, but they often cook it. They may not grind the wheat, but they can surely make the bread. They may not make their own candles, but they always know where the candles are when the lights go out. Moms are creative, resourceful, and amazing.

You probably would have a hard time making a list of all the things you do in a day. Even so, it's always a good day to give God thanks for making you so flexible and talented, so clever and skillful. If you're running around a little too much today, slow the pace and stay in the present moment. Your contribution to your home and family is awesome, and God is pleased with all you do for the ones you love.

Let your light shine, even if you do have to make your own candles.

Light shines on those who do right;
joy belongs to those who are honest.

PSALM 97:11 NCV

Mom's Prayer

Lord, thank you for filling in the gaps and being my strength when I'm too tired to figure things out. Thank you for all the people in the world who create the products I need so that I don't have to start from scratch just to have a good grilled cheese sandwich. Amen.

Wonder-Full Mom

Since the day you became a mom, your life has been busy. In fact, you've probably had many days when the thing you craved most was sleep. You simply wanted to slow down and relax and not have so much responsibility. You may have even wondered if you'd ever have anytime that's your own again.

Today, as you look in wonder at the things you accomplish each day, and as you stand in awe of the One who created you and designed every detail of your heart and mind so you can do all that you do now, stop and pray. Give thanks for a life that is full of wonder. Give praise for all that God does to fill you up with love from your family. Rejoice in all that you are as you live and breathe in the fullness of joy and grace. Everything about your life today is wonder-full.

Many, LORD my God,
are the wonders you have done,
the things you planned for us.
None can compare with you;
were I to speak and tell of your deeds,
they would be too many to declare.

PSALM 40:5

Mom's Prayer

Father in heaven, you surely have given me a full life and I am truly grateful. Help me to also remember that there is nothing I can do without your love, mercy, and grace. For all of those things, I am eternally grateful. Amen.

A Mother of Great Kindness

Constant kindness can accomplish much. As the sun makes ice melt, kindness causes misunderstanding, mistrust, and hostility to evaporate.

ALBERT SCHWEITZER

Sometimes moms have to referee the squabbles that pop up like thunderstorms in the desert and try to calm everyone down. Sometimes moms have to listen tenderly to hurtful words that indicate that all she attempted to say or do was very much misunderstood. Moms have the goal of treating others with kindness. It's just what they do.

A kind heart is a blessing, a gift from God. Though you may discover people who don't understand the concept of genuine kindness along the path of life, you must never allow yourself to be deterred. You serve God and the people you know most effectively when you are kind. Think of all the times you've helped to melt the icy sting of harsh words and brought warmth and understanding to a situation again. A good mom's job is often to simply set an example of what it means to be kind to others.

"May the LORD show you kindness and faithfulness."

2 SAMUEL 15:20

Mom's Prayer

Lord, I thank you for all the years of kindness that you have shown me. Give me the strength, the patience, and the energy to do all I can to melt the chilling tentacles of heartless actions and words that can occur even in my own home. Amen.

Moms Always Use the "L" Word

Love is a natural response to parenting. Love is the reason you wanted a baby in the first place, and love is what motivates you to do a good job guiding your child into adulthood. Moms are lavish about using the "*L*" word. They know how important it is to give and receive love.

Other "*L*" words are important to moms as well. One might be "laughter." Moms want their families to recognize the importance of having fun. Another word might be "lazy." Moms know that most of life requires work and that loafing won't take you very far. Finally, a fourth "*L*" word is Lord. Moms want to share the Lord of their hearts. They know that nothing can work well in this world without the gift of Jesus.

Today, love your own mom and love yourself. Most of all, love the Lord your God with all your heart, soul, and mind. He'll help you do everything better.

Jesus replied: "'Love the Lord your God with all your heart and with all your soul and with all your mind.'"

MATTHEW 22:37

Mom's Prayer

Lord God, thank you for teaching me how to love and how to give. I am grateful for all that you have taught me about love and laughter and you. Let me never be lazy in my efforts to love others better. Amen.

Having a Heart for God

Be strong and take heart, all you who hope in the Lord.

PSALM 31:24

As a mom, you encounter a lot of things in life that give you pause—things that make you feel fearful or uncertain. You watch protectively over your children, and your heavenly Father watches protectively over you.

Having a heart for God means that you know where your strength truly comes from and you know that you don't bear the difficult things—or even the good things—that happen in your home all by yourself. You always have a place to go when troubles come, because you put your hope in the Lord. As you go through life today, stop many times to give thanks to the One who cares so much for you and your family. Offer Him your heart, and He will always take care of your soul.

Today, be strong in the Lord.

Acknowledge and take to heart this day that the LORD is God in heaven above and on the earth below. There is no other.

DEUTERONOMY 4:39

Mom's Prayer

Dear Lord, I thank you that you help me to stay connected to you at all times. I ask that you would teach me to love you with my whole heart, holding nothing back, so that I may acknowledge you in every way and approach life without fear. Amen.

Mom's Work

To simply say "Mom's work" probably makes you smile. Of course, we could be talking about the fact that moms work all the time—in the home, outside the home at a job, or as a volunteer. We could talk about what kind of work moms do and describe all the ways that moms work. We could even talk about the fact that the whole notion of putting moms in a family is part of what makes that family work well together.

Mom's work today—your work—is to stop everything and surrender every shopping list, every to-do list, and every plan to God. Your work is to hand it all over so you aren't trying to do everything yourself, carrying a load that's way too heavy. Your work is to put everything on the various lists at God's throne. When you work that way, God can bless you more fully.

Today, put your lists aside and seek God's help with all you need to do. He'll make everything lighter because He loves you.

Depend on the LORD in whatever you do, and your plans will succeed.

PROVERBS 16:3 NCV

Mom's Prayer

Lord, sometimes I'm a bit too independent. I think everything depends on me to get it done. Thank you for reminding me that you are willing to help me carry the load. Amen.

God's Promises for Moms

When you became a mom, God didn't intend for you to take on such an important task all by yourself. He planned to be there with you through the good times and the bad times. Let this Scripture remind you that God wants to help you in the work you do as a mom.

Do not worry about anything, but pray and ask God for everything you need, always giving thanks. And God's peace, which is so great we cannot understand it, will keep your hearts and minds in Christ Jesus.

PHILIPPIANS 4:6–7 NCV

When you're a mom, there are many days that don't feel very peaceful. In fact, the greatest joy of the day may be when you get to slide into bed and turn out the lights. But the good news is that God is with you through the chaos and the noise of life, and He is always ready to cover you with a blanket of luxurious, sweet peace. Hand over all your worries today and get a good night's sleep this evening. You'll be so glad you did.

Mom's Prayer

Lord, please help me to give you the worries of my heart, those things that feel too complicated and make too much noise in my head. Grant me your kind and much needed peace. Amen.

Hearts and Flowers Day

You may not celebrate Valentine's Day, but for many moms, it's the day we receive those awesome handmade cards from little ones, the thoughtful sweet cards from older ones, and maybe even some flowers from the kids who have already moved out into the world. Valentine's Day is our official day to celebrate our love for each other.

The beauty of this holiday is that it's a reminder that we must celebrate love every day of the year. All we have to do is start with our Creator and remember how loved we are. Then we can thank Him for giving us the amazing things we have and let Him know that we truly do love Him with our whole heart. From there, we can send up prayers for our family members and friends who are so dear to us and let God know how much we love them too.

Hearts and flowers are always part of life, always something to celebrate, because love has no time or season. It exists and is to be treasured every day of the year.

I trust in your love. My heart is happy because you saved me.

PSALM 13:5 NCV

Mom's Prayer

Lord, thank you for days like Valentine's Day, when I can stop for a moment to simply remember how important love is to me. Thank you for your love. If I could send a valentine to you today, it would say in big letters, I LOVE YOU WITH ALL MY HEART. Amen.

Mom Boot Camp

Being a first-time mom may be a bit like going to boot camp. Nothing is familiar, you never get to sleep in your own bed, and you haven't had a good meal in weeks because someone is always demanding something of you. You answer to everyone else, primarily the one little voice that keeps you hopping every minute.

The good news that comes with any kind of training is that once you're through it and look back on it, you forget the difficult parts. You forget those things because you proved you're strong and brave. You showed that you're worthy of the amazing job you have been given.

Life is always a boot camp in one way or another. You're always learning something new, being trained to do a task you didn't do before. You rise to the occasion and discover your inner strength. Whether it's becoming a mom for the first time, or getting through a family crisis, you're never intended to rely on your own strength to get the job done. God is with you every step of the way.

God used his great strength
and his powerful arm.
God's love never fails.

PSALM 136:12 CEV

Mom's Prayer

Father, I appreciate the training you give me to handle the ups and downs of life. I know that I can't juggle all the issues that arise, and so I rely on your strength. Help me to lean on you every day. Amen.

Mom and the Weatherman

Moms watch the weather. They need to know whether it's going to snow ten inches and keep the kids home from school, or whether the Little League game will get rained out. It's hard when the weatherman gets it totally wrong. When the snow doesn't come and childcare has already been arranged, or when the game gets rained out and mopey little future stars are hanging around the house, the tone of the whole day changes.

Like the weather, much of life is not predictable. When we make our own plans, we know that things may change and everything might not work out. There's only one real solution.

We have to put all of our plans and all of our concerns about the weather, our finances, our health, and anything else that might cause us stress, in the hands of the One who created the weather in the first place. Make your plans, but give God the opportunity to guide the direction of every step you take.

Who has the wisdom to count the clouds?
Who can pour water from the jars of the sky
 when the dust becomes hard
and the clumps of dirt stick together?

JOB 38:37–38 NCV

Mom's Prayer

Father, I thank you for being in the midst of all the changes that happen each day. Though I may feel a bit put out with the weatherman when his predictions are incorrect, I know that he has no control over anything. Thank you for being in charge of all that happens in my life. Amen.

Mom's Friends

As much as you love your family, you also need good friends. A variety of friendships helps create joy in your life.

Some of your friends may have children about the same ages as yours, giving you a common bond. Other friends may have no children, so you can talk about life and things that matter to you as women. You may also have friends who are older and provide great wisdom, and friends who are just part of your work environment or volunteer life.

The beauty of it is that God knows you need companions to walk the way with you. He knows you need people who help feed your spirit, who love to chat over coffee, and who simply give you a chance to laugh. Your friendships matter to God, and it's by His design that very special people come into your life.

Thank God for each special woman in your life. Bless your friends and pray for abundance, opportunity, and peace in each of their lives. You're blessed to be a blessing.

"I will bless those who bless you....And all the people on earth will be blessed through you."

GENESIS 12:3 NCV

Mom's Prayer

Father, you know that I would not survive long without my dearest friends. I appreciate and honor each one of them. Bless each of them in a big way today. Amen.

Mom's Guidance

Henry Ward Beecher once wrote, "The mother's heart is the child's schoolroom." Moms are teachers; they help sort things and classify them so children learn the difference between rocks on the ground and cookies in a jar. Moms encourage kids to listen to the birds sing or notice the clouds in the sky before a storm. Moms are the reason that most kids learn 90 percent of what they will ever learn, before they are aged five; they have Mom as a loving guide.

The same is true for you in the relationship you share with your heavenly Father. He has been teaching you about Himself and about the world since you were born. He has been helping you determine the difference between what's good and what's not good, whether they're things that your head can figure out or things that are simply a matter of the heart. Your Teacher will never retire.

Today, thank your mom for her guidance, find joy in the direction you're able to give your own children, and then thank God for all He has taught you so far.

For this God is our God for ever and ever;
he will be our guide even to the end.

PSALM 48:14

Mom's Prayer

Lord, I'm so grateful for your continued guidance in my life, especially as you help me to be a better mom and a loving parent. I pray that the things my children learn from me will bless them always. Amen.

Are You Going to Wear That?

Children have opinions. If you wear an outfit that your children believe to be less than fashionable, they may burst out with something like, "Are you going to wear that?"

As the mom, you don't have to explain your taste in clothing, but the question helps you see that your children are growing up and discovering their own likes and dislikes. They're becoming more confident about their relationship with you.

In a similar way, you may not always understand how God shows up in your life. You might question what He's going to do. You only began to question God once you had a relationship with Him.

Today, you may find comfort in realizing what a good job you've done helping your children to voice the things that matter to them. In the same way, remember that God is not offended when you question Him. He welcomes your questions because you have a loving relationship.

"Ask and it will be given to you; seek and you will find; knock and the door will be opened to you."

MATTHEW 7:7

Mom's Prayer

Lord, all I know is that I love my relationship with you and I'm certain that I have many things to learn. Help me to appreciate my children's attempts to grow up in ways that will only serve to strengthen our relationship. Amen.

Mom Is Such a Wise Woman!

She speaks with wisdom,
and faithful instruction is on her tongue.
 She watches over the affairs of her household
and does not eat the bread of idleness.
 Her children arise and call her blessed.

PROVERBS 31:26–28

As a mom, you may have wondered whether your actions were wise on some occasions. After all, you're only doing your best. You attempt to look at all sides of any issue that arises, and you try to listen with love to everyone's concerns. You're a good mom, and everybody would affirm that truth.

God knows it's not always easy for His daughters to be wise. He knows that we do better when we seek His help, but that we often simply plunge ahead, making one decision after the other and doing what needs to be done as quickly as possible. Today, as you go about the things that must be done, ask God to grant you wisdom in your choices, help you with important decisions, and guide you as you help your children and your family.

Mom's Prayer

Lord, I don't know if I'm wise or not, but you know I often seek
your direction for my life and for the help I need to raise my
children. I want to be a wise woman and a faithful wife and mom.
Most of all, I want to please you. Amen.

Mom, the Coupon Clipper

Since moms try to live within their means, they often become vigilant coupon clippers. The local paper and a cup of coffee over breakfast can save them a lot of money. Moms are good at getting great deals, shopping for the bargains, and finding the little things that please their families.

Of course, you know that not all the things you need will come with a coupon or be offered on a two-for-one deal. When you've exhausted the options to find a good bargain, there's one more place to try.

Take your list to God and seek His guidance on those things that are most treasured. Ask Him to help you find the right retail outlet to make the purchase, or ask that He simply take away the desire for any of the things you don't need at that moment. If you're looking for something special, put it at the top of the list and seek God's help. After all, He is the God who is in the details. The little things that please you, please Him as well.

There's nothing that is too small for you to take to God in prayer.

Rejoice always, pray without ceasing, in everything give thanks;
for this is the will of God in Christ Jesus for you.

1 THESSALONIANS 5:16–18 NKJV

Mom's Prayer

Lord, thank you for giving me good habits when it comes to spending my money wisely. I know that it seldom feels like I'll have enough for each thing on my list, but you always provide for me. Thank you. Amen.

Mom Knows Best

Years ago there was a television show that depicted the kind of father few of us had but most of us envied. It was called *Father Knows Best*, and it seemed that the actor in the series always had the solution to whatever difficulty arose. Of course, there were never real life-changing things that happened, because this show was way before reality TV.

As a mom, you may not feel that you always know best, but the fact is that when you put your heart and mind into any situation, things get better. You know your children better than anyone else. You know your family culture. You know what brings a smile to the face of each person under your roof. You really are a mom who knows best.

Today, as you look at your family, remember one more thing: God knows best! He always knows what you need. He's always there to guide you and give you counsel as you deal with any family situation. Thank God for knowing you so well.

You have looked deep
into my heart, LORD,
and you know all about me.

PSALM 139:1 CEV

Mom's Prayer

Lord, I'm certain that I don't always know best when it comes to taking care of all the needs of my family. But I trust and believe that you know best, and that you will guide my steps. Bless each person in my household today. Amen.

Nighty Night, Mom!

Moms are busy! They get up early, starting with the lists they made the night before to make sure everyone has what they need before they go out the door. They check the refrigerator to see if they need to stop at the store, and they check the laundry to make sure the team uniform for the game on Saturday is clean and ready to go.

Some moms go off to a job. Some moms are involved in church organizations where they donate endless hours for the good of others. Other moms are trying to finish college degrees or are learning a skill that will provide for their family in the future. Ultimately, moms are busy and they are tired. They seldom get the rest they need for the work each day brings.

If you're a mom who's overextended—too many obligations, too many chores, too many demands on your time—then it's more important than ever for you to make time for a few moments with God each day. Take the time to breathe in the peace of the Savior, because He's the only One that can give you the strength you need. Get some rest today, and get a good night's sleep tonight, Mom.

Come to me, all of you who are tired and have heavy loads, and I will give you rest.

MATTHEW 11:28 NCV

Mom's Prayer

I hate to admit when I'm weary, Lord, but it's really hard to get a full night's sleep. Tonight, I ask that you would grant me that perfect rest that only comes from you so that I can be strengthened for the work I have to do tomorrow. Amen.

Mom Needs a Hug

A Mom's Hug

A mom's hug can change the way
Any child sees the day,
And when a mom is slightly blue,
An extra hug can cheer her too.

Moms are huggers. They give out endless hugs and encouragement to their children and the people they love simply because it brings them joy. But when moms need a hug, they seldom mention it. They don't ask for hugs; they simply wait for them.

As a mom, you know what you need. You're good at making sure everyone else in your family feels loved and cared about, but you're not always good at letting the family know your own needs. It's okay to ask for a hug, whether you need a joyful moment or some encouragement. Hugs keep families together.

Today, as you hug each person in your family, let them know how much they mean to you and how much their love and comfort make a difference to your day. Love is a gift of God, and He wants you to embrace every opportunity to be filled with His love all day long.

Greet one another with a kiss of love. Peace to all of you who are in Christ.

1 PETER 5:14

Mom's Prayer

Lord, I love to hug and kiss the people in my family. It does my heart good to connect with each of them. Please help me be willing to say when I need a hug too. Help me not to forget the little things that let you know I love you as well. Amen.

Mom Lifts Weights

Moms are natural-born weightlifters. They lift the weight off the backs of their children. They do their best to strap on another load and carry the burdens of raising a family. They can lug huge bags of groceries into the house, sling heavy book bags over their shoulder, and still carry a toddler. They are that strong.

Whether you're a single mom or have someone to help you with the load of parenting, you are incredible. You have taken on a task that is formidable, because you lift weights every day.

When you feel like you're getting weak in the knees or wondering how long you can hold everybody else up—including yourself—it's a good idea to seek more strength from your heavenly Father. He doesn't expect you to be Atlas and shoulder the whole world. He will gladly help you carry the burdens. In fact, He prefers that you rely on Him, because He doesn't want you to take on the world all by yourself.

Today, before you lift one thing, ask God to be with you to help carry any potential burden that comes your way. If you do, your heart will feel much lighter.

"Fear not, for I am with you;
Be not dismayed, for I am your God.
I will strengthen you, Yes, I will help you,
I will uphold you with My righteous right hand."

ISAIAH 41:10 NKJV

Mom's Prayer

Lord, I do feel a bit like a weightlifter, and a lot of the things I have to deal with are pretty heavy. You know the burdens that I carry, and so I ask you to be with me each day and strengthen me. Amen.

Mom, the Beauty Queen

My mother had a slender, small body, but a large heart—
a heart so large that everybody's joys found welcome in it,
and hospitable accommodation.

MARK TWAIN

Chances are you don't rush to the mirror just to gaze on the beauty of your face. Of course, in God's eyes, you could because you're always beautiful to Him. For some reason, though, it's harder for you to see what God might think is beautiful about you. You've just never thought of yourself as a beauty queen.

God sees you from the inside out. He looks to see what's happening in your heart. When He sees how much love you hold there, how often you pour out that love on your family and friends (and even on strangers you meet), He is pleased. He looks at you and blesses you further because He sees the beauty within you.

Today, as you brush your hair to leave the house, take a deeper look at the woman in the mirror. When you do, you're sure to see the glow that God has put there, the shimmer of beauty that you possess because of your great love for others. In fact, God will meet you there to remind you that you're looking good to Him all the time.

Charm is deceptive, and beauty is fleeting;
but a woman who fears the Lord is to be praised.
Honor her for all that her hands have done,
and let her works bring her praise at the city gate.

PROVERBS 31:30–31

Mom's Prayer

Lord, I pray that you'll help me to maintain a beauty that only you can give me, the kind that others can see because it comes from the love I share. Thank you for being with me always. Amen.

Professor Mom

You have omitted to mention the greatest of my teachers—
my mother.

WINSTON CHURCHILL

You may not have an advanced degree in education, but you're one of the greatest influences your child will ever have. You guide the values that are embraced and listen when things don't go well, and you share your heart in loving ways. You could easily have a Ph.D. in being a mom.

Your influence on your children is brilliant. You instill a sense of unequaled self-worth. You teach them how to think ahead and how to organize their time. You teach them how to love others and consider another person's needs even ahead of their own. They have you as a beautiful example.

You're an excellent teacher because you help your children grow up to be honorable and loving adults. You are an example, a woman they will always honor and look up to with great respect no matter how old they are. Bravo for you, Mom!

Train up a child in the way he should go,
And when he is old he will not depart from it.

PROVERBS 22:6 NKJV

Mom's Prayer

Lord, thank you for providing me with good judgment and wisdom as I raise my children. I ask that you would bless my children to grow stronger each day in all that life brings their way and that they too would embrace your teachings. Amen.

Moms Are Tigers

Moms can seem pretty quiet and laid back. They take things in stride and stay calm through most of the everyday chaos of life. But look out! That's not all there is to a mom.

Moms can be ferocious. They charge into battle when they think someone is trying to harm their children. They arm themselves with every bit of ammunition they can muster to bring strength to any situation. Moms will not let anyone take advantage of their children. If that happens, they turn from gentle felines to absolute tigers.

God is that way about you too. He remains calm through most of the things that happen in your life, knowing that you grow through experience and that He can't always step in or you wouldn't understand the lesson to be obtained. However, all that changes when someone does something that might harm you. Then God is there in full armor ready to defend you. He guards your life and will do so until the day He calls you home.

Today, be glad for that tiger that lurks within you, defending your children and your home. It's something you may have learned from your heavenly Father.

The LORD will protect you from all dangers;
he will guard your life.
The LORD will guard you as you come and go,
both now and forever.

PSALM 121:7–8 NCV

Mom's Prayer

Lord, I know that I depend on you to protect me and my children. I ask that you would keep the people I love from any danger and guard their lives. Thank you for giving me the strength to take care of them each day. Amen.

Mom's Treasures

Moms love the little treasures they get from their children through the years. Most moms keep the first handwritten love notes, the imitation gold pin, and the handkerchief with an initial on it. These items retain the feeling of being loved forever and ever. Some moms keep their treasures in a special box, while others simply hold the memory close in their heart.

Our treasures are seldom things that have monetary value or can be displayed on walls. Our heirlooms may be lovely and appreciated, but the real treasures are the ones we hold in the heart. Jesus reminded us to store up our treasures in heaven where moth or rust cannot devalue them.

As you think about the things you treasure today, may some of those thoughts carry you back to the sweet poem in the hand of your little one, or the violet that was picked in the yard. Those are treasures nothing can replace.

But store your treasures in heaven where they cannot be destroyed by moths or rust and where thieves cannot break in and steal them.

MATTHEW 6:20 NCV

Mom's Prayer

Father in heaven, I have a heart full of the gifts that have come my way over the years. Though I love having my grandmother's lace tablecloth and my mother's pendant, there is nothing in the world quite like the treasured memories I have of when my kids were growing up. Amen.

March

Walking in Mom's Shoes

Moms with toddlers get used to being followed around all through the day. As little ones grow to be more independent kids and then teenagers, the need to follow Mom around diminishes. Interestingly, even adult children would love to be able to walk in Mom's shoes, especially when life's burdens are all on their shoulders.

You may not hear your kids talk about the ways they aspire to be more like you, but you can be sure that if the question came up, they would heartily admit the things they admire most about you as their mother. They'd probably talk about your ability to stay on top of a lot of different things at once, or about the creative ways you make ends meet when times are tough, or about the way you always come up with a positive solution to most any problem. Yes, they'd have plenty to choose from.

Your kids may not say it out loud, but they are very proud of you and aren't so sure they could ever fill your shoes.

And what does the Lord require of you?
To act justly and to love mercy
and to walk humbly with your God.

MICAH 6:8

Mom's Prayer

Lord, I don't know if my kids would say they want to walk in my shoes or not, but I do know that I want to walk with you. I want to live in ways that please you, keeping you ahead of me, behind me, beside me, and everywhere that I happen to be. Amen.

Moms Always Have Hope

Youth fades;
Love droops;
The leaves of friendship fall;
A mother's secret hope
Outlives them all.

OLIVER WENDELL HOLMES

From the moment a tiny newborn is placed in its mother's arms, an avalanche of hope spills out of the mother's heart. She comes alive with hope about the gifts this new baby can bring to her life and the world. She hopes to raise her child well and to give her baby great love and guidance. And she hopes that the world will be good to this little one she loves so much.

That kind of hope never goes away. When children fall down, moms pick them up again and hope they'll do better next time. When children make poor choices, moms share their pain and hope that together they can find better solutions. Almost nothing a child can do will cause a mother to lose hope that something better will indeed come.

As a mom who believes in God, you have infinite hope because you trust that with God all things are possible. As you think about your children and the things you most hope will happen in your life and in theirs, reach out to God and seek His direction. He will renew your hope even in the darkest hours. Let His light shine on your life each day.

But the eyes of the Lord are on those who fear him,
on those whose hope is in his unfailing love.

PSALM 33:18

Mom's Prayer

Father in heaven, I could never give up the hope I have in you. When I'm at a loss to understand the complexities of life that affect my children, I can only seek your face and the sweet peace you offer. I thank you that I can always trust and hope in you. Amen.

Mom's Amazing Spirit

Moms are resilient. They bounce back. When they have an off or bad day, they look ahead to better times. They expect good things to happen because they trust that God is going before them and will smooth out the road ahead.

God has put a special spirit into the heart of loving moms. He gives them a fierce sense of loyalty to their families, a warrior's spirit for when troubles come, and an angel's sweetness to keep things positive and calm. God knows it's not an easy job to be a mom, and that there are many tough times, hard decisions, and tiring days.

When the tougher parts of being a mom seem to strike your home or your heart, seek the presence of the Lord. Rest at His feet and share every detail of what's not going as it should. Let Him revive your spirit and get you back on your feet. If there's one thing that your family counts on, it's your amazing, beautiful spirit.

You surely know that your body is a temple where the Holy Spirit lives. The Spirit is in you and is a gift from God. You are no longer your own.

1 CORINTHIANS 6:19 CEV

Mom's Prayer

Lord, you have given me a vibrant spirit and I am grateful. Renew me and energize me for all the tasks ahead of me. Amen.

Sometimes Moms Cry

Maybe you remember a time when your mom was in tears. Perhaps you found it confusing, wondering if it had anything to do with you. After all, moms aren't supposed to cry, or so you thought.

Moms work hard to stay upbeat and happy, but now and then the tears spill down their cheeks. As an adult, you understand that it's a good thing to be able to cry.

Being strong isn't about not shedding tears. Being positive about most things doesn't protect you from difficulty. Tears are a gift from God, one of the ways we release the sadness or hurt deep inside. They're also a way we can be refreshed again. Oftentimes we feel better able to cope with life after shedding tears.

Jesus wept. He was sad when His friends died or when someone's life circumstances broke His heart. He shared His emotions, and He wants us to do that too. It's okay to cry. It's good to cry. Cry when you must and then take your sorrow to the only One who can help you deal with it.

Now as He drew near, He saw the city and wept over it, saying, "If you had known, even you, especially in this your day, the things that make for your peace! But now they are hidden from your eyes."

LUKE 19:41–42 NKJV

Mom's Prayer

Lord, I feel bad when someone else sees me cry. I try to keep all those emotions inside, but sometimes they simply come out. Thank you for drying my tears and helping me see things more clearly, through the eyes of love. Amen.

No One Cares Like Mom Cares

Caring about someone means that person really matters to us. It means we're willing to have him or her placed in our care. We care because we've learned how to care from God.

Oftentimes we hear the phrase "I don't care." It might mean we don't care about someone, or it might just mean we don't care about an event, a movie, a book, or a kind of food. Not caring comes with a little bit of attitude and has become an almost prideful statement. Not caring means we've chosen to step around or step aside from something.

Fortunately, moms care. You not only care for your children in the sense of raising them up and giving them what they need on a physical level, but you also care about them on an emotional and spiritual level. As a mom, you care about your children like no one else can.

Today, remember that God feels exactly the same way about you all the time. He cares for you like no one else can.

Therefore humble yourselves under the mighty hand of God, that He may exalt you in due time, casting all your care upon Him, for He cares for you.

1 PETER 5:6–7 NKJV

Mom's Prayer

Lord, thank you for keeping me always in your care. Hold me accountable for any way I can shine your light and help my children to grow. Keep me and my family close to you always. Amen.

Mom's Plans, Procedures, and Policies

As the mom, you get to lay down the rules of the house. You teach everyone how to fill the dishwasher, do the laundry, and take messages for you when you're out. You set the dinner menu and keep a calendar of where everyone is at any given time during the week. It's a big job, and nobody else really wants to do it.

When the family makes an effort to abide by the house rules, things run relatively smoothly. You feel pretty confident about what to expect. You don't worry about getting your favorite white blouse washed with the new red tablecloth because you have taught each person how to properly sort the laundry. Ah, it's a nice idea. If only things were that simple.

If we follow God's plans, procedures, and policies, we'd live by the Ten Commandments. However, with those rules being somewhat difficult for people to remember, Jesus reduced them down to two rules.

As you think about the plans and policies you set down for your family, remember to keep them in light of the ones God Himself authorized. Love the Lord and love each other, and things will surely run more smoothly for your household.

"'Love the Lord your God with all your heart, all your soul, all your mind, and all your strength.' The second command is this: 'Love your neighbor as you love yourself.' There are no commands more important than these."

MARK 12:30–31 NCV

Mom's Prayer

Lord, having a few house rules helps keep things organized.
I appreciate it when my family tries to go by the rules. I try to remember your commands too. I want to please you and do the things that make you proud of me. Amen.

Mom's Little Joys

The little things in life keep most moms going. Moms appreciate the hugs they get when they bake cookies or the little smiles of appreciation when they make the best lunch for school. With a little attention and affection, moms can keep going, keep doing, and keep strong.

Other little things that bring joy are having everyone in the household get along or knowing the laundry and the dishes are all done. When the people in your family recognize what brings you joy, they can provide little ways to make you smile. A second cup of coffee, a few minutes to read a book, and playing the kind of music you like can all be part of the little things your family can do for you.

Sometimes we forget to tell others how they can make a difference in our lives. Happiness is not so much about the big things, but it is often wrapped in little pleasures. God knows you enjoy having a few treasured moments each day. Let your family know that too and then every day will seem like Mother's Day to you.

It takes knowledge to fill a home
with rare and beautiful treasures.

PROVERBS 24:4 NCV

Mom's Prayer

Lord, I do enjoy the little things in life—a chance to read a book for a few minutes or to chat with a friend on the phone, or even sit with a quiet cup of tea. Thanks for giving me a family that cares about what brings me joy. Amen.

A Psalm for Mom

If you like to read the Psalms, you may be familiar with those that are written like poems or songs. Some have beautiful imagery and others offer words of praise. Many of the psalms are attributed to David, and they were meant to show how God was worshipped and adored.

With that in mind, you might recognize that a psalm for Mom is not a bad idea. After all, moms deserve to have their children offer love and adoration. Moms deserve to have kind and loving things said about them.

Today, try your hand at writing a little love note to someone who is a mom—perhaps to your mom, or maybe even to yourself, and offer genuine heartfelt thanks and praise for the things that woman does. God will be pleased to have you borrow an example like this from His Word.

Speak to each other with psalms, hymns, and spiritual songs, singing and making music in your hearts to the Lord.

EPHESIANS 5:19 NCV

Mom's Prayer

Father, it's always good to give thanks and praise to you, and so I thank you for the love of my children, for the work I do as a mom, and for the joy that being a mom gives me. Amen.

The Proverbial Mom

Proverbs 31 sets up some pretty lofty ideals for women. It creates a picture of a woman who is accomplished, organized, successful, gracious, and loving. It's a wonderful portrait of what a woman can be.

As you think about what kind of woman you'd most like to be, both for your family and for the Lord, perhaps it would be helpful for you to go back and read through Proverbs 31. It may give you some guidance into ways you'd like to grow closer to the Lord.

There's no question that you always strive to do your best when it comes to being a good mother, a faithful wife, and a devoted woman of God. Remind yourself today just how special it is to have all of those things be such important aspects of your daily life. You have every reason to be pleased with your amazing efforts to take care of your family.

Charm is deceitful and beauty is passing,
But a woman who fears the Lord, she shall be praised.
Give her of the fruit of her hands,
And let her own works praise her in the gates.

PROVERBS 31:30–31 NKJV

Mom's Prayer

Lord, I don't know if I can hold up the banner of the Proverbs 31 woman. She seems to be able to do it all. Help me to become what you most want me to be as a woman and as a mom. Amen.

Slow Down, Mom!

In a hurry? Does it always feel like you're running from one task to the next? Are there any free spaces at all on the calendar that marks the hours of your day? The chances are good that you lead a pretty hectic, fast-paced life. You may feel like you're lucky to get the dishes done and the kids off to school. Taking time for morning devotions seems like a nice idea, but there just aren't enough hours in the day as it is.

Having dedicated time to spend with the Lord each day is a powerful way to feel His guidance for your life and to renew your spirit for the work you have to accomplish. If you can't take a lot of time, try to find a few minutes to do a devotion, read a Scripture or two, and then say a prayer. If you try that first thing, before the demands of the day get too loud, you'll be surprised at how much more calmly you'll get everything done. Give it a try. It can't hurt.

Rejoice always, pray without ceasing, in everything give thanks; for this is the will of God in Christ Jesus for you.

1 THESSALONIANS 5:16–18 NKJV

Mom's Prayer

Lord, I know that I hurry my way through the day. Please help me to slow down enough to thank you for all I have and to wait on you with patience, seeking your direction for the things that must be done. Amen.

Grateful for Mom

Step back and think about the things your mom did to make your growing-up years easier. She probably made sure you had a decent dinner, helped you get your homework done so you'd have some free time, and made you laugh now and then with her sense of humor and quirky ways. After all, moms can be a lot of fun too.

All those thoughts make your heart smile and make you grateful for the years you were able to spend with your mom. Now think about yourself. Your children may have similar thoughts. They like to think about the things you did or still do that make a difference in their lives. They realize how grateful they are to have you as their mom.

Since we're being grateful for the ones who love and take care of us today, how about including God in the mix? Think about all He does to give you a life that is loving, challenging, and full of blessings. Give God your gratitude for the gifts that fill your home.

Sing and make music from your heart to the Lord, always giving thanks to God the Father for everything, in the name of our Lord Jesus Christ.

EPHESIANS 5:19–21

Mom's Prayer

Lord, I am truly grateful today for the gift you've given me in being a mom. I know that my family appreciates me and the things I do to take care of each one of them. Amen.

The Mom Market

What a marketing target you are as a mom. You're offered a whole new world of retail delight the day you sign up for baby diapers and toy catalogs. Before your baby was born, people started advising you about the best neighborhoods to live in, the best schools, and even the best colleges. It was probably overwhelming. After the first baby shower, when you discovered there were gadgets for every possible baby need, you could see that keeping the advertisers away from your door could be a problem.

As giddy as being in the mom market made you feel early on, by now you've managed to temper the e-mail and newspaper ads so you receive only what you're interested in. When you come up for air after reading the latest pitch from a parenting magazine, remember that you're special as a mom primarily because God is with you, watching over your efforts and the raising of your child. He knows that you have the most important job in the world and that no product on the market can do more for your child than the bushel full of love you give every day. The good news is that love doesn't cost you anything at all.

Jesus said, "Let the little children come to me, and do not hinder them, for the kingdom of heaven belongs to such as these."

MATTHEW 19:14

Mom's Prayer

Lord, I guess we've been conditioned as moms that if we're choosy, we'll buy the best products we can. I'm glad that you're choosy about me and my family and that your love is free to us anytime at all. Amen.

Moms and Dads

We live in a culture where children often live with Mom or Dad, but not both. Whether or not children are raised in traditional families, the need for parental love exists. Because there are so many alternative and blended families today, it is even more important for families to rely on the eternal Father. God always watches out for them.

As you think about this, take a moment to pray for all the moms and dads who raise children together, and then pray God's blessing in lavish ways on the moms and dads who are trying to raise children all on their own. Whatever style family you have, know that God longs to share in all that happens in your home.

Children, obey your parents as the Lord wants, because this is the right thing to do. The command says, "Honor your father and mother." This is the first command that has a promise with it—"Then everything will be well with you, and you will have a long life on the earth."

EPHESIANS 6:1–3 NCV

Mom's Prayer

Father, thank you for watching over me and my children. I pray that all family relationships may be strengthened in you and that children will be blessed by loving parents all the time. Amen.

Would Mom Do That?

Moms surprise their kids sometimes. They might get a new haircut that makes everyone wonder what they were thinking. They might buy an outfit that's a bit too retro for the family at large. They might even book a cruise or unexpectedly get a part-time job at the zoo. The thing is, as a mom, you can still chase the dreams that are important to you. Those dreams don't have to be important to anyone else. It's okay to simply be you.

It's not a bad idea to do things that make your family ask, "Why would Mom do that?" When you give them a chance to question what you've done, it means they're getting to know you a little better. After all, you may be the mom, but your kids at every age and stage get to know you better when you do things that really reflect who you are.

Today, as you go about your routine, try to imagine one little thing you might do that will cause your family to take notice. Have a little fun with it. Surprise them!

"Now, my children, listen to me,
because those who follow my ways are happy.
Listen to my teaching, and you will be wise;
do not ignore it.
Happy are those who listen to me,
watching at my door every day,
waiting at my open doorway."

PROVERBS 8:32–34 NCV

Mom's Prayer

Lord, I don't mind surprising my kids sometimes. Thank you for inspiring those little things in me that keep me being true to myself. Amen.

What Would Mom Say?

If your kids are asking the question "What would mom say?" it's almost certain that what they want to do is something they know won't garner your approval. Most likely they want to know how to explain themselves if they move forward with their plans and things go sour.

It's an age-old problem. Adam and Eve experienced the same dilemma in the garden of Eden. After all, they let the snake charm them into forgetting what God would say if they took a bite of the tempting fruit from the Tree of Knowledge of Good and Evil. Of course, Adam and Eve had their excuses all ready when God came around to question them. But it was too late for them to do the right thing.

Perhaps this question is still pertinent for all of God's children. Your kids may want to know what you would say about their plans. In the same way, you do best when you consider what God would say. When you seek God's voice first, you're more apt to make a wise decision.

Now the snake was the most clever of all the wild animals the LORD God had made. One day the snake said to the woman, "Did God really say that you must not eat fruit from any tree in the garden?"

GENESIS 3:1 NCV

Mom's Prayer

Father, I ask that you would keep prompting me to think first about what you would say before I take any action today. Help me and my children to do the things that are right in your eyes always. Amen.

This Is Your Day, Mom!

If you declared "mom day" in your house, what would it look like? Would you be served breakfast in bed and have your favorite bagel and a long-stemmed rose in a vase? Would you go out to brunch at your local pancake restaurant and order the works?

Mother's Day is one event on the calendar year, and for some moms, ideas like the ones above make the day really special. The good news is that you can declare any day to be "mom day," and when you do, the ways to celebrate are endless. You can spend all day in a bookstore, drink your favorite beverage, read the magazines, and listen to music. You can declare that everyone has to treat everyone with kindness and extra love because it's "mom day."

The overall idea is to stop every now and then to celebrate who you are as a mom and allow your family to pay special attention to you simply because of the awesome job you do. When you do that, also stop and give God the praise for giving you a wonderful home and family. It will be like an early breath of spring!

I will praise you, Lord my God, with all my heart;
I will glorify your name forever.

PSALM 86:12

Mom's Prayer

Father, I don't suppose I really need a "mom day," but this idea is a good one to consider. Remind me that it's okay to take a little break sometimes and that it's good to take some breaks even in the job of being Mom. Amen.

A Special Prayer for Mom

Moms everywhere need someone to pray for them. They need the assurance that they're not alone in their efforts and that someone knows how hard they try to shape the lives of their children in positive ways. They need to feel empowered to do the things they believe are important as they nurture and love the people God gave them to raise.

A special prayer for moms today might look like this:

Father in heaven,
Thank you for all the moms who devote themselves to doing a good job each day in raising their children. Bless them with wisdom, insight, and courage to do the things that need to be done. Grant them stable income to provide for the needs of their family, and give them support to do the job well. Most of all, Lord, let moms know that you see them, that you love them, and that you are there anytime they call your name. Amen.

But as for me, it is good to be near God.
I have made the Sovereign LORD my refuge;
I will tell of all your deeds.

PSALM 73:28

Mom's Prayer

Lord, I join in the prayer for moms everywhere and ask that you would strengthen their spirits when they are tired and renew them with fresh insights as they guide their children. Amen.

Mom's Birthday

What if today you celebrated the joys all around you as if it were your birthday? Maybe you'd call a friend and have lunch, laugh together, and then do a bit of shopping just to breathe in the fabulous array of fun things to be purchased in the world. Or maybe you'd grab the kids and take a picnic to the park, enjoy some lemonade, and let all the other cares of life fade into the background.

The idea here is to remember that your candle is always glowing and is meant to be lit with joy and shared with others. You alone hold this amazing candle, because it is the light that God placed within your heart. You are His light in the world, in your neighborhood, and in your family. Shine on today with your brightest birthday kind of smile and share the love all around you.

"You are the light of the world—like a city on a hilltop that cannot be hidden. No one lights a lamp and then puts it under a basket. Instead, a lamp is placed on a stand, where it gives light to everyone in the house."

MATTHEW 5:14–15 NLT

Mom's Prayer

Lord, I'm not always thrilled when my actual birthday comes around, but help me to remember that whatever I do and no matter what age I am, I need to shine my light for you. Amen.

Exercise for Mom

For some moms, the very idea of the word "exercise" makes them cringe. They imagine those work-out clubs where every woman looks like a Barbie doll and they don't. They can't quite see the "fun" in putting on tight little spandex pants and a big T-shirt and smiling while they do crunches at the gym. All this makes more than a few moms a bit uneasy.

Perhaps you can take a good walk around the neighborhood with a friend for exercise. You could also count the twelve times a day you go up and down the stairs to clean, do laundry, and get something for somebody else as a stair-step program. Maybe hauling in the groceries and bending and stooping to pick up the baby works for weight lifting. It's starting to look like getting in some exercise really isn't difficult at all.

One exercise that always helps to strengthen you as a mom is to be connected heart to heart with your Father in heaven. When you are, He can help you take care of yourself—body, mind, and soul. Yes, the best possible exercises might start there, with lifting your heart and mind to God in prayer. No doubt you'll feel refreshed and fortified once you do.

My health may fail, and my spirit may grow weak,
but God remains the strength of my heart;
he is mine forever.

PSALM 73:26 NLT

Mom's Prayer

Dear Lord, I don't necessarily stay away from exercise, but it isn't always easy to make it a priority. Help me to always reach out to you in prayer and to seek your Spirit to keep me healthy in every way.
Amen.

Mom's Good Book

If you're a mom who likes to take a little break from the world and curl up with a good book, you probably do all you can to make reading time possible. After all, reading a good book gives you a chance to peek into worlds that others have created and take a fantasy trip to anywhere your heart might want to go.

Of course, you might have to fight for the opportunity to simply sit and read, negotiating other people's schedules and getting your chores done early, but it's all worth it to you.

In the same way, you might have to build in time with God, reading the Good Book He has provided to guide your life. You may have to manipulate, reorganize, and plan ahead to find a few quiet moments in the day to make that happen. Sometimes if you're seeking to read more about courageous men and women, or supernatural and miraculous deeds, the Good Book will satisfy your need. In fact, it's a book that is very much alive. May reading the Good Book be one of your best times of the day.

These were more fair-minded than those in Thessalonica, in that they received the word with all readiness, and searched the Scriptures daily to find out whether these things were so.

ACTS 17:11 NKJV

Mom's Prayer

Lord, I do like to read, and there are many days when I don't get to do so. Sometimes when I do, I'm so tired that I fall asleep instead. Help me to stay awake and alert to your Word, giving myself a little time each day to simply breathe in your spirit and your love. Amen.

Mom Is Brilliant

Moms are brilliant! They have quick minds and are the absolute queens of multitasking. They can remember when a school report is due, how many days it is until finals, and when to pull the plug on the TV to make sure everything gets accomplished. They know all the aspects of running a home, and they know how to pay the bills and budget the family income.

Moms also know about relationships. They know how friendships are formed and kept. They know how to say the right thing at the right moment. They have uncanny abilities, and they get it right most of the time.

As a mom, you may not always remember that you're incredibly brilliant. You may not recognize that your ability to keep the household running smoothly, get the kids to the various extracurricular activities, and still get your own work done makes you amazing, but it does. You are the one everyone else leans on, the foundation stone of the house and the linchpin that holds it all together. Bravo for you, Mom!

Seek God's direction for all that you do today, and give it all over to Him to help you carry the load.

If you would earnestly seek God
And make your supplication to the Almighty,
If you were pure and upright,
Surely now He would awake for you,
And prosper your rightful dwelling place.

JOB 8:5–6 NKJV

Mom's Prayer

Lord, I don't know how brilliant I am, but I do seem to keep everything moving in the right direction. It seems like my whole family depends on me to know what is happening when and what needs to be done right away. I count on you the way they all count on me. Amen.

Mom's Light Shines

Moms are brilliant lights who are always willing to be the helping hands and feet of other moms, friends, and family. They join school organizations that will help their children thrive. They become actively involved in programs that are important to the lives of their children and their neighborhood. And even though moms are busy people, they find ways to give of themselves to others.

Some moms volunteer to care for children on their street so other moms can work outside the home. Some moms make cookies for the school bake sale and drive neighbor kids to their track meets and swim classes when their parents can't.

As a mom, it's easy to see that your light is always shining. It's a beautiful light that helps your children grow in strong and healthy ways, and it's a light that often reflects the love in your heart for others. Today, as you go about doing all the amazing things you do, give God thanks and praise that you are strong, capable, healthy, and willing to be a light for Him wherever you are.

So let each one give as he purposes in his heart, not grudgingly or of necessity; for God loves a cheerful giver.

2 CORINTHIANS 9:7 NKJV

Mom's Prayer

Lord, I'm willing to help others in my neighborhood. Forgive me when I don't notice the needs of those around me, and help me remember to turn up the light you put within me. Amen.

Moms Are Humble

Most moms aren't very good at thinking about themselves. They're so used to taking care of others that they forget to notice whether they're being taken care of as well. They put themselves at the bottom of the list. In a word, most moms are humble.

God wants women to be humble when it comes to realizing that they need His help for all they do and that without Him they'd have a tough time. He wants them to be humble in their relationships, because He doesn't like arrogance or pride. Humility suggests that you know that no matter how much you can do on your own, you can't do it all and you can do everything better with God's help. Humility suggests that you recognize your need for God.

Today, as you do your work, spend time with your children, and move forward with the important things on your list, be sure to do so with a gentle spirit and joyful attitude. God will always reward your humble heart.

Do nothing out of selfish ambition or vain conceit. Rather, in humility value others above yourselves, not looking to your own interests but each of you to the interests of the others.

PHILIPPIANS 2:3–4

Mom's Prayer

Father, I'm humbled by your presence in my life, touched that you find me worthy of your love, and honored that you stay close to me. Help me to graciously share your love with others. Amen.

Just Keepin' It All Together Today

Some days, it's hard to keep it all together. It feels like things pile up and you're standing at the bottom of the heap trying to figure out how to climb out of the mess. For whatever reason, there's too much on your plate and you're not sure how you got there or how to clean it all up.

When you're trying hard to keep it all together, the idea of simply "keeping on keeping on" doesn't offer enough direction. Those are the days when you really need to sit down and separate the important and the practical from the wait-another-day stuff.

God will help you sort things out because He loves you and wants to renew your strength. He does that when you choose to start the day with Him, sitting at His feet and listening to His advice. He knows what's on your list, and He won't let you get knee deep into things you can't take care of on your own; He'll be with you through every mundane chore and must-do activity.

Go ahead and put that list at God's feet. You'll be able to keep it all together with a lot more strength and grace afterward.

May the Lord, the God of your ancestors, increase you a thousand times and bless you as he has promised! But how can I bear your problems and your burdens and your disputes all by myself?

DEUTERONOMY 1:11–12

Mom's Prayer

Lord, I thank you for being willing to walk through this list with me today. It looks pretty overwhelming, but I believe that together we can keep it all moving forward. Help me to set the right priorities today. Amen.

Mom Sees Everything

God built a radar system into moms to help them discern the smallest details of what's going on in their family. They can sense when something is wrong and begin to work toward a solution before anyone even admits there's a problem.

You're one of the best moms when it comes to staying connected to that dynamic system. Your radar is on full time. It sometimes surprises the members of your household when you act on the things they need before they even ask. This part of you is a gift that emulates God's Spirit.

God is there for you in the same way. Even before you ask, He is ready to answer your need. He sees everything, and He already knows what you're going to need in the future. It's His way of always being prepared to help you with whatever life brings your way.

Of course, unlike God, you can miss a signal now and then, but He has given you a special gift of awareness that is designed to equip you to do a better job. Ask God to help you grow in awareness of Him and in keeping your radar working in every good way for the needs of your family.

Don't be like them, for your Father knows exactly what you need even before you ask him!

MATTHEW 6:8 NLT

Mom's Prayer

Lord, thank you for always being one step ahead of me. Help me to be as aware as possible of the unspoken concerns of my family and the real needs that must be addressed. Keep us all strong in your care and love. Amen.

Mom's Car

If your car could talk, it would probably amaze you with what it has learned on its travels with your family. After all, this is the vehicle that transports everyone to their destination many times a day, keeping track of the miles you go and the wear and tear on its very being. Your car is your ally, the one thing that keeps so many things moving in your life.

But as good as your car may be about getting you where you need to go, it takes a backseat to the things that God can do to keep your life running efficiently. Your car runs on fuel and oil, and you do too. Your oil is the anointing oil of God's presence in everything you do, and your fuel is the bread of life. God feeds you all that you need to keep going in the right direction.

Today, give thanks for the car that gets you around and makes sure you show up at every destination safely, and then give God the praise for helping you get where you need to go. God gives you the continual spark to clear the bumpy roads and makes it easier for you to find your place in the world.

The Lord went ahead of them. He guided them during the day with a pillar of cloud, and he provided light at night with a pillar of fire. This allowed them to travel by day or by night.

EXODUS 13:21 NLT

Mom's Prayer

Father, I do thank you for the car that keeps us all going. I ask that you would help me stay close to you so I can be continually fed and refueled by your gracious Spirit. Thank you for going ahead of me wherever I travel each day. Amen.

Mom's Mad

Moms vary in their willingness to display anger. Some moms rarely let the family know that they're offended or truly upset about something. Other moms will raise their voices and let everyone know when they aren't happy. It's okay to be mad now and then. Being angry is a God-given emotion and even a protective one. You have a right to your feelings.

While being a little angry can be a gift, it must be treated with "kid" gloves. Your anger must be centered on a loving spirit, and sometimes the only way you can get there is to let the anger dissipate before you erupt like a volcano. Sometimes you have to walk away—literally take a walk and pray for God's Spirit to direct your angry feelings in a way that will allow you to have a positive effect on the situation.

You don't have to step away from angry feelings; you just have to direct them at the right time and in the right way. After all, Jesus showed His anger with the moneychangers at the temple in a very real way. He let them know in no uncertain terms what was bothering Him: He wanted God's house to be a house of prayer. Perhaps for you, turning your house into a house of prayer will be one solution to those moments when you simply want to turn over all the tables.

Then Jesus entered the Temple and began to drive out the people selling animals for sacrifices. He said to them, "The Scriptures declare, 'My Temple will be a house of prayer,' but you have turned it into a den of thieves."

LUKE 19:45–46 NLT

Mom's Prayer

Dear Lord, I am not always good at handling anger. Sometimes I speak too soon or too loudly. Sometimes I get so frustrated that I cry. Show me the best ways to deal with momentary anger. Amen.

Mom's Tender Talk

Perhaps you find it difficult to talk tenderly to yourself. You may have a tendency to criticize yourself a whole lot more than you say those nice things. It's important to develop your ability and willingness for tender talk. After all, you do a lot more that is right than you do that isn't right. You're a shining example of what love really is to the people in your family.

Today, make an effort to be kind to yourself. Start by looking at your beautiful face in the mirror and telling yourself that you are indeed a unique and special woman. Why? Because God designed you and He doesn't make anything that isn't a beautiful original. You are one of His best creations.

If you struggle with being able to say something nice to yourself, then at least follow the old adage, "If you can't say something nice, don't say anything at all." Then you'll be ahead on those days when you seem to find fault with anything you do. This is a good day to thank God for all that you are and all that He has given you. Start with a little tender talk to God, and then try again to talk tenderly to yourself.

And be kind to one another, tenderhearted, forgiving one another, even as God in Christ forgave you.

EPHESIANS 4:32 NKJV

Mom's Prayer

Lord, I have to admit I'm much better at listening to my critical self than I am to listening to the self that has something good to say about me. Help me to be better at being tender to myself. Amen.

Can-Do Mom

One of the best things about moms is that they have a can-do spirit. When something comes up that they haven't done before, they don't hesitate. They simply think, *I can do that!* Moms may not be able to do everything, but moms with that can-do attitude make a huge difference in the lives of those around them.

If you're a can-do mom, that's awesome. One other thing to remember, though, is that when you don't feel like you can do something, there's still hope. Remind yourself, *When I can't, God can!*

When you have a God-can attitude, you have no worries. Together, you and He are a force to be reckoned with because He will always help you with the things you can't do on your own. You have an amazing and willing spirit and you can do a lot of things, so rest assured that God will bless your efforts and step up beside you when there's even the smallest thing that you can't do without Him.

But Jesus looked at them and said to them, "With men this is impossible, but with God all things are possible."

MATTHEW 19:26 NKJV

Mom's Prayer

Father, I recognize that you are the One who's behind even the things I can do. I want to thank and praise you for the skills you've given me and for the reassurance that you're right there when I can't manage something on my own. Amen.

BFF Mom

It takes a lot of living and learning before most kids realize that Mom is so much more than a mom. Mom is a best-friend-forever kind of person. She's the one who will never desert them, always love them, and forever hope, pray, and root for the best for them. There's no greater friend or cheerleader than Mom.

No matter how old your children may be, you're always building on the friendship you share with them. Sometimes when life has taken you some distance from each other, either in physical miles or emotional miles, you may not be able to sense the closeness or the camaraderie you once enjoyed, but it's still available to you; it's still something you can cultivate when you're ready.

Remind your kids as often as possible, that no matter what, where, why, or when, they can depend on you to be their BFF Mom. You will always be a friend in their corner, just like God is in your corner. Think of God as your BFF, and emulate His love to your children. You will share a beautiful relationship forever.

No longer do I call you servants, for a servant does not know what his master is doing; but I have called you friends, for all things that I heard from My Father I have made known to you.

JOHN 15:15 NKJV

Mom's Prayer

Lord, help me to act like a friend when a friend is what my children need most. Help me to respect their ideas and protect their feelings as a good friend would do. Help me to lean on you when I need a friendly voice for myself. Amen.

Mom's Apron Strings

We might talk about a child who hides behind his mom's "apron strings" as one who is afraid to get out and face the world. This comment rarely serves to build confidence and trust in the child. On the other hand, if you need a little more comfort, you may also seek a safe place.

On certain days, you may wish that you actually could hide your kids behind your apron strings, keeping them safe from an all-too-violent world. You would do anything to protect them from any type of harm. This is part of the job a mother does.

As you look at that idea and your desire to protect your children, remember that God also has a desire to protect you. In fact, He would keep you tucked under His wings like a mother hen. He wants you to know that just like you, He wants what's best for His children.

Put your life and the lives of your children in God's hands today. That is the safest place to be.

He shall cover you with His feathers,
And under His wings you shall take refuge.

PSALM 91:4 NKJV

Mom's Prayer

Father in heaven, I thank you for keeping me under your protective wings. I'm sure there are many times that you've protected me and I didn't even realize I needed your help. You guard my spirit and guide my life, and I am grateful. Please watch over my beloved family today. Amen.

April

Mom Needs a Vacation

Don't you love all the colorful travel brochures that show up in your mailbox and all the ads that jump out at you from the newspaper? Those alluring advertisements want you to take a vacation. Of course, they neglect to emphasize that most of those vacations will cost you a pretty penny. So what do you do? Do you just ignore the fact that you really do need a vacation and that you've earned one without question?

Maybe. Or you might consider the options that are more affordable for you. Give yourself a mini vacation by taking the day off on Friday for no reason at all. Doing that may mean that you need to manipulate schedules or hire a babysitter, but you'll be planning something special just for yourself.

Remember that God wants you to relax and breathe in the miracles of life, the special things He designed just for you. Take Him up on it soon and plan a little vacation break to enjoy some quiet time exactly as you'd like. Cut out a colorful ad from your favorite magazine, post it on the refrigerator with the date of your mini vacation, and go for it. Your family will support you in the effort and God will too.

And He said, "My Presence will go with you, and I will give you rest."
EXODUS 33:14 NKJV

Mom's Prayer

Lord, I would love a little vacation time. I'll leave mini vacation ideas in your hands and thank you for all the moments you give me to take a breather. Amen.

Mom's Lookin' Good!

As a mom, you're not always focused on if your hair is perfectly coiffed or if your outfit would be appropriate for the cover of *Woman's Day*. You're just thankful to be in relative order when you head out the door to begin the mountain of errands that keep your household functioning well.

Every now and then, maybe you do get to go out on the town and have an adult kind of evening, perhaps a nice dinner at your favorite restaurant or a night at the theater. It can feel so good to dress up, put on your face, and head out, leaving all the mom responsibility behind the door. Yes, at that point you're really looking good.

Just as a reminder, you're always looking good to God, because when you rise in the morning, dressed in your jeans and a smile, He's delighted with the beauty of your soul. When you brush your hair, He sees you as crowned in royalty. You're always brilliant and amazing in His sight.

So if you're having a day where you feel slightly bedraggled and not exactly like a princess going to the ball, just hold your head up high and thank God for seeing you from the inside out. You have the most beautiful heart He's ever seen!

Do not let your adornment be merely outward—arranging the hair, wearing gold, or putting on fine apparel—rather let it be the hidden person of the heart, with the incorruptible beauty of a gentle and quiet spirit, which is very precious in the sight of God.

1 PETER 3:3-4 NKJV

Mom's Prayer

Lord God, I know that sometimes I'm anything but good looking. Some days I feel lucky to brush my teeth and run a comb through my hair. I have to look down to make sure I don't have yesterday's lunch on the shirt I pull over my head. Help me to always look good to you. Amen.

The One, the Only, the Amazing Mom!

Moms are mysterious. They can pull off some pretty magical feats and hold the family spellbound. How do they do it?

Moms have personal magic tricks. Some take the contents of a nearly empty refrigerator and put a delicious dinner on the table. Others put special ingredients in a bowl and only minutes later pull freshly baked cookies out of the oven. It's truly amazing.

Many moms cast a spell over the household with their peaceful demeanor and talent for keeping everything and everyone organized. Though moms don't really have a magic wand, they somehow manage to keep everything in perfect order, never missing an important moment in their children's lives. Yes, moms have a variety of talents and all of them are somewhat mysterious to their families.

Think about all the amazing things you do for your family with your own touch of magic. You make everyone so proud.

She must be known for her good works—works such as raising her children, welcoming strangers, washing the feet of God's people, helping those in trouble, and giving her life to do all kinds of good deeds.

1 TIMOTHY 5:10 NCV

Mom's Prayer

Lord, sometimes I feel like I could use a magic wand to get things done, or maybe just to tidy up the house quickly. I know that if I do anything that my family would call amazing, it's because you've given me the talent and the time to do it. Please help me to use the resources I have to your glory. Amen.

Mom's Advice

Your kids will come to you for advice many times in their lives.

When they're little, the kind of advice they need is usually the practical sort. Should they invite a friend to play, or should they make a card for grandma? As they get older, the need for advice may be different. They seek your help as a friend more than a parent. They hope to build on the wisdom you've always possessed and the voice of assurance you've always offered.

Thank God for giving you a wise heart. Seek His help anytime you need to give advice to your children or to others. He will help you understand the best direction for the concerns you all share. May God fill your heart and mind with a spirit of wisdom today.

Wise children take their parents' advice,
but whoever makes fun of wisdom won't listen to correction.

PROVERBS 13:1 NCV

Mom's Prayer

Lord, help me to be wise when it comes to giving advice to my children or anyone else. Remind me that you're always near when I need your advice as well. Amen.

Thankful Mom

Moms were born with a gratitude gene. They learned early on how important it is to let others know that they're grateful for the special things done for them. They don't take anything for granted because they appreciate the little treasures that come their way.

Moms are not only thankful for the things and people in their lives; they're also thankful for the chance to be moms in a variety of ways. They like having the chance to plan menus, routines, and rules of the household. They like knowing they're respected and loved.

You're probably aware of the many things that make you feel grateful for your own home and children. You recognize that everything in life is a cooperative effort and that it takes a lot of people, both inside and outside the home, to help raise your children.

As you look at the things you have to be grateful for today, share your joys with God. Let Him know that you're well aware that you couldn't be a successful mother without Him. Thank Him for giving you wisdom and ideas that work to make your family happy.

Let the message of Christ dwell among you richly as you teach and admonish one another with all wisdom through psalms, hymns, and songs from the Spirit, singing to God with gratitude in your hearts.

COLOSSIANS 3:16

Mom's Prayer

Lord, I'm grateful to you from the bottom of my heart for my precious children. My life is filled with possibility and joy because of your grace and mercy. Thank you so much. Amen.

Mom's Blackboard

A blackboard is an interesting device. It can give a quick reminder about the need to buy milk, or it can announce to family members how much each of them is loved. In mom's hands, a blackboard can be a remarkable tool.

Some moms keep tabs on their kids with a blackboard. They write down all the appointments for the week, and all the chores to be done and which person is responsible for each job. They write down any events the family will attend and phone messages that need to be returned.

There's nothing quite like Mom's blackboard, because she uses it to clarify the direction of all those in the household. If God had a blackboard, what do you suppose He'd write on it for you this week?

Perhaps He'd like to make an appointment with you to have some one-on-one time. Maybe He'd give you a little list of chores He'd like you to get done for Him. Maybe He'd ask you to visit someone in the hospital or make a welcome cake for the new neighbor.

God might also remind you how much you're loved. See if you can imagine God's blackboard list for you today.

Do to others as you would have them do to you.

LUKE 6:31

Mom's Prayer

Lord, help me to be more mindful of your work this week so I do what I can for you with great joy. Amen.

Moms Bend without Breaking

You're probably aware that you've been made from some pretty flexible stuff. After all, you're often called upon to break the rules a little, to bend the options slightly, and to do all of this without breaking. You're actually pretty limber when you stop to think about it. You're not exactly made of rubber, but you're pretty willing and able to bounce back when things get tough.

God designed you so you could bend. It's important to be able to do that, because being too brittle could cause you to break—and that doesn't serve Him or you in any way. Where are the areas in your life that you might be able to bend a little more, perhaps be flexible in ways that would help move a project along or give one of your children the room they need to grow?

When you're looking at options and ways to make decisions today, be sure to include the things that make you stretch and bend and grow. Most of those things will be good for your spirit, your soul, and the very foundation of your home. It's okay to bend a little.

Teach us to realize the brevity of life,
so that we may grow in wisdom.

PSALM 90:12 NLT

Mom's Prayer

Lord, help me to be more flexible and willing to bend when change is needed. Keep me from breaking. Amen.

I'll Tell Mom!

Remember when you were growing up and one of your siblings did something you didn't like—something you knew Mom wouldn't like either. You might have been the one to say "I'll tell Mom!" or you might have heard that from one of your siblings or a friend you were playing with. Chances are once Mom got in on whatever had gone wrong, the game was over because Mom would send everybody home or at least to their own room. Yes, telling Mom didn't usually have the hoped-for end result.

It's funny, but as an adult you may have times when you wish you could fix an issue by shouting, "I'll tell Mom!" The problem is that you're the mom, so there's no one to tell.

When you have a feeling like that again, try this. Go tell God! Let God know that you're frustrated or tired, or that you feel taken advantage of or otherwise used in some unfair way. Let Him know that you need some help to get through the situation. When you do, you'll feel better. While Mom can sometimes help settle a problem, God can always do so. Go tell God! It will do your heart good.

Always be joyful. Never stop praying. Be thankful in all circumstances, for this is God's will for you who belong to Christ Jesus.

1 THESSALONIANS 5:16–18 NLT

Mom's Prayer

Lord, there are moments when a situation doesn't seem fair and I wish I had someone to tell. Please remind me to come to you, the only One who can really fix the things that matter. Amen.

Wishes for Mom

If you could cover a mom with good wishes, what kinds of things would you wish? Imagine that every word you speak is going to come true. Speak those good wishes for moms everywhere and even for yourself.

Perhaps you would wish for moms to have boundless energy, to be healthy and strong in body, mind, and spirit, and to live fully and well, thriving on the energy of children and sharing in their songs and laughter. Perhaps you would wish her prosperity, enough of this world's material goods to keep her feeling secure, and not worry over financial matters.

You might wish that moms would have good friends to support them and strengthen their courage, to offer good advice, and to keep their spirits positive and joyful. Think about moms you know and make today a day when you send to them, in thought or deed, an abundance of good wishes.

Keep in mind that every thought can be a prayer—and your prayers are powerful.

Let everything you say be good and helpful, so that your words will be an encouragement to those who hear them.

EPHESIANS 4:29 NLT

Mom's Prayer

Lord, I pray for good things to come true, in my own life and in the lives of women everywhere who strive to be good mothers, doing all they know how to make life a positive journey. Amen.

Stand Tall for Mom

When you were growing up, did your mother ever tell you that you needed to stand up straight? Did she tell you that if you didn't stand up straight, you might be hunched over for the rest of your life? Mothers will sometimes tell you almost anything to get you to do something they think is good for you, regardless of whether they're reasoning is totally accurate. You've probably had that experience yourself.

Besides standing up straight, though, there comes a time when we understand that we can stand tall for Mom because we're so proud of her. We're proud of the way she handles being a mother. We're proud of her optimism and her efforts to keep everything we do in line. We're proud that she never gives up even when her kids do nothing but challenge her.

Today, stand tall for your mom. Remember all the amazing things she did to give you the best possible options in life. Remember her warm smile when you did well and her guidance when you needed more direction.

Stand tall for Mom and bless her in every way you can. After that, be proud of your own work as a mom. You deserve that too.

She takes her stand on the top of the high hill,
Beside the way, where the paths meet.

PROVERBS 8:2 NKJV

Mom's Prayer

Lord, bless every memory I have of my mother's kindness and love. Help me to stand tall for her, speaking kindly of her to others and remembering the gifts she brought into my life. Help me to walk in her positive footsteps. Amen.

Springtime Serenade for Mom

Hundreds of dewdrops to greet the dawn,
Hundreds of bees in the purple clover,
Hundreds of butterflies on the lawn,
But only one mother the wide world over.

GEORGE COOPER

You're the kind of mom who dispenses smiles and warmth wherever you are. You make everything seem a little brighter, a little cheerier, and a whole lot more possible. Your kindness and your attitude bring a special joy to each day.

Does this sound like you today? You may not feel like a breath of fresh air as you go around the house doing the daily chores, making dinner, and taking care of your kids. You may not look in the mirror and give one thought to being anything at all like "mother nature." The joy of it is that you're the heart of all that happens in your home and your family appreciates your gentle guidance and the special touch you bring to everything.

When you think about the rebirth of springtime and the beauty of all that surrounds you today, give God praise for the great joy you're experiencing because of all He has done to refresh the earth and bring it back to life.

He is your praise, and He is your God, who has done for you these great and awesome things which your eyes have seen.

DEUTERONOMY 10:21 NKJV

Mom's Prayer

Lord, help me be willing to plant new flowers wherever weeds have grown, both literally and in the ways that I think. Bless my home with your creative and loving spirit. Amen.

Will the Real Mom Please Stand Up?

It's not always easy to be a creative, loving, ever-patient, always hopeful, somewhat-less-than-perfect mom. You want to do the right things, and most of the time you do, but now and then you can feel like you're just going through the motions. You do what must be done. You're neither good nor bad at being a mom in the process, but you're a bit removed from the blissful scene you'd like to create at home.

When you feel like checking out from all the responsibilities of motherhood, even for a few minutes, it's okay to admit that to God. Seek His guidance and wisdom as to the best way to get your mojo back. Sometimes you're just tired and He can refresh you with His living water. Real moms need to rest a little too. You're sure to hear Him when He calls to you, *Will the real Mom please stand up.*

May the God of hope fill you with all joy and peace as you trust in him, so that you may overflow with hope by the power of the Holy Spirit.

ROMANS 15:13

Mom's Prayer

Lord, some days I'm drowning more than I'm flourishing. When I have those days, please grab my hand and help me stand again so I can be the kind of real mom you would have me be. Amen.

Worst Mom Ever

Yipes! You never imagined you would be a candidate for the Worst Mom Ever award, but today you're not so sure you wouldn't qualify and maybe even win. You lost your temper with the kids, you sent a neighbor kid home, and you forgot all about the PTA meeting. You're just not on top of the whole parenting thing right now.

What's going on? Maybe you need to sit in the stillness, perhaps in your garden, or take a walk and find a great place to be alone for a while. Tell God all the things that have been piling up and closing in on you, making you feel short tempered and ill prepared for the little frustrations that come up at home.

God will calm your spirit and lead you to a brighter day. He'll help you sort through what's causing you more angst than you want to cope with, and He'll help you carry the load. Sometimes your worst days are His best days. He gets stronger when you let Him know how weak you feel.

You're not the worst mom ever. You're one of the best moms anywhere, but when things are getting to you, stop and spend time with the only One who can truly make things better.

"I have no peace, no quietness;
I have no rest, but only turmoil."

JOB 3:26

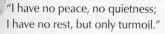

Mom's Prayer

Lord, you know I don't like it when I can't seem to pull myself together. I really don't like to be grumpy or have a short fuse. Sit with me awhile and help me to listen for your sweet voice to ease my cares. Amen.

Picking a Mom

You may have never given any thought to whether your kids would have picked you to be their mom if they'd had a choice. After all, you're the mom and that's just the way life worked out. Imagine for a moment that they could choose a mom though.

What would they say are the most important qualities a mom should have? It seems likely they would choose a mom who would love them, and one who would give them good things and make sure they had all they needed in terms of food, clothing, and shelter. Then they might pick a mom based on her sense of humor or willingness to forgive them when they made a mess of things.

No doubt, if they could choose the mom of their dreams, they would come right back and choose you. They would look at you and remember how loved they are and how much your kindness and smile make them feel safe and secure. They would choose you because they know they're a priority for you, that they are number one on your list.

Some days you might wonder how you got yourself into this parenting thing, and other days you're probably unable to imagine being anywhere without your kids. God knew what He was doing when He placed you in the midst of your choosy kids.

You did not choose me, but I chose you and appointed you so that you might go and bear fruit—fruit that will last—and so that whatever you ask in my name the Father will give you.

JOHN 15:16

Mom's Prayer

Lord, I'm glad there isn't a "mom store" where my kids might be tempted to shop around and see if they could get a better deal. I love them so much, and I know they love me right back. Thank you for giving us to each other. Amen.

Who Does Your Hair?

God may have meant for your hair to be your crowning glory, but there are probably days that get so frantic that you can't even remember if you brushed your hair, much less whether it could be considered glorious. Moms are usually a little too busy to spend a lot of time fussing with their hair and make up when they're simply going to be around the house with the kids.

Though you may not have time to preen in front of the mirror and make the most of the face and hair God gave you, you can be sure that nothing detracts from your beauty in the eyes of the Lord. You're always a treasure to Him, and He doesn't worry about who does your hair.

No doubt you do your best to keep up appearances, but every now and then try to remind yourself that whether your hair is windswept and wild or well coiffed and lovely, all that matters is that the One who counts every hair on your head knows you by name and personally beams at the very sight of you.

God even knows how many hairs are on your head.

MATTHEW 10:30 NCV

Mom's Prayer

Lord, thanks for loving me even when I'm not exactly gorgeous. There are days when I realize I'm not doing all I can about my appearance, but I'm always interested in doing the best I can as a mom. Amen.

Mom Shines...Everything!

As a mom, it's a given that you shine at a lot of things, and it's also possible that you shine everything you can to make your house sparkle. You like things to be neat and orderly and even dust-free. It's not always easy to maintain that shiny aura you'd like your house to have, but the effort is worth it to you.

Perhaps you fantasize about everyone in the house willingly pitching in to get the jobs done with a dust cloth, mop, and laundry basket. Yes, it's a fantasy but one that you wistfully long for.

Even so, the real reason your house shines is because you brighten it up with love. You dust off the past and move things into the present and the future. You mop away the cares of each person and dry their tears. You keep everything so shiny that your family loves being at home. For each of them, home is where they can hang their hats and the place where you can hang your heart.

It's great when everything can be clean and shiny, but it's even better when it shines with love. Thanks for all you do every day.

Anything you decide will be done,
and light will shine on your ways.

JOB 22:28 NCV

Mom's Prayer

Father, help me when I get a little frustrated by the continual chores around the house. You've blessed me enormously with a great family, and I'll put up with a little dust as long as I have each of them. Amen.

Mom, the Church Lady

As a mom, you may not always find it easy to pack everyone up and get to church every Sunday, but God loves your effort and blesses your life. He trusts you to influence and teach your kids about Him so that they too can grow in His love and grace.

As the church lady, you have an opportunity to come together with others who place their faith in God and work to live a life that is pleasing to Him. You grow in your own awareness of all the gifts God has for you and the blessing you are to your family. God enjoys the time you share with Him so He can get to know you better.

This year, make it a special effort to be a significant presence in your church—the woman who graces others with a smile and serves as an example of God's goodness. When you do, your light will shine for them, but it will also shine for you. Walk in God's presence every day of your life.

Then your goodness will shine like the sun,
and your fairness like the noonday sun.

PSALM 37:6 NCV

Mom's Prayer

Lord, I may not always make it to the church door on a given Sunday, but please help me make that effort. Remind me that I can draw close to you in prayer at anytime and that I don't have to wait for a Sunday service to do that. Amen.

Mom's Singing

Whether you're a mom who leads the church choir and sings at weddings, or you're a mom who only sings in the shower, God loves to hear you sing.

Singing comes not only from your mouth, but also directly from your heart. It's a way you can connect your spirit to God's Spirit in joy and praise. Your songs of love are always melodious and beautiful when they're directed to your Creator. There's nothing more beautiful to Him than when you let your heart sing.

Maybe your kids will tease you if you open up in joyful song while you're driving in the car. Or, maybe they'll join in. Whatever you do and wherever you are, make it a practice to allow your heart to sing. If the only one who ever hears you is God Himself, then you'll be communicating with Him in a way that will fill your soul with joy. Lift up your voice today.

I will sing to the LORD,
Because He has dealt bountifully with me.

PSALM 13:6 NKJV

Mom's Prayer

Lord, I'm not so sure the world is ready to hear me belt out a song, but I like the idea of singing my heart out to you. Thank you for the gift of song and for those with beautiful voices that bring us to our knees in praise. Amen.

Mom's Daily Bread

Moms are often in need of special provision from the hand of God. Whether they're single moms striving to make ends meet or moms blessed with spouses and financial stability, they still need God's provision. Sometimes you need God to provide more ways to pay the bills, while other times you simply need God to provide your spirit with new energy and enthusiasm for all the things you have to accomplish. God is your provider in every way. He knows your needs, and even before you ask for His help, He seeks to come to your aid.

Thank God for your daily bread and all the ways He sustains you and your family. Thank Him for the things you may not usually recall as His provision, things like good friends who support you with love and the car that takes you wherever you need to go. Give God the glory today for taking such good care of your every need.

"Therefore do not be like them. For your Father knows the things you have need of before you ask Him."

MATTHEW 6:8 NKJV

Mom's Prayer

Father, thank you for my daily bread. I'm so grateful for the many ways you provide for our needs. Please be with all the people who await you to supply their basic needs right now. Amen.

The Good News for Mom

Do you ever think about the way the news gets reported on television or in the newspapers? It seems like the attention-getting news is the bad news, the tragedies around the world or in your neighborhood. Since the media depends on news to get people to buy into their time spot on TV or purchase their newspapers, they pick the news that is most likely to do that—the hyped-up, somewhat-larger-than-the-truth kind of news. It sells papers and causes us no end of despair.

When you compare that kind of news with the Good News, the truth of the gospel, it's a wonder we even bother trying to keep up with the news of the world. We need the Good News! As a mom, you need positivity and joy in your life. You need to know that there is Good News so your children can be blessed and safe in the world.

Today, as you read the morning paper, seek out the positive news—the Good News that might make a difference in your day. If you can't find any in the paper, you'll surely find it in your Bible.

And the Good News about the Kingdom will be preached throughout the whole world, so that all nations will hear it; and then the end will come.

MATTHEW 24:14 NLT

Mom's Prayer

Lord, thank you for being a source of positive and uplifting news. I pray for all the people caught in devastating circumstances, and I ask that you would protect my home and family and keep sharing the Good News with us. Amen.

Mom Acts

As a mom, you're probably a tough act to follow. After all, you're on the run for a large portion of the day. Most of the time, you do a number of things that aren't even on your list because they still need to be done.

Interestingly, there's a book of the Bible called Acts. It shares some of the actions and activities of the Holy Spirit and the people who were affected by Jesus' life, death, and resurrection. It's a pretty incredible account of miracles and opportunities that were recorded by Jesus' followers as they learned more about Him and His ministry.

Perhaps no one will write a book about your acts and actions, but for today, think a bit about those followers of Jesus, the ones who were looking for ways to uplift others and provide encouragement and love. That's what you do as a mom every day. Let God lead you into the kinds of actions that please Him and benefit your loved ones.

Commit your actions to the LORD,
and your plans will succeed.

PROVERBS 16:3 NLT

Mom's Prayer

Lord, I want all my actions to please you, and I pray that the things that I do will benefit my family. Help me to desire more of you and to be ready to take up the activities that will make a difference in the lives of others. Amen.

Thoughts of Mom

If you stop to think about your own mom and the things she did or said as you were growing up, what comes to mind first? Do you think about her sense of humor and the twinkle in her eye? Do you think about her kindness and warm advice? Maybe you think about how she always seemed to know when you were up to something you knew she wouldn't like. Whatever thoughts come to mind, you probably have conflicting feelings about the things you understood about her and those you didn't.

Now that you're a mom, you might wonder what thoughts your kids will or do have about you. One thing you know is that they often have very loving thoughts about you. In the Bible, the psalmist talks about the way God thinks about you, and the writer of the text says that all God's thoughts are loving. In fact, He thinks amazing things about you and believes you to be one of His most beautiful creations.

Today, think loving thoughts about your own mom, and know that your family and your heavenly Father are thinking loving thoughts of you.

How precious also are Your thoughts to me, O God!
How great is the sum of them!

PSALM 139:17 NKJV

Mom's Prayer

Lord, I thank you for the loving thoughts you have of me even when I more than likely don't deserve them. Thank you for my own mother and all she did to be a loving example. I praise you and thank you in Jesus' name. Amen.

Think about This, Mom!

No one in the world can take the place of your mother. Right or wrong, from her viewpoint you are always right. She may scold you for little things, but never for the big ones.

HARRY TRUMAN

One of the great things about being a mom is that you quickly learn to pick your battles with your children. You understand when they bend the rules a bit, and you remind them why those rules are important. You help them when they fall down, either literally or figuratively, so they can get back up again with dignity and keep trying.

But when something big happens—something that has a greater consequence than they expected or than you ever dreamed would come their way—you always do the same thing. You pray and you help them. You love them through it. You seek to give them room to grow and find their way again.

You're a great mom, and you do all you can to guide your children. Every now and then you have to leave the guidance in God's hands so they can build a stronger relationship with Him.

When you think about all of this, Mom, you can be sure you're right where God wants you to be in each of your children's lives.

Train up a child in the way he should go,
And when he is old he will not depart from it.

PROVERBS 22:6 NKJV

Mom's Prayer

Lord, when my children get into something that's over their heads and mine, I have only one choice. I come to you and ask you to help us take care of things in the best way. I can work with them on the little things, but I need your help for the big things. Amen.

Mom Is Real

When kids are young, they don't often give much thought to why Mom does what she does, or even how she does what she does. They just know that she's the one who's there for them, taking care of their needs and making sure they get their homework done. She's just Mom.

Then one day, they get old enough to see Mom in a whole new way. They discover that Mom is real. She's a real person with real needs, hopes, and dreams. They start to understand how to treat her when she doesn't feel well, when she's too busy, and when she's having a hard day. They learn to give something back to Mom in the same way she has always given to them.

You may remember when you discovered that your own mom was real. You might have even been a bit surprised to realize that she had more things to worry about than just taking care of you. In the children's book *The Velveteen Rabbit*, we discover that moment when the skin horse realized he was real. He was real because all his fur had worn off but he was loved anyway.

It's nice to know that when your kids discover you're a bit weary and worn, you're still very lovable to them. In fact, you're even more lovable because you're their mom.

This is what real love is: It is not our love for God; it is God's love for us. He sent his Son to die in our place to take away our sins.

1 JOHN 4:10 NCV

Mom's Prayer

Lord, thank you for teaching me that I can be myself with my family and that no matter what state I'm in, they still love me. Thank you for your love too. Amen.

Mom's Big Love

When moms love their kids, there's no middle ground. They don't just acknowledge their children, kind of like their children, or simply deal with the fact that they have children; they love them all the time, and they love them in big ways.

The love you have for your family never needs to be replenished, because when it comes to your kids, there's no end to what you'll do to provide for their well-being. You love them in great big ways because that's what they need to grow strong and healthy and be prepared to go out into the world. They do best when they're rooted in an understanding of what it means to be loved.

Oh, sure, there are days when you question whether it's enough, or whether there's more you could do to show your love. There are moments when you're somewhat put out with them for the little irritations that happen in any household, but those things have nothing to do with love. Your love will never be just a halfway affair. Your love will be big forever.

This is how we know what real love is: Jesus gave his life for us. So we should give our lives for our brothers and sisters.

1 JOHN 3:16 NCV

Mom's Prayer

Lord, I do love my children with big love. I don't know what it would mean to love them even more than I do, but if more love is required, I'm ready to give it. Amen.

If Mom Only Knew

Most kids have had the thought, *If Mom only knew what I did, she wouldn't be very happy.* Part of growing up includes testing the boundaries and flirting with things we feel pretty sure Mom wouldn't be very pleased about. It's a natural thing, and all of us have been there.

When you imagine your own kids today, you may wonder what may have already transpired that would bring that thought to their conscious minds, or you may wonder what could cause that thought down the road. As long as testing the boundaries doesn't do emotional or bodily harm to them, it's all good. It's part of growing up.

Imagine, if you will, how God might feel as you test the boundaries He put up for you. Do you think, *If God only knew I did…?* Of course, the problem there is that unlike Mom, who may or may not know what you did, God does know. He knows everything about you now, back then, and into the future. There's no need to hide in the bushes like Adam and Eve, hoping He'll pass by.

Today, forgive yourself for any of the little things you might have done to push the boundary lines while you were growing up. Forgive your kids when they do those things now. Then ask God to forgive you when you still do those things with the boundaries He's set for you. It will do your heart good.

He has taken our sins away from us
as far as the east is from west.

PSALM 103:12 NCV

Mom's Prayer

Lord, protect my children when they step over the boundaries,
and forgive me when I do that to you. Amen.

Mom's Keepsakes

Moms like to keep things. They save their baby's first tooth and a lock of hair from the first haircut. They have the little mold of their child's hand from when he was in kindergarten and the picture from her first ballet class. No matter what the event might be, moms like to have keepsakes.

Your favorite keepsakes might well be some of those described here or you may have a few others, perhaps pictures from your baby shower or your child's baptism. You may have a journal you kept as the kids were growing or that you still keep now. It's a blessing to have these bits and pieces of memorabilia as your children grow, because time passes so quickly. In fact, the problem is that we can't hold on to time or to our little children long enough. Everything slips through our fingers.

If God had a baby book for you, what keepsakes do you think He might put into it? Perhaps He would keep a picture of the first time you touched the velvety petal of a flower and were in awe of His creation. Maybe He'd keep a memo of your first prayer or the first time you admitted to Him that you'd made a mistake.

Today, imagine what you'll do that will be worth putting in a memory book. There's always an opportunity to discover a new keepsake.

"In the future, when your children ask you, 'What do these stones mean?' tell them that the flow of the Jordan was cut off before the ark of the covenant of the LORD. When it crossed the Jordan, the waters of the Jordan were cut off. These stones are to be a memorial to the people of Israel forever."

JOSHUA 4:6–7

Mom's Prayer

Lord, thank you for giving me so many beautiful memories of my life as I was growing up, and thank you for the lives of my children now. I know that these little treasures from life will always mean the world to me. Amen.

Mom's Hats

Of course, moms wear a lot of hats. When we say that, we don't usually think of wide-brimmed Easter bonnets, although some moms wear them too. Most moms wear a lot of hats in the sense of all the different chores they do.

One minute they're the general housekeeper and overseer of the grounds. Another moment they become the chef and the clean-up crew. At any given time, they can become the nurse taking care of a nasty cold or the teacher helping with a homework assignment. Whatever they're asked to do, moms do their best to keep things moving along.

God put a lot of amazing traits inside the women He calls to be moms, and so He put those traits in you. Some of the hats you wear require a lot of patience and thoughtfulness. Some of them require specialized skill and talent. Others require that your heart be totally fixed on what God would have you do.

Whatever hat you wear the most often today, wear it proudly knowing that you do your work in honor of the Lord.

The Lord your God has blessed you in all the work of your hands.

DEUTERONOMY 2:7

Mom's Prayer

Lord, I don't often think of myself as wearing hats, but I do a lot of different things during the day. Thank you for giving me patience and flexibility to do my best for you. Amen.

Moms Believe in You

When it came to establishing your faith when you were a child, you probably had a number of teachers. You may have had a grandmother who influenced you because she prayed or read the Bible. You may have had a Sunday school teacher who told you Bible stories and encouraged you to think about the ways of God even before you could understand what the stories truly meant.

Another way you might have been influenced to believe in God was because your mom believed in you. Your mom trusted you to do the right things. She had faith in you when you tried hard to complete a task, and she encouraged you to keep being kind even if someone wasn't kind to you.

The faith that your mom had in you, and the faith you have in your own children, is part of the reason you understand what it means to have faith in God. Faith requires that you trust and believe and let your heart do the rest.

The blessing of all this is that in the same way you had faith in your mom and she had faith in you, you have faith in God and He has faith in you. Keep trusting and believing in God's goodness and mercy.

Faith is the confidence that what we hope for will actually happen; it gives us assurance about things we cannot see.

HEBREWS 11:1 NLT

Mom's Prayer

Lord, I did learn about you from my grandma and even my mom. I didn't know exactly what they believed back then, but over time I understood that you are real and that you love me. I pray for my own children, that you would be real to them and help them to always have faith in you. Amen.

Mom's Trials and Errors

By now you've learned that being the mom is not an easy job. There are times when you have to do things by trial and error. You try something and hope you don't make a serious error.

Kids don't come with how-to manuals and so the things they say and do are not simple or black and white. Sometimes you have to choose the direction of what'll happen next. You have to choose between what appears to have happened and what actually happened. It's all trial and error.

Fortunately for us, God gave us a lot of flexibility in the rules. He tells us to love Him and to love our neighbors as ourselves. When we break those rules, there are consequences. But before He decides how to handle it, He does one more thing. He looks at the heart to see what motivated the action. Then He deals with us with love and forgiveness.

When you're raising children, it's important to remember this concept. God sees the heart, and you need to see the heart too. When you seek the truth of the situation based on actual motives, you won't often suffer with pure trial and error. If you do, then love and forgiveness are still options.

Don't excuse yourself by saying, "Look, we didn't know."
For God understands all hearts, and he sees you.

PROVERBS 24:12 NLT

Mom's Prayer

Lord, thank you for seeing my heart first. Help me to use that kind of mind-set with my own children when they do something wrong. Thanks for your steadfast love. Amen.

May

Mom's Support Group

You're often the superhero of your own adventure story. You're on top of the world, managing beyond belief all the tasks to be accomplished. You look back at the day and are amazed at what you've been able to get done.

Other days, the superhero flies away and you wonder how you'll even get the kids off to school or pull out the vacuum cleaner. It's a lot of work to do one simple thing. Everything about the day seems cloudy even though the sky is clear blue.

What do you do? One way to handle the off days is to remember your support groups. You may not have a formal mom support group out there, but you have options for getting a little extra encouragement. Here are a few things to consider when you need extra support.

- Let your family in on the fact that you need a little more cooperation.
- Look at your calendar and intentionally schedule a break—and take it.
- Call a friend to meet for coffee right now.
- Step away from the to-do list and sit with God for a few minutes; read your devotional books.
- Call your mother and commiserate.
- Delete from your to-do list two things that can wait until tomorrow.

Give yourself a pat on the back for all you do each day and then allow others to offer a bit of extra support whenever you need it. You can jump into the suit with the red cape with the big M on the front again tomorrow.

Your words have supported those who were falling;
you encouraged those with shaky knees.

JOB 4:4 NLT

Mom's Prayer

Lord, thank you for all the people who give me moral support when I need an extra boost. Thank you for hearing me when I deliver my stress load to your door and for helping me keep things together. Amen.

The Mom Challenge

Being a parent certainly comes with challenges. There's no such thing as a totally smooth ride for anyone who takes on the role. Challenges come from every direction—the kids, your job, your friends, your family, and even your spiritual life.

Your children may challenge you when they're ready for another independent step but you're not quite ready for it. They want more independence; you want them close to you. When they behave in ways that aren't appropriate and dispensing discipline is not your sweet spot, that's a challenge.

The fact is that loving anyone is a challenge, but as a mom you've been highly equipped to win out over the obstacles. God loves you so much that He stands ready to help you anytime a challenge comes your way. Thank God in the midst of the challenges and for the strength He gives you to work your way through them.

We know that in everything God works for the good of those who love him. They are the people he called, because that was his plan.

ROMANS 8:28 NCV

Mom's Prayer

Lord, please stay near me in the challenging times and let me hear your sweet voice as I meet every difficulty with love. Amen.

Mom's Obedience School

You may have wondered what happened to the training manual you thought would come with being a mom. After all, there are training manuals for nearly everything else. Somehow, there seems to be no manual for this parenting thing or for your child in particular.

If you were a puppy, there would even be obedience school. That would be the place where they would teach you the rules and you would be rewarded for doing the right thing.

Actually, you don't really need mom obedience school or help with the rules. All you need to learn is to sit close to your heavenly Father and lean in. Let Him guide you through all that develops in your household. You'll be lovingly taken care of for this one act of faithful obedience.

Now that your obedience to the truth has purified your souls, you can have true love for your Christian brothers and sisters. So love each other deeply with all your heart.

1 PETER 1:22 NCV

Mom's Prayer

Lord, I don't suppose I need to attend obedience school, but you certainly know all the times I've fallen short of your rules. Help me to draw near to you as I try to train my children in positive ways. Amen.

Because Moms Care

Of course, moms care about their homes and their families. Moms care about everything that matters to their children.

When your child gets excited about learning how to run a cross-country race, you get excited too. Whey your child recites a poem, you realize you've always liked poetry. Whether you enjoyed cross-country racing or poetry before you had children no longer matters, because now all that matters is your child. You care about what they experience in the world.

Jesus often reminded people that it's important to care about things that matter to other people. He wants us to embrace each other right where we are at the moment. Your ability to care is a very real influence over the ways that your children will also learn to care about those around them. Thank you for being such a caring mother.

Today, thank God for all the ways He demonstrates His caring love for you.

Cast your cares on the LORD
 and he will sustain you;
he will never let
 the righteous be shaken.

PSALM 55:22

Mom's Prayer

Lord, I do care about the things my children get excited about, even when I don't know much about the topic. Thank you for caring enough to learn more about me as I keep moving forward. Amen.

Mom Can Dance

You may be thinking that you're not really a dancer. Sure, you may have never taken a formal dance class. No one will confuse you with a cast member of one of the great dance shows on TV. But not having any formal training doesn't mean you can't dance.

You can dance because you have the music within your spirit. You hear the beat of a drummer, and that beat will get your toes tapping and your heart jumping before you can move across the floor. You're a dancer because God has lifted you up and swirled you around to hear His tempo. He has you swaying to and fro when you hardly realize you're dancing.

Today, as you move about doing all the activities on your list, make sure you've included a little time to dance to the tune that only God can play. You'll hear the sound anytime you listen closely. It will be a melody of love just for you.

Then young women will dance and be glad,
young men and old as well.

JEREMIAH 31:13

Mom's Prayer

Lord, I can move back and forth to the music, but you know I'm not really a dancer. Thanks for putting your melody in my heart. I love moving through the day with you. Amen.

Mom Will Understand

Women know the way to rear up children (to be just).
They know a simple, merry, tender knack
Of tying sashes, fitting baby shoes,
And stringing pretty words that make no sense,
And kissing full sense into empty words.

ELIZABETH BARRETT BROWNING

Moms just seem to know things. Life have changed since Elizabeth Barrett Browning's day, since few children have to wear sashes or be fitted for baby shoes anymore. Yet the idea remains true that as a mom, you can spin a simple loving thought anytime it's needed. You inspire a child's imagination as you bandage a hurt finger or help him to see a world of beauty in a butterfly's wing. You have a way about you that no one else in your child's life will ever have.

Your words make a difference, and they've been doing so since your child was born. You were singing songs, telling little stories, and sharing the softer side of the world even before your child presented you with a sweet baby smile. Ever since, no matter how old that baby is today, your kind words linger, still making a difference in the way everything else is perceived.

God blessed you with a kind and sweet voice, and it serves your family well.

Whoever loves pure thoughts and kind words
will have even the king as a friend.

PROVERBS 22:11 NCV

Mom's Prayer

Father, I thank you for all the simple ways you've given me to shine a light on a sweet moment with my child. I can only imagine how such moments make you smile as well. Thank you for inspiring my voice with your love. Amen.

Fabulous Fatherly Mom

If you're a single mom, then you understand the idea of being both Mom and Dad to your children. Even if your children's dad is actively involved in their lives, there are many times when you have to act or make decisions on your own.

If you're not a single mom, you may still need to take a fatherly role when your spouse travels or simply works too late to interact with the kids in the evening. You may be the one who has to tell all the bedtime stories and take them to soccer games and basketball practice. Sometimes, under any circumstances, moms play both roles.

When you have to be Mom and Dad, even temporarily, the good news is that you have a remarkable option. You can go to your heavenly Dad anytime at all and seek His help and direction. He will offer you wisdom and remind you that even in that moment you're not alone. He is always available to you. He never lets His work get in the way of His love.

Wise children take their parents' advice.

PROVERBS 13:1 NCV

Mom's Prayer

Lord, there are times when I've done all I can as the mom and had to step up to be the dad as well. I pray for your strength in my own life and in the lives of all moms who raise kids largely on their own. Amen.

The Jobs Mothers Do

Have you got troubles that won't go away?
Are people depending on you?
We specialize in impossible things,
Doing jobs only mothers can do!

It's a big job! Some days it even feels like an impossible job. What was God thinking, leaving children in your hands?

The fact is that God put children in your hands because He knows you so well. He knows your heart and your ability to look at everything with love. He sees that you don't give up easily and that you fight for what matters. He sees that you face impossible things every day and still take them in stride.

God sees you as the woman who can be His hands, feet, arms, and legs in a very busy world. He sees you caring for the children He loves, and, no matter how exhausted you feel, opening those arms again the next time you're called.

He sees you doing the jobs that only mothers can do, and He knows you do it well.

"I am the LORD, the God of every person on the earth. Nothing is impossible for me."

JEREMIAH 32:27 NCV

Mom's Prayer

Lord, being a mother takes all my strength some days, and then just when I need it most, a soft hug will surround me. Those hugs often feel like they have come directly from you. Thank you for being with me all the time. Amen.

Moms Worry

If you're a mom who worries—and what mom doesn't?—then God has a message for you. He wants to remind you that even though it seems like a little worrying might impress Him more, He doesn't need your worries; He only needs your prayers.

The worries you may suffer almost never come true, and when they do, they happen differently than you suspected. God is with you even in the midst of the things that cause you to worry, and even before you pray, He seeks the solutions on your behalf. He's not far from you, but He has a desire for you to seek Him out anytime you feel concerned or troubled.

God knows that raising children isn't a simple task and that mothers everywhere worry about the safety and well-being of their children's hearts, minds, and bodies. The answer is to pray. Pray protection over your children, and pray for wisdom in guiding them through life. You have so much more to do today than worry. You pray and God hears. It works every time.

Can any one of you by worrying add a single hour to your life?

MATTHEW 6:27

Mom's Prayer

Lord, help me to pray without ceasing so that worry never has a chance to crowd into my thoughts. Amen.

Moms Forgive

Moms sometimes get angry at the behavior of their children. After all, they set rules and boundaries to help their kids grow up responsibly. When troubles walk through the door, as they do in every household, moms can react with anger.

Even so, moms also always forgive. As a mom, you've probably had more than one occasion when you felt a bit angry or unhappy about your kids' choices or behaviors. You probably then had to take on the task of finding appropriate consequences for those actions. Even so, you began to forgive them right after the momentary anger faded. Your children may break the rules, but since you don't see yourself as perfect either, you realize that everyone needs to be forgiven sometimes.

Maybe it helps if you reflect on a moment or two from your own childhood when you were reprimanded for something that didn't meet your mother's approval. Then look at what she did later to let you know you were forgiven, and, even more than that, to let you know you were still loved.

"Therefore, I tell you, her many sins have been forgiven—as her great love has shown. But whoever has been forgiven little loves little."

LUKE 7:47

Mom's Prayer

Lord, remind me that when I get a little angry at my kids, you feel the same way about me too when I behave badly. Help me to always let my kids know that I love them no matter what, in the same way that you love me. Amen.

Mom Plays

Your friends probably don't drop by these days to see if you can come out and play, although it might be nice if they did. Sometimes you need to be reminded that a little playtime is a good thing. It's good for you and it's good for your family because it makes you happier and gives you a greater sense of being valued and loved.

Playtime is a necessary ingredient to a life that feels contented and full. You need to put down the laundry, the stack of bills, and the shopping list now and then and simply give yourself permission to enjoy the present moment. Whether you meet friends for coffee, go to a movie, or simply go out window shopping, that bit of time to yourself will make everything else easier to handle.

Today, thank God for the people who encourage you to play a little, and then go out and do something special. You'll be able to do the laundry later.

Do not conform to the pattern of this world, but be transformed by the renewing of your mind.

ROMANS 12:2

Mom's Prayer

Lord, I know I don't get out to play nearly as much as I wish I could. Help me to create some spaces in my day that are just for me, ones when I can breathe in your warmth and love and take a break from everything else. Amen.

Mom Sweeps

Moms make a clean sweep at the start of each day. They like to let yesterday go and begin again. It's a good approach to life that makes a difference in how they perceive the world.

Sometimes, though, it's tempting to try to sweep things under the rug. But when we sweep things under the rug, they aren't really gone. In fact, the dirt is still there; it's just hidden. When we hide the things that are troubling us, they end up making everything else feel a bit bumpy.

As a mom, you may not always feel like it's easy to make a clean sweep with each new day. Maybe a disagreement with one of the kids is still on your mind, or maybe an offhand remark about your parenting skills put you a little on edge. A lot of things can make it difficult for the dust to settle, and so the best thing to do is to hand yesterday to God and move on to today.

When you simply don't know what to do, put down the broom and spend time with your Creator. He'll help you have a clean heart and start again.

Create in me a pure heart, O God,
and renew a steadfast spirit within me.
Do not cast me from your presence
or take your Holy Spirit from me.
Restore to me the joy of your salvation
and grant me a willing spirit, to sustain me.
PSALM 51:10–12

Mom's Prayer

Lord, sometimes it seems easier to simply sweep something under the rug rather than deal with it directly. Help me know when I should try to clean up a mess from yesterday and when I should just bring it to you. Amen.

Mom's Counting Sheep

Do you ever find it difficult to sleep? You have so much on your mind that the stories just won't stop playing out in your head. There seems to be no off switch. When that happens, you probably try things like counting sheep or perhaps creating lists for the things that need to be done.

Those activities can be helpful, but maybe you'll settle down into a good healthy sleep simply by turning your worries over to God. Tell Him that since He's up all night anyway, you've decided to spend more time talking with Him. It's pretty likely that once you have a good conversation with your Lord, He'll bless you with sweet slumber. If you finish the conversation and you're still wide awake, you might turn your thoughts to counting the things that are really good in your life.

When life makes you feel like you're left to wander around in the pasture, don't look for the sheep; instead, simply relax and talk to the Shepherd. He sees you right where you are.

He will not let your foot slip—
he who watches over you will not slumber.

PSALM 121:3

Mom's Prayer

Lord, I often struggle with getting to sleep. Help me to listen to you in the nighttime hours when sleep is eluding me. Cause me to rest in you. Amen.

Mom's Pet Peeve

You may have noticed that when you've been clear with your children or other members of the family about the things that bother you, it almost feels like they pet your pet peeve on purpose. If you tell the kids it really bothers you to be late in the morning, getting ready for work or school, they seem to sleep later and later. If you tell your spouse you really don't like it when shoes are left in the living room, you'll find shoes all over the floor.

What is it about petting your pet peeves? Why don't they all understand the little things that bring you frustration and irritation?

Perhaps the issue you face is that what bothers you doesn't bother them, so they don't realize its importance. It might mean that you simply have to be clear about why you're making your requests. You may even address these issues with God. Share your pet peeves with Him. Then go a step farther and seek His voice in helping you understand how you might be doing a few things that He asked you not to do—His pet peeves, if you will. It might bring a smile to both of you.

O God, You know my foolishness;
And my sins are not hidden from You.

PSALM 69:5 NKJV

Mom's Prayer

Lord, help me to see those things that I do that might make you feel slightly peeved at me. Forgive me when I don't notice things that need to be corrected in my own life. Amen.

Call Your Mom

You probably have a general house rule that when someone is going to be late or when they're not going to be at the place you thought they were going to be, they need to call. Giving you a call is a matter of respect, and it also provides important information that keeps you from worrying.

If your children are all grown now, you probably still appreciate it when they give you a call to keep you up to date on what's going on in their lives. It's just one of the ways your hearts stay connected to each other.

The same thing is true for you and your relationship with God. God really likes it when you give Him a call. He loves to hear your voice, and He's always open to offering advice. No matter how old you are, there's never a time when He doesn't want to hear from you. It's good to give God a call many times a day.

The next time you think of calling your mom, or when your kids call you, also think about calling your Dad, your Father in heaven.

As for me, I will call upon God,
And the LORD shall save me.

PSALM 55:16 NKJV

Mom's Prayer

Lord, I do love to get calls from my kids. Help me to call more often on you to seek your guidance and your help, and simply to hear your voice. Amen.

Love Letters

Moms begin writing love letters to their children the moment they realize a baby will be born. Oh, they may not always write them in a journal or a baby book, but they write them on their heart. They spend countless hours imagining this new life and how they will do everything they can to give their baby a sense of worth and of being loved.

This same thing is true of God and you. God started His love letter to you even before you were a twinkle in His eye. He knew you'd come along one day and that He'd have a plan for your life and your salvation. He knew you would need guidance and direction, and so He started writing love letters. Many of His letters were captured for you in the Bible. To help you as much as possible, He even sent the Holy Spirit to influence you as you read His word. It brought Him great joy to do this for you.

Keep writing your love letters to the special people in your family, and keep reading God's love letter to you.

"I am with you always, even to the end of the age."

MATTHEW 28:20 NKJV

Mom's Prayer

Father, I thank you for writing your love letter to me. Thank you for your Son, Jesus, who brought that letter to life and who even now gives me grace and guidance. Amen.

Mom Steals Home

If you're a baseball fan, you've probably seen runners steal home base, edging their way across the playing field. The runner is hoping to get to home base before he can be tagged with the ball and cause an out for the team. Stealing home means he can add to the scoreboard and everyone will cheer. It's good to steal home.

Moms are always at the home base encouraging their kids to steal home at anytime. Moms watch out for everyone else's interests, making sure each person gets a fair chance at bat and that the games are fair. Moms run the bases if need be and protect their own little runners all the way from one base to the next until they get home again.

Moms create the joy and love that makes home base the best place to be. Because of all the things a mom does, most of the family can't wait to steal home.

Thank God for you and all you do to create homeruns for your family.

"Go back, each of you, to your mother's home. May the LORD show you kindness."

RUTH 1:8

Mom's Prayer

Father, help us all to stick together, watch out for each other, and enjoy every chance we get to be at home. Bless my children wherever they have to run today. Amen.

Mom's Magic Hug

Imagine yourself wrapped in a great big warm hug. You feel safe and content, and everything seems right with the world. That's the kind of hug God has for you and the kind that you offer your kids. Your hugs are simply magic. Your hugs make a difference to all that goes on in the day. There's no place that is quite as beautiful as Mom's embrace.

Some people say that a person needs at least twelve hugs a day to just survive. Imagine, twelve hugs! If you need twelve hugs to simply survive, what do you need to thrive? If you're a little short of your hug quotient today, take a little time and go collect hugs from the various members of your family. While you're at it, embrace each one with a blessing and a prayer. Offer them one of God's hugs through your arms so they can have an incredible day, totally loved and protected.

Your hugs are a little bit of magic. God's hugs are a little bit of heaven. May God's love bless your life today.

Dear friends, let us love one another, for love comes from God. Everyone who loves has been born of God and knows God.

1 JOHN 4:7

Mom's Prayer

Lord, thank you for giving us two arms to hug the people we love. There's nothing quite as comforting and loving as a big hug. Thank you for wrapping your arms around me even when I don't seem aware of it. I love knowing you're always close to me. Amen.

Mom's Very Inquisitive

Moms ask a lot of questions. Kids might say that they ask too many questions. Moms always want to know where you've been, what you're doing, and if you have any homework. They want to know why you said what you did or acted in a certain way. Moms are just so inquisitive.

The funny thing is that no matter how old you are, if you have a mom near you, she probably asks a lot of questions. If you're the mom, you're probably the one doing the asking. Questions are a good way to show that you care. When you ask your kids for details about what's going on with them, it lets them know that their lives matter to you. When you ask with a loving heart, it's always a positive form of communication.

From the time we're little children, we understand that when we want to learn something about the world, the best thing we can do is ask. In the same way, when you want to know more about God, you ask Him questions too. When you're not sure what questions to ask, just lean in and lean on Him. After all, inquiring minds just want to know things. No question about it, God wants you to ask Him anything at all.

Until now you have not asked for anything in my name. Ask and you will receive, so that your joy will be the fullest possible joy.

JOHN 16:24 NCV

Mom's Prayer

Lord, I'm certain that I ask more questions than my kids probably think are necessary. Help me to be sensitive to them so that I ask the right kinds of things with a loving heart. When I don't know quite what to ask, let me come to you for guidance. Amen.

Quiet, Mom Is Thinking!

Do you have little fantasies about spending a few quiet moments to yourself? You know, when everything is peaceful and you're having a steaming cup of your favorite beverage, looking out at a pastoral scene, and all is right with the world. You aren't responsible for anyone or anything at that very moment. You can just sit and relax in the presence of God and all that He created.

This fantasy moment was created just to remind you that it's okay to seek a little peace and quiet. It's okay to send the kids to play with friends or do homework while you spend a few quiet moments on your own. Relaxing is what gives you renewed energy.

Another way to spend quiet time is with God. Take a look at a favorite Scripture and pray your way through it. Read a devotional book and spend time renewing your spirit with the idea being presented or with the Scriptures you see there. Apply those principles to yourself. In just a few moments, you'll feel stronger and better equipped to handle the day.

"For the joy of the LORD is your strength."

NEHEMIAH 8:10

Mom's Prayer

Lord, I know that I need more thinking time, time to just spend with you and consider your Word and the things that you would have me know. Bless me with times to spend just with you. Amen.

Mom, Teacher and Tutor

Since you've been your children's teacher from the beginning, you know your children better than anyone else. You know what motivates them to learn, what keeps them from learning, and what's easy or difficult for them. You not only teach them about life and personal care and things of the Spirit, but you tutor them when the lessons are more difficult.

When you look at it that way, being a mom is a big deal. Being a mom means you are directly aligned with how your children think and act and participate in the world. You are and you aren't, that is!

The truth is that while your influence is powerful, it's also limited. You can only teach them certain things. You can only share your life perspective. At some point, they will go out into the world and take the God-given personalities they have, and their minds and hearts, and do what they were called to do. God gave them a unique spirit.

You will always be their first teacher, but the mastery of life comes from the gifts God has given them, and so He will guide them on their way as adults. Pray for your kids to listen to His voice as they grow in wisdom.

We continually ask God to fill you with the knowledge of his will through all the wisdom and understanding that the Spirit gives, so that you may live a life worthy of the Lord and please him in every way.

COLOSSIANS 1:9–10

Mom's Prayer

Lord, I thank you that my children are open to my ideas and the things that I would teach them. Bless their minds and hearts, and fill them with truth and knowledge of you. Amen.

In Mom's Eyes

In your mother's eyes, there is no one in the world who compares with you. She sees you for all that you are, and all that you can be. She looks beyond what is and helps you grow into what seems impossible. In your mother's eyes, you are indeed a gift from God.

Moms have a way of looking at their children through a positive lens that is not easily changed or distorted. No matter what anyone else might say, a mom will believe in her child with steadfast love and resolve. She will always seek the best, knowing full well her child is brilliant and kind.

A mother's eyes for her child may be a bit like God's eyes for you. When He looks at you, He sees what you can be and loves you into being it. He sees the light that is glowing from within you. He sees you choosing the path of love to brighten the lives of others.

When you think of the ways you perceive your children with such love, imagine too the ways that God sees you and invests His love in your life. Ask God to help you see your children through His eyes as well.

For God understands all hearts, and he sees you.

PROVERBS 24:12 NLT

Mom's Prayer

Lord, thank you for my children and the beautiful people that they are. They have achieved at life in so many ways, and so I give you thanks for creating them so well. Bless their lives in every way. Amen.

MAY 23

The Joy of Moms

As a mom, you may not actually sit down and make a list of the things about parenting that bring you joy. But if you could put together a recipe for a happy family or for what might make joy in a household, what do you think would be on the list?

Perhaps you would note all the special times your children have given you sweet surprises, like flowers from the neighbor's yard or a butterfly that they caught and put in a jar. Maybe you'd remember the first words they ever said or the first steps they took. No doubt those things filled you with joy.

Another measure of joy may be just in realizing what a good mother you are. After all, without any particular mom training, you've managed to help your kids grow up. Let that thought make you smile, and remember that you can also have joy in the Lord. In fact, the joy of the Lord is your strength. Thank God for all He does to give you the gift of joy.

The LORD is my strength and shield.
I trust him with all my heart.
He helps me, and my heart is filled with joy.

PSALM 28:7 NLT

Mom's Prayer

Lord, I do remember the little things my children have done or do to make me smile. Thank you for the ways families express love and bring joy to each other, and thank you for your great love too. Amen.

If It Weren't for Mom

Moms hold it all together! They manage this heroic feat not just for themselves but for everyone else in the family too. It can even be echoed throughout the house, "If it weren't for Mom…we'd be eating cereal for dinner, or we wouldn't get to school on time, or we wouldn't have clean clothes."

You're an amazing force to be reckoned with and everyone in the house knows life wouldn't work quite as well if you didn't do all that you do each day. Your family rejoices in that about you, and your Father in heaven does too. God sees what you do. It doesn't go unnoticed. He knows that He chose the right woman for your particular family for this time in history. He appreciates your work and your effort on behalf of His children.

Today, be willing to accept a little credit for being such an amazing mom and then give God the glory for giving you such an abundant life. It will do your heart good.

A thief comes to steal and kill and destroy, but I came to give life—life in all its fullness.

JOHN 10:10 NCV

Mom's Prayer

Lord, I appreciate how much you've blessed my life in every way, so believe me when I say I couldn't do it without you. If it weren't for you, Lord, I'd be lost. Thanks for loving me so much. Amen.

Wanted: Good Moms

If kids could post ads for moms, they would most likely ask for "good" moms. What "good" might mean to each of them would probably vary, but chances are they would want a mom who is a lot like you. They would want a mom who has a positive spirit and brings a smile with her early-morning hug. They would want a mom who listens to their concerns or plans and gives them ideas about what might work well. They would want a mom who invests her time and energy in simply being a loving person and who sees the best in them.

You're a good mom! It's not hard to imagine that your kids want you to be in their lives forever no matter what age they are.

God may not have given all moms the same skill sets, but He gave them the common ingredients focused on love. You love because God first loved you and gave Himself for you. Good moms everywhere seek God's help in raising their children. Draw near to Him anytime you need a little more advice on how to be a great mom.

We love because God first loved us.

1 JOHN 4:19 NCV

Mom's Prayer

Lord, you've given me good kids, so that makes it easy to be a good mom. I thank you for them with all of my heart. Amen.

Another "Momism"

Moms have been dispensing little tidbits of wisdom since the beginning of time. Your grandmother probably sat on her front porch and predicted the weather by the color of the sky or talked about some idea that wouldn't amount to a hill of beans. She probably said it was so dirty behind her kids' ears that she could plant potatoes. Your mom may have also told you there was no use crying over spilt milk or that you had to eat your beets because there were starving children all over the world who wished they had those beets to eat.

Whatever they were, your mom was fond of pet phrases. These phrases usually had a ring of truth to them, and that's part of the reason they seem to move from one generation to the next.

Think about what you say to your kids. Are there any "momisms" sneaking into your conversations? It's okay if there are, because those ideas have a familiar ring that makes everyone feel connected, one generation to the next.

Thank God today for all the wonderful women who've added a bit of color and delight to your life through their special ways of saying just the right thing.

My child, listen to your father's teaching
and do not forget your mother's advice.
Their teaching will be like flowers in your hair
or a necklace around your neck.

PROVERBS 1:8–9 NCV

Mom's Prayer

Lord, my mother shared a lot of folk wisdom. Bless those phrases that connect my heart to her and that will connect my own children to me. Amen.

Neighborhood Mom

Some women don't become moms in the traditional sense. They don't have their own children, but somehow they end up in a "mom" role with many children in their neighborhood. They become the mom with a kind heart and good advice, who listens with patience and offers gentle solutions. They're the moms who bake cookies and keep the porch light on for kids who play tag in their yard.

Today, let's honor all the moms out there who don't have their own children, but who help support the healthy growth and lives of many kids simply by being available to them and offering a sweet spirit of love. The gifts they bring to kids last a lifetime.

Think of women you know who are like a mom to others, and bless them with your prayers. Thank God that in His wisdom He planted a few "moms" in neighborhoods so kids could benefit from their kindness. Maybe you're a mom like that.

And be kind to one another, tenderhearted, forgiving one another, even as God in Christ forgave you.

EPHESIANS 4:32 NKJV

Mom's Prayer

Lord, please bless the women who take on the mothering role simply because they want to serve others with kindness and love. Amen.

Heartstrings

If your heart were a kind of tapestry, it would probably have bright yellow stars for the brilliant moments in your life, pink flowers for the sweet events that brought you great joy, and blue violets sprinkled about to represent the moments when everything seemed more quiet and uncertain. Your tapestry would have texture created by laughter and tears through the years and probably a few very special hearts tied with strings. You're tied to your children by heartstrings, and nothing on earth can break those connections.

A tapestry is a beautiful thing, and yours is being woven together by your Master, the One who created every aspect of you and the life you now live. He's given you a wealth of sentimental heartstrings that are graciously tied to others and mercifully tied to Him. Anytime you need Him, you can just tug at the string and He'll be right there.

Thank God for creating your personal tapestry with such love.

You made all the delicate, inner parts of my body
and knit me together in my mother's womb.
Thank you for making me so wonderfully complex!
Your workmanship is marvelous—how well I know it.

PSALM 139:13–14 NLT

Mom's Prayer

Lord, you have blessed me with so many beautiful life experiences.
Please continue to work with me, shaping my heart so that with
each gentle tug from you, I feel our connection. Amen.

Mom's Little Lullaby

Remember when you used to sing softly to your precious babies as they nodded their little heads and drifted off to sleep? It was one of the sweetest moments of the day and one that gave you a few minutes of much-needed rest yourself.

You may be past the stage when someone will sing you a little song to help you go to sleep, although our ancient ancestors engaged flute players to help them quiet down and slip off to dreamland. You deserve a peaceful night's sleep too.

As you go about the day, see if you can anticipate the soft music that will allow you to let go of the stress of the day, and the warm blankets that will cradle you as you slumber. Imagine your heavenly Father looking at you, holding you close, humming a gentle song to ease your rest. Or, try humming your praise to God, thanking Him for all the precious moments in your life and in particular those that bring you perfect peace in Him.

And each morning and evening they stood before the Lord
to sing songs of thanks and praise to him.

1 CHRONICLES 23:30 NLT

Mom's Prayer

Lord, be with me as I go to sleep, and help me to see myself simply nodding off, listening to your gentle voice and resting in your loving arms. Amen.

Mom's a Good Sport

Moms are really good sports. They step in to pitch the baseball when the neighborhood kids get together. They bake cookies for the 5K runners when they come back from crossing the finish line exhausted and victorious. They even sleep in a tent sometimes just to give kids the experience of the great outdoors. Yes, moms are really good sports.

You're a good sport because you want your kids to enjoy their lives and have the chance to try things that you may have never gotten to do. You want them to understand what it means to be a team player and what healthy competition looks like. You're a good sport because you've been in training most of your life for the job at hand.

The good news is that God is a good sport too. God gives you lots of chances to get off the bench and get into the game. He wants you to feel free to try new things and to discover what you're really good at in the process. Today, your life may not literally revolve around sports, but most situations require you to be a good sport anyway. Let God know you're so glad to have a chance to keep playing.

All the believers devoted themselves to the apostles' teaching, and to fellowship, and to sharing in meals (including the Lord's Supper), and to prayer.

ACTS 2:42 NLT

Mom's Prayer

Father, I try to be a good sport and not back down when it comes to participating with my kids in things they enjoy. Help me to do all I can to nurture their interests and to protect them as they grow. Amen.

Stand by Your Mom

Moms have to make a lot of decisions that aren't always easy for kids to understand. Even when a mom can't explain her choice, she's doing her best to use good judgment. Kids figure out that Mom is a pretty smart woman, and they look to her to set the example and guide their steps. Kids stand beside their mom.

Now that you're a mom, your kids trust your judgment and stand beside you. They may not always agree with your choices and they may overstep the boundaries, but in truth they want to do what you feel is best.

You may have a similar feeling about God. You may not always understand what He wants from you or why His answers aren't exactly what you hoped for, but you trust Him and you know that if you stand beside Him, things will work out for the best.

Seek God's help with any stand you have to take and walk with Him each day, and He'll guide your choices.

So I will walk with the LORD in the land of the living.

PSALM 116:9 NCV

Mom's Prayer

Lord, please help us to stand together in the decisions we make in our house, supporting each other in love. Amen.

June

Second Chances

We're grateful anytime we get a second chance. We may have fallen flat on our face the first time we tried something, or for some undefined reason, we just weren't able to make a good first impression.

Our kids are also glad when we give them another chance to do something better than they did it the first time. Whether we encourage them to do a section of their homework over again or whether they want us to forgive them for breaking one of the house rules, they want another chance.

When you think about it, human beings are always doing that to God. We're always seeking His face knowing we need a do-over because we didn't do something the way we should have and we recognize we can do a lot better. We want mercy and grace to prevail when we need another chance.

Today, remind yourself that you live each day in amazing mercy and grace, and that is why you can offer the same grace to those around you.

May the LORD show you his kindness
and have mercy on you.

NUMBERS 6:25 NCV

Mom's Prayer

Lord, I know that I often need second (and third and fourth!) chances, and each time I come back to you, you forgive me again. Help me to give another chance to everyone who needs that from me as well. Amen.

Mom's Top Ten Gratitude List

If you could make a list of the top ten things you are especially grateful for as a mom, perhaps you would note some of these:

Number 10: You're grateful to have noisy, happy kids.

Number 9: You're grateful that you have a good home.

Number 8: You're grateful for the wisdom you get from other moms.

Number 7: You're grateful for good health.

Number 6: You're grateful for a sense of humor.

Number 5: You're grateful for friends who sustain you when things are too crazy.

Number 4: You're grateful for bedtime stories and hugs.

Number 3: You're grateful for school and school activities.

Number 2: You're grateful to God for His strength and blessing.

Number 1: You're grateful to be such a loved mom.

No matter what your top ten looks like, the number one reason you love being a mom is because your family loves you right back. Give God the thanks and praise for the love you all share today.

I lavish unfailing love to a thousand generations.

EXODUS 34:7 NLT

Mom's Prayer

Lord, I love being a mom. Even on days when I'm a little tired or restless, I know that there's nothing more important for me than to be a good mom to my children. They are my number one joy. Amen.

Spiritual Refreshment

On a hot summer day, there's nothing quite as lovely as a refreshing glass of iced tea or sweet lemonade. It appeals to your senses and satisfies your thirst. What a delightful thing that is!

Sometimes your spirit needs a little special nourishment as well. It craves something that will tickle the senses and enrich the taste buds. It longs for a satisfying and refreshing blend of something that is simply divine. When your spirit is calling for an infusion of joy mixed with a hint of praise and celebration, give in to the moment and give God the glory! Stop everything and simply praise God. He will refresh your heart and mind like nothing else can do.

God wants to give you a fresh taste of His love and goodness every day. He longs to inspire your days with His peace and fullness. Look to Him when you need some spiritual refreshment.

When doubts filled my mind,
your comfort gave me renewed hope and cheer.

PSALM 94:19 NLT

Mom's Prayer

Lord, you seem to know when I'm running on empty and when I need a little more time with you. Help me to draw closer to you to always keep my spirits from sagging. Amen.

Mom's Not Feeling Well

Moms get puny sometimes, drained of all their energy. They keep everything and everyone else running smoothly, and then they finally fall over in a heap and their batteries are shot. They have no more go power.

When you're having one of those days, it's not easy to be the perfect mom. You have to call for a time-out and get your family to fend for themselves. You may think it isn't possible for the household to actually run well without you. You may think that taking a nap or resting is just not something you can do. The thing is you need to rest. You need to set yourself as a priority, even mother yourself. Do for yourself all those things you would do for the other members of your family.

Take a break when you're not feeling well. Rest and relax in the care and keeping of God and the people who love you. It will do your body good.

But those who hope in the LORD
will renew their strength.

ISAIAH 40:31

Mom's Prayer

Lord, thank you for taking care of my family when I'm not feeling up to par. I don't like being sick, and so it's hard for me to give in to those times and simply rest. Amen.

Blue-Ribbon Mom

Country fairs and craft markets often give blue ribbons to the winners of contests. Sometimes the ribbon is for having the prize rooster or for the best blueberry pie. It's a simple gesture but one that brings a real sense of pride to those who receive the ribbons.

You may not have received your official mom blue ribbon yet, but it goes without saying that if there was a contest this very day, you would win. Your kids would vote for you without fail.

How did you get to be a blue-ribbon mom? Well, that's easy. You raised your kids with love and kindness and helped them learn what it means to be part of a family and a community.

Today, no matter how old your kids are, think about what it means to get the blue ribbon for being a great mom. No doubt, there's one hanging in your house somewhere already.

Give God a big blue-ribbon thank-you for all He does to help you each and every day.

I press on toward the goal to win the prize for which God has called me heavenward in Christ Jesus.

PHILIPPIANS 3:14

Mom's Prayer

Lord, I'm not sure I would win a blue ribbon for my pies or for raising a great rooster, but I can raise blue-ribbon kids. Thank you for giving me the strength and inspiration to do a good job. Amen.

Mom Is So Strong

You're a master at rearranging all the boxes in the attic to make room for more boxes to be stored, and you're probably pretty impressed with being able to move all that stuff around. After all, it's clumsy and heavy. You also might amaze yourself with how many bags of groceries you can successfully carry from the car into the house in one trip. Fortunately, you're a strong woman.

But you're strong in a lot of ways, and few of them have anything to do with powerlifting. They all have to do with the strength God gives you. You're a strong woman in His sight because you love His Son, Jesus. You serve Him with honor, and you do all you can to make His name great to those around you.

As you look at all that needs to be lifted and carried and moved about in your life today, remember that while it's good to be strong, it's best to be strong in the Lord.

The LORD is my strength and my shield;
My heart trusted in Him, and I am helped.

PSALM 28:7 NKJV

Mom's Prayer

Lord, I thank you for giving me physical strength to do the things I must do. I also thank you for the strength you give me, through your Spirit, to rise with joy each day and answer your call. Amen.

Mom Unabridged

Can you imagine what the unabridged book of your life might look like? It would have every detail, every thought, and every version of you recorded for all posterity.

The unabridged version of you would recall stories you long ago put behind you and even hoped were gone. Fortunately, there's only an abridged version of you. The best version of you is the one that God keeps in His record room. It's the one that shows grace and forgiveness given to you by Jesus. It shows some gaps where misdeeds have been blotted out and better actions have been recorded.

The abridged version of your life tells of the wonderful woman you are. Your path may not have always been smooth, but the result is awesome. Thank God for removing any stains that would ever appear on your soul and for giving you a beautiful book that speaks so well of who you really are.

"I, even I, am He who blots out your transgressions for My own sake; And I will not remember your sins."

ISAIAH 43:25 NKJV

Mom's Prayer

Lord, I know I have a few blotches on my book of life, and so I thank you that you're the only One who knows every one of those details. Be with me and help me to do the things that cause you to smile. Amen.

Mom Hopes

Hope takes shape in a mom from the moment she knows a new life is forming in her womb. There's a sense of wonder and anticipation that is unequaled in any other life experience. Moms hope to be good moms. They hope the world will treat their children well.

God is with you every step of the way and guards your hopes and dreams. He already knows the story of your child and how you will strive to be a good mother. He chose you from the beginning to be the mother of one of His precious beings.

You have hoped for many things for and about your children since you became a mom. Your hopes may not always come to fruition, but keep on striving to be the person who plants the seeds of hope and possibility. You and God together make all the difference.

But the LORD looks after those who fear him, those who put their hope in his love.

PSALM 33:18 NCV

Mom's Prayer

Lord, in you I put my hope for the welfare of my children. I know that you're watching over us all the time, and I'm grateful for your guiding hand. Thank you for your love. You are the hope of our lives. Amen.

Mom Mixes and Fixes

As a mom, you learn to be very creative. You do your fair share of fixing little mechanical things that break down. You may have learned to fix more things than you ever dreamed you could, even changing your own flat tire.

One way or another, you manage to fix little problems, offer the right kind of encouragement, give the best word of wisdom, and do it all with a smile and a hug. You're great at fixing things.

You're also good at mixing things. You might mix up a cake just to please the family, or mix up a special frozen fruit smoothie. You can mix and fix and balance a lot of things because you have a wise heart and strong faith.

Today as you fix the little problems that arise, thank God for fixing His gaze on you and taking care of those big problems. Mix your joy with some songs of praise and do a happy dance. God is with you always.

The Lord helps those who have been defeated
and takes care of those who are in trouble.

PSALM 145:14 NCV

Mom's Prayer

Lord, I'm so relieved to know that you're walking with me all the time. There are so many things that happen every day that take far more than the kind of fixing and mixing I can do by myself. Amen.

Mom's Example

You're the first example your kids have for how to treat others. You're the guide to relationships and making friends. You're the one who demonstrates kindness, love, and patience. It's great to be that kind of guide, at least sometimes.

But what do you do when you need an example to follow? You may not have had the best parents, or you may have missed the workshop on how to raise amazing kids. But whatever you feel you might have missed in your training to be a mom isn't lost. It's still possible to pick up a refresher course or actually learn some new things.

You learn each time you reach out for advice or seek someone else's method for dealing with an issue that's new to you. You can also look to Jesus and ask Him for guidance and direction. Follow His example and you'll always be on solid ground.

Today, be an example of a woman who knows right where to go when difficult situations arise. Go right to Jesus, the One you follow each day.

Jesus said to him, "Follow me," and he stood up and followed Jesus.

MARK 2:14 NCV

Mom's Prayer

Lord, please help me when I fail to be a good example for my children. Inspire my decisions when I'm faced with difficulty. Please be my example and help me learn from you with an open and willing heart. Amen.

Mom Is Wrong Sometimes

Yipes! You're not used to having to admit to being wrong. You're not used to it because you're pretty careful about the things you do. As a mom, you do your best to stay the course through difficulties and to follow your heart and trust your intuition. You're good at those things, but now and then you still discover that you've made a mess of things. What do you do?

If your first response is one of regret, then that regret needs to go directly to your prayer chair and seek God's face. He is the divine forgiver, and He will help you cleanse the mistake with grace and mercy. From there, He'll also guide you through the steps to remedy the situation.

Everyone is wrong sometimes. Moms are vulnerable, and life can be overwhelming. When or if that ever happens to you, seek God's help as quickly as possible. It's a new day. Forgive yourself, let God forgive you, and move on!

"Therefore, my friends, I want you to know that through Jesus the forgiveness of sins is proclaimed to you."

ACTS 13:38

Mom's Prayer

Lord, I hate to admit when I'm wrong. It's hard to acknowledge that I can be foolish sometimes. Give me a right spirit and bless my foolish heart to make it wise again. Amen.

Mom Is Super!

You're about to meet a fascinating woman. She's really amazing. She can manage a household, create gourmet delights, attend the parent meetings at school, bake those brownies, and still have time to read a good book all in the same day. She can hold down a full-time job, run a couple miles each morning, get the laundry done before work, and keep a smile on her face.

Who is this super woman? She's you! You're an amazing woman, no matter how many of the things you do that are listed in this little fantasy story. You have a real story and a real commitment to your family that makes you a super woman and a super mom.

If you ever get weary, feel the need for a little rest, or want an extra dose of positive energy to renew your spirit, stop and put away your Super Mom cape, then sit with your super Father in heaven. He'll always fortify your soul and give you super strength—His strength—to keep going. He's so proud of you.

I can do all things through Christ who strengthens me.

PHILIPPIANS 4:13 NKJV

Mom's Prayer

Lord, thank you that I don't have to try to be Super Mom all the time. Being a mom is a pretty exhausting job as it is, and so I gladly come to you to renew my strength and my energy to get things accomplished. Amen.

Good, Better, Best Mom

Sometimes moms feel the pinch from who they imagine to be the "better" moms. These are the moms who never miss a soccer game, keep gourmet meals flowing from the kitchen, and plan the party of the year for their child's birthday. They just don't miss a thing when it comes to being awesome.

But the "best" moms aren't in a competition with each other. They simply have two goals in mind. They want to please God with the way they raise their children, and they want to help their children be strong, loving, and contributing members of society as they grow up. The best moms leave a lot of things in God's hands because they're prayer warriors and they know they do best with God's help.

Today, know that you're a good mom, and in fact, you're the best mom your children could ever have. The only thing that could possibly make you a better mom is having more time for prayer.

Hear my prayer, O LORD,
Give ear to my supplications!
In Your faithfulness answer me,
And in Your righteousness.

PSALM 143:1 NKJV

Mom's Prayer

Lord, please bless my family today. Grant me wisdom in all the ways that I work to be a good mom, and let me always make you proud of the things I do. Amen.

Getting to Know Mom

One of the biggest challenges of any relationship is knowing the heart and mind of another person. How do we truly get to know each other, or, for that matter, how do we get to know God?

God's request to you is expressed in a desire that you would know Him. He says in the Psalms, "Be still and know that I am God." Perhaps one thing to get from that message is that you need to spend quiet time with God if you want to know Him better. You may also need to spend more "getting to know you" time with your kids if you want to know more about them and give them a chance to know you.

Reflect on what it means to make more of an effort to know your kids, your friends, or even God in a better way. All your relationships may benefit from that reflection.

Be still, and know that I am God;
I will be exalted among the nations,
I will be exalted in the earth!

PSALM 46:10 NKJV

Mom's Prayer

Lord, I'm not very good at spending quiet time with you. I seem to always be so busy running from one thing to the next. Help me try harder to spend more time with you and to also find ways to spend more focused time with my children. Amen.

Coffee with Mom

You may enjoy having coffee or your favorite beverage as you talk with your mom. If your kids are older, you may also find that it's nice to go out for coffee and a chat with them. In the daily grind, we don't seek the chances to talk one to one with the people who mean the most to us. We send a quick e-mail or a text, or have a cell phone chat as we run out the door. We don't take time to be together face to face.

As you think of your mom today, or of your kids who might enjoy spending a little coffee chat time with you, make a space on your calendar so you can create the opportunity. Give yourself a chance to laugh out loud with the people you love most in the world.

Once you've done that, make another note; pencil in some time to have a coffee chat with God too. He'll be happy to hear more about what's brewing in your life.

Tell these people to come to me.
Let them talk about these things together.

ISAIAH 45:21 NCV

Mom's Prayer

Lord, please help me to set up face-to-face time with my mom and with my kids. Bless our laughter and sharing, and help us to build some new memories over a little cup of coffee. Help me to set up more time with you too. Amen.

Mom's a Bit like Grandma

It'll surprise you, but it will happen. In some way, a part of your personality or your style will remind you of your mother. About the time you realize it, the kids may even tell you that you've become a bit like Grandma.

Chances are that what your kids see is that you reflect the very best things about your mom. They see your smile and your energy for life. They see your willingness to help others or to bake cookies for the neighbors. They see that kindness is something that goes from one generation to the next in your family, and they like to see that.

As you think about those aspects of your personality, just smile and say a little prayer of gratitude. Thank God that the very best things about you as a mom are some of the best things that your kids see in Grandma too.

I remember your true faith. That faith first lived in your grandmother Lois and in your mother Eunice, and I know you now have that same faith.

2 TIMOTHY 1:5 NCV

Mom's Prayer

Lord, thank you for giving me a good mom and for letting me be a reflection of her. Help me to honor her and you in all that I do today. Amen.

Mom Is Full of Surprises

Wherever you go, people find reasons to smile. Your energy and enthusiasm are hard to match, and you're not predictable. Nobody knows what you'll think of next because you're always full of surprises. You have the kind of heart that invites people into your inner circle and makes them feel glad to have met you.

You are the same way with your kids. You find little ways to treat them to special things that they never expected. Sometimes it's easy things like making fresh pizza for dinner or calling out for delivery. Other times, it's your charming way of being able to help them chase the blues away.

God gave you some incredible gifts that are making your life as a mom more fun and exciting. He blessed you with a heart that cares about everyone around you. Give God a heartfelt prayer of praise and gratitude today.

May the LORD show you his kindness
and have mercy on you.

NUMBERS 6:25 NCV

Mom's Prayer

Lord, I'm blessed with good friends and with loving children.
I'm blessed with a sense of joy that permeates everything I do.
I am truly grateful. Amen.

Mom Makes Things Happen

Moms are go-getters. They don't let any grass grow under their feet as they work their way through the endless lists of things to do. They know what has to be done, and they make it happen. Sometimes it's best to just stay out of the way.

You've probably had days when people just stepped aside to let you through. You had things to accomplish, and nothing was going to prevent you from getting them done. Your attitude, your heart, and your mind were poised on taking care of the business at hand.

When you think about it, you have all the energy and focus that God needs His people to have to get His work done in the world. Is there anything that you might do for Him with equal enthusiasm and joy?

Seek His direction in your prayers today and get it done!

The LORD your God has blessed you in all the work of your hands.

DEUTERONOMY 2:7

Mom's Prayer

Lord, I ask you to help me do more for you and for others. Give me the same spirit and desire to see your work accomplished as I have for the work I do for myself. Amen.

Mom Makes the Best Pancakes

There's nothing like walking into the kitchen to the fresh and unmistakable aroma of pancakes and warm maple syrup. It's a treat, and when you're a kid you can't have pancakes too often. Chances are your mom made the best pancakes ever.

A beautiful part of pancake making is that you can also add intriguing and tasty things like chocolate chips, blueberries, or cinnamon. You can pile pancakes high with syrup, whipped cream, or anything else your imagination might put together. Yes, pancakes must certainly be the food of angels.

It's fun to consider the simple things that make life feel warm and cheery. God knows us so well that He made sure we were treated to those tasty delights that would make us smile. He wants us to enjoy the little things and share them with each other. Moms like you know how to make little things seem like heavenly things.

Take delight in the LORD,
and he will give you the desires of your heart.

PSALM 37:4

Mom's Prayer

Lord, we love the fresh and homey things that make the whole day more wonderful. Bless all the moms who delight their children in simple ways. Amen.

Mom's Favorite Kid

Sometimes kids think they're in a competition. Oh, it's not the competitive spirit they might have with their peers to see who can do the best on the soccer team or who can be the team captain. It's the competition for Mom's love and favor. Some kids strive to be Mom's favorite.

Moms love all their kids and don't intend for them to compete for attention or affection. But it's interesting to note that some of Jesus' followers had the same struggle. Two brothers who followed Jesus wanted to know if they could sit on either side of Him in the kingdom of heaven.

Though they were following Jesus as part of a group, they wanted to compete for the chance to be closest to Him in heaven. Jesus told them only His Father knew for whom those spaces were prepared. The good news is that we don't have to compete for God's love. Our ticket into heaven was signed at the cross. May that love bring you peace all your life.

They said to Him, "Grant us that we may sit, one on Your right hand and the other on Your left, in Your glory."

MARK 10:37 NKJV

Mom's Prayer

Lord, I don't want my kids to think they compete for my love. Help me to adore them all so much that they never have to question the relationship we share. Amen.

Mom Is Prepared

As a mom, you're on the alert for the unexpected, the things that come up and need to be dealt with in a hurry. It's important to be prepared. You never know when a tot is going to throw a toy in the toilet bowl to watch it swim or when a teenager is going to have a fender bender coming home from school. You're continually alerted to the possibilities so you can act fast.

It's good to be prepared for emergencies, and it's good to be prepared for living fully and well. You're alerted to God's plans and desires for you by reading His Word and spending quiet time with Him.

Today, seek God's guidance on what else you need to do to be truly prepared for the days ahead. Then embrace all that He has for you and give Him thanks and praise.

"Prepare yourself and be ready."

EZEKIEL 38:7 NKJV

Mom's Prayer

Lord, I may not be as prepared as a Girl Scout, but I'm certainly trying to be ready for whatever might come my way during the day. Please watch over the people I love and help us to rely on you. Amen.

Mom Tells Good Stories

Moms love to tell stories. Raising kids gives them lots of opportunities to share events and situations that could actually make a good book. Sometimes they share tales of laughter and those funny things that kids say, and other times they share moments of success, when they feel so proud of something their child has done. They may even share stories of concern when they hope for a friend's feedback to guide their thinking.

It's helpful to know that God knows all the stories you have to share too. When He listens to your stories, He feels your joy and your pain. He laughs with you and cries with you, and He does all He can to sustain your heart and mind. He's always there for you when you need Him, and He invites you to tell Him the stories that most affect your life and your children anytime at all.

He told many stories in the form of parables, such as this one: "Listen! A farmer went out to plant some seeds."

MATTHEW 13:3 NLT

Mom's Prayer

Lord, I love to share the stories of the amazing things my kids do. Sometimes it gives me courage for the days ahead. When my stories are full of concern, I love to share them with you. Amen.

Mom Jogs

Jogging is a great outlet for moms these days. They can walk part of the way or run as much as they can and have a little time to themselves. It helps to keep their bodies in shape and their minds alert. Whatever form of exercise works best for you, it's helpful to stay active in ways that give you time for yourself and offer opportunities for reflection and prayer.

It might be a good option for you to run a little, walk a little, and say a few prayers as you go. Jogging time could also be your Jesus time. It could be your chance to think about the things that concern you or the situations in your life that feel a bit shaky. Whether you can go a mile or five miles, see if it helps you to offer up some prayers as you work out. It will do your body good, and it will do great things for your spirit.

You can be sure God will be running alongside you wherever you are.

Always be joyful. Never stop praying. Be thankful in all circumstances, for this is God's will for you who belong to Christ Jesus.

1 THESSALONIANS 5:16–18 NLT

Mom's Prayer

When I get out to walk or jog, I ask you to go with me and help me to become healthier in every way. Bless my efforts to do the things that are good for me to do. Amen.

Mom Blogs

Blogs are becoming a normal part of our culture, and a lot of moms share their parenting joys and frustrations through the Internet. They have a great resource and a great network for sharing problems and getting ideas about how to have a better experience as a mom.

You may not blog yourself, but it could be worth your time to check out some of the blogs of women who are also trying to be good moms. They can help you get a new perspective, offer some ideas for dealing with particular issues, or even suggest a prayer that will help you through the day.

Blogging is all about sharing ideas and helping others to do things better. See what you can find that might inspire your heart today.

Get wisdom; develop good judgment.
Don't forget my words or turn away from them.

PROVERBS 4:5 NLT

Mom's Prayer

Lord, I don't know if I'm a blogger, but I can certainly appreciate the efforts of other moms who are. Sometimes those stories help me feel encouraged. Thanks for supporting my parenting efforts every day. Amen.

Mom Likes People

It stands to reason that most moms are interested in people. After all, they have to guide their children to get along in the world with all kinds of people. The more a mom respects and enjoys others, the more her children learn to model that behavior.

More importantly, though, is that God commanded us to love one another and to love our neighbors as ourselves. We have to like people and do our best to live in peace with them. We have to reach out when others are in need, and offer compassion and sympathy when a crisis looms.

You're a "people" person. That means you offer to pray when others need help, lend a hand when you can, or simply listen with a loving heart. When you do those things, God is pleased and honors your work and your willingness to love in ways that give you a full and abundant life.

I have come that they may have life, and have it to the full.

JOHN 10:10

Mom's Prayer

Lord, thank you for giving me a sense of compassion and genuine interest for other people. Help me to reach out wherever I'm needed with love. Amen.

Mom A to Z

If we chose words for moms, walking through the alphabet, we'd probably go from "awesome" and "blessed" to "zany," and we'd be able to see how Mom is all those things. Moms like you are the people who define day-to-day living, and the things you do make a huge difference to your household.

Some days you might not think you have the energy, wisdom, or strength to be the alphabet mom, but the truth is that being plugged into the source of your strength all the time makes it possible.

You're connected to a lifeline that will never be put on hold or snapped in two. God is ready any moment of the day to pick you up and restart you on the path to all that is awesome and blessed. Give God thanks and praise today for all He does to keep you moving in the best direction.

Unfailing love surrounds those who trust the Lord.

PSALM 32:10 NLT

Mom's Prayer

Lord, I can't always take on the tasks that might get me from "awesome" to "zany" on any chart, but I know with you I can do all things. Help me with the impossible things according to your will and purpose. Amen.

Mom's Aspirations

Moms aspire toward many forms of achievement. They want to raise happy and healthy children. They want to enjoy positive relationships with their spouse and their friends. They also want to achieve personal goals that they set long before they became moms. Moms are multidimensional, and God knows every side of their personality.

If you wonder whether God remembers that you had plans long before you became a mom, such as plans to finish a college degree, learn a new skill, or even spend more time reading your Bible, just ask Him. Seek His help to getting the time and opportunity to work toward your personal dreams and goals. After all, you're more than a mom. You're a woman designed to live a full life.

Seek God's help with any of the aspirations you have put on the back burner. It may just be time to heat some of them up.

The Lord sees the good people
and listens to their prayers.

1 PETER 3:12 NCV

Mom's Prayer

Lord, I have dreams, but I try not to think about them. When my children were born, I thought I had to leave most of those things behind. Help me know what dreams to still pursue and when the time will be right to go after them. Amen.

Mom Smells Trouble

Did you ever notice that when you come across a deer standing near the side of a road, its ears go straight up? It's listening for trouble. It knows when something just isn't right. The same thing happens with rabbits and other animals.

Moms are like that too. They can sense trouble even before it hits. They have all their senses poised to protect their children and keep guard on all that happens. And when good moms smell trouble, they know what to do. They move immediately to prayer.

You may be sensing some difficulty in your own family today. If so, stop what you're doing and step out of the clearing. Get closer to God and speak to Him of the things that are weighing on your heart. He'll be there for you, ready to listen and to offer guidance.

What do you want? Shall I come to you with a rod, or in love and a spirit of gentleness?

1 CORINTHIANS 4:21 NKJV

Mom's Prayer

Lord, thank you for keeping me alert to the bumps in the road that can slow things down or stop them entirely. I pray for your guidance in all things. Amen.

Summertime Mom

June is the month when many kids heave a sigh of relief that school is finally out. It's also the month when moms heave a sigh because school is finally out. Now the kids are home every day, and within minutes of facing the slower summertime pace, they will be bored.

If you still have kids at home in the summertime, you may need a little extra refreshment time for yourself. It may be harder to find moments of quiet when you can sip a little lemonade and watch the garden grow. Be more intentional about finding moments to renew your spirits.

The joy of being God's child is that His schedule doesn't change with the seasons. He's available to you anytime of the year, so pull up a lawn chair for Him anytime you're a wee bit frazzled.

Anyone who is having troubles should pray. Anyone who is happy should sing praises.

JAMES 5:13 NCV

Mom's Prayer

Lord, thank you for giving the kids a break in the summertime. Help me to create the time and energy needed for them to have a good summer with me and for me to have a good summer with you. Amen.

The Mom Beatitudes

Blessed are the moms who understand the need for kids to laugh and play, for they shall be light hearted.

Blessed are the moms who create a chore contract so that kids know exactly what home chores are to be done and what the consequences are if they are not, for they shall be less busy.

Blessed are the moms who create afternoons at the park and take along a picnic basket, for they shall be filled with tasty treats.

Blessed are you for making every day special, for you shall be known as a woman of great joy.

God blesses those who work for peace,
for they will be called the children of God.

MATTHEW 5:9 NLT

Mom's Prayer

Lord, thank you for blessing my life and my children with your grace and mercy. Bless all that we do over the summer months to create joy and love and to grow closer to you. Amen.

July

Mom Never Gives Up

Moms love their kids past the scraped knees and the bruised elbows. They walk with them into the classrooms of life and make sure they learn the important things that will sustain them as adults. They allow their kids room to grow and strive to give them wings to fly, and at the same time, they impart confidence to do things themselves. Moms never give up on their kids.

No matter what the circumstances might be, you believe in your kids. You believe in their dreams and in their abilities. You believe in their good hearts and in their efforts to achieve in the world. When something happens that causes a delay in their progress, you press on. You encourage them to press on as well.

You're an amazing influence on your kids, and your faith in them does wonders. God has that same kind of faith in you. Even when you fall and scrape your knees, He picks you up again. He watches each step you take to boldly try again, because God never gives up on you.

He will also keep you firm to the end, so that you will be blameless on the day of our Lord Jesus Christ. God is faithful, who has called you into fellowship with his Son, Jesus Christ our Lord.

1 CORINTHIANS 1:8–9

Mom's Prayer

Lord, thank you for believing in me. It makes all the difference as I strive to encourage my own children and stay strong in my faith. Amen.

Why Won't Mom Give In?

By now you've learned some secrets about when to give in to the demands of the kids (or even of the day) and when to hold out for the way you want things to go. It's an art form really, and you've become good at "giving in" on your terms.

Kids can see the struggle to get Mom to change her mind as a bit exasperating. They want Mom to do what they want Mom to do—right now! They don't want to wait for anything.

The truth is we're all like that. We all have that same motivation when we present the things we really want to God. We want God to give in the first time we suggest an alternative to what's going on in our lives. We want God to take our side on things and just do what we ask. We want that, or so we think, but we also know that what we want may not be the best thing for us in the long run. The kids may want to eat dessert before dinner, but generally they also recognize that doing so is not really good for them.

Yes, there are times when you hope God will answer your immediate needs as you suggest, but seeking His will is the best answer for anything you need anytime at all.

Instead of worrying, pray. Let petitions and praises shape your worries into prayers, letting God know your concerns. Before you know it, a sense of God's wholeness, everything coming together for good, will come and settle you down.

PHILIPPIANS 4:6–7 MSG

Mom's Prayer

Lord, I know that the kids often hope I'll give in to what they want, just like I secretly hope you'll give in to what I want. Help me to seek your will in each area of my life and offer you thanks and praise. Amen.

A One-in-a-Million Mom

You're a unique woman and a one-in-a-million mom! Why? Your kids could probably give a lot of reasons, but some of the reasons are likely to follow these lines.

You have a style that your kids have come to know and appreciate. They like knowing that you don't easily get angry and that you laugh spontaneously. They like knowing that you'll offer them your opinion on everything from what to wear to what goes on in the world today. They like knowing they can trust you to be there for them, willing to go the distance.

You're the only mom who loves them unconditionally, sees past their more challenging sides, and looks for opportunities to praise their best sides. You're a one-in-a-million mom!

God didn't make you from a cookie-cutter pattern. He created you in a unique and wonderful way, knowing every fiber of your being as you were knit in your own mother's womb. He made you special and gave you the chance to be perfectly you—and yes, one in a million!

"Live out your God-created identity. Live generously and graciously toward others, the way God lives toward you."

MATTHEW 5:48 MSG

Mom's Prayer

Lord, thank you for designing me just as I am. Thank you for giving me unique and wonderful kids as well. Amen.

If for Moms

If you can keep your head

When all about you,

The kids are screaming louder than before.

If you can trust yourself

When others doubt you,

And stop yourself from running out the door.

If you can keep a dream

That looks all broken

And know that dreams are still meant to come true,

Then you'll be a mom

Who's loving and soft spoken

No matter what your kids can ever do.

You're one amazing mom!

Supplement your faith with a generous provision of moral excellence, and moral excellence with knowledge, and knowledge with self-control, and self-control with patient endurance, and patient endurance with godliness, and godliness with brotherly affection, and brotherly affection with love for everyone.

2 PETER 1:5–7 NLT

Mom's Prayer

Lord, with you by my side, I can do anything. Amen.

Mom's Gotta Get a Life

If you've been spending a little too much time with a dust cloth and an ironing board lately, it might be time to explore some other options. You may have the cleanest socks in the galaxy and the kids may have glistening smiles and well-scrubbed ears, but something may still be at a loss. It might be you.

When even the kids suggest that maybe you should go out for lunch with friends or go get your nails done, they've noticed you're a bit too tied to them and the house. Sure, they want your attention, but every now and then they want you to get a break, whether they verbalize that or not. Your friends may even be wondering when you're gonna get a life.

How about today? How about giving yourself permission to do something wonderful just for you? It's time to turn your world around and get a blessed few moments with laughter and friends. Give yourself a break. It's okay. The dusting will still be there tomorrow.

I said to myself, "Relax,
because the LORD takes care of you."

PSALM 116:7 NCV

Mom's Prayer

Lord, I do need a little break in my routine. Help me to schedule
some time to just relax with some friends. Amen.

Bless You, Mom!

A little girl was sitting with her mom when the child happened to sneeze. Her mom said, "God bless you." At that point, the little girl asked why her mom said that just because she sneezed. The mom said it was just a nice thing to do.

The fact is that saying God bless you when someone sneezes dates back to the plagues in Europe when people were admonished to pray without ceasing so they would stay healthy. The sneeze was considered to be one of the first signs of the plague, and the blessing was meant to ward it off.

Today we still say God bless you when people sneeze and also at other moments when we want to seek the best for another person. As you go about your day today, may God bless you tenfold each time you offer this warm blessing to others on your path.

"Please, bless my family. Let it continue before you always. Lord GOD, you have said so. With your blessing let my family always be blessed."

2 SAMUEL 7:29 NCV

Mom's Prayer

Thank you for blessing my life in so many wonderful ways. Help me to always seek to bless the lives of those around me. Amen.

Taking the Mom Test

Imagine that you had to study up and take an exam and pass it in order to be a mom. What kinds of things would that entail? Would there be a course on managing tantrums of two-year-olds? Perhaps there'd be a listening course where you had to repeat back all the things that your ten-year-old said in an hour. What if part of the test meant you had to hold a baby, start dinner, and console a friend all at the same time? The tests could be endless, including everything from rocking babies all night long, to staying up till three waiting for your teenager to come home from the prom. Yes, it would be a strenuous test and you might wonder if you'd pass or not.

Fortunately, you didn't have to get an advanced degree to learn how to be a good mom. You simply had to sign up for the job, be willing to share your heart, and have faith in yourself and in the woman God designed you to be. When you do that, you can pass any test with flying colors. You're an excellent mom!

"Now I am putting you in the care of God and the message about his grace. It is able to give you strength, and it will give you the blessings God has for all his holy people."

ACTS 20:32 NCV

Mom's Prayer

Lord, please help me pass the mom test with you. Let me be smart and able to do the right things in your eyes. Amen.

It's Good to Be the Mom!

One of the lines from a Mel Brooks movie repeats the words "It's good to be the king!" Whenever the king wants anything in the movie, he's able to get it. He's in a very enviable position.

It's good to be the mom too. You may not always be able to get everyone to do your bidding the first time you ask—or even to pretend that's possible—but you have an honored position in your house just the same. You're the center of what makes each person in your house feel safe and confident, and you're the comfortable place where everyone else goes when they need special attention and love. You're always respected, and your ideas are valued by the whole family.

A mom may not be a king demanding to be obeyed, but she's definitely the queen of her domain. Reflect on all the things in your life that make it good for you to be the mom.

Get wisdom, get understanding;
do not forget my words or turn away from them.
Do not forsake wisdom, and she will protect you;
love her, and she will watch over you.

PROVERBS 4:5–6

Mom's Prayer

Lord, it's good to be the mom, but it's also good to know that anytime I don't get it right or I need some wisdom, you'll be there to redirect my steps and help me be a good mom. Amen.

What's on Mom's Refrigerator?

You can tell a lot about a mom by what's on her refrigerator. Many moms have shopping lists to remind them of what they need to pick up at the store. Sometimes they have chore charts or appointment schedules there. And oftentimes, they have kid stuff, pictures, drawings, and handprints.

Moms love to display their kids' creations on the refrigerator. It's a place they visit often, and every time they walk by it, they get a fresh reminder of how much they're loved and of the blessing it is to be a mom.

It's been said that if God had a refrigerator, your picture would be on it. He might even have a love note that you sent Him. Home is where the heart is, and sometimes hearts are expressed by those very love notes we find on the refrigerator door.

Express your love to the people nearest you today.

Each of you should give what you have decided in your heart to give, not reluctantly or under compulsion, for God loves a cheerful giver.

2 CORINTHIANS 9:7

Mom's Prayer

Lord, thank you for the beautiful love notes I receive from my kids. No matter how old they get, let me always enjoy the special ways they share that love with me. Amen.

What's *in* Mom's Refrigerator?

Kids are always hungry, or at least they think they are. No matter what age they may be, one of the first things they do when they arrive home is take a look in the refrigerator. They always want to know if Mom made anything special that they can nibble on before dinner or late at night for a snack.

Some moms take a lot of pride in being sure they have a well-stocked fridge. They want to be prepared for hungry munchkins anytime they might appear. They even like having a few things for themselves on those shelves.

In today's culture, moms are a bit more conscious of having healthy snacks that are good for growing kids, like carrots and apples, but every now and then something especially nice like a chocolate brownie might appear behind that large cool door.

It's great to plan ahead to please the people in your family. As you go about your day, plan some time with God so He can nourish your spirit. It will do you both good. Be sure that you offer God thanks and praise for providing for you so well.

And this same God who takes care of me will supply all your needs from his glorious riches, which have been given to us in Christ Jesus.

PHILIPPIANS 4:19 NLT

Mom's Prayer

Lord, you often inspire my thinking about what to have available in the fridge that will please my family. Thank you for your great provision beyond our needs. Amen.

Mom's Favorite Places

We appreciate favorite places where we can revive memories, take a break from the day, or simply have fun with friends in a familiar atmosphere. One of your favorite places may be someplace where you can have lunch with a good friend, enjoy great conversation, and just be yourself. It might be a place that is kid friendly and therefore a great outing for the family as you seek an opportunity to get a little change of scenery. Your favorite places may include those you love to share with your husband or that you remember from when you were a kid.

Another favorite place might be when you imagine sitting with Jesus and enjoying a warm conversation. Perhaps you would meet Him on the beach and listen to the waves, or you'd go down a mountain trail and look out over an amazing vista that reminded you of all God has done in your life.

Think about your favorite places today, and thank God for every spot where He created warm memories just for you. Then seek to enjoy a place where you might talk more closely with Jesus. That may become your most favorite place of all.

As often as possible Jesus withdrew to out-of-the-way places for prayer.

LUKE 5:16 MSG

Mom's Prayer

Lord, thank you for giving me such wonderful places to share with friends and family. Thank you for the quiet spaces we share together as well. Amen.

When Mom Was a Girl

Depending on where you grew up, you may have fond memories of a certain street, park, or school. You may remember the house where your parents created warm memories for you.

Sometimes those days can seem like a long time ago, yet other times they walk vividly through your mind as though they happened yesterday. It's amazing to reflect on the changes that have happened over time, both in your family dynamics and in the culture of your life. Perhaps you moved from the country to the city or from one state to another, but something will always call you back to where you lived when you were just a girl.

Share some of those stories with your kids, because they won't be kids forever and someday they'll think back on all the ways you've enriched their lives from moment to moment, day to day simply because of your roots and who you were as a girl.

Give God the glory for all that has been and all that will be as you move forward in His mercy and love.

A good and honest life is a blessed memorial.

PROVERBS 10:7 MSG

Mom's Prayer

Father, you have blessed my life so much that I couldn't possibly recount each thing you've done or give you proper thanks and praise. Please bless my children all the days of their lives so they create great memories. Amen.

Dream On, Mom!

Do you remember the first time you were conscious of a dream you wanted to explore? If you dreamed of being a ballerina, for example, you may have read everything you could about what it was like to dance on the stage, or maybe you read biographies of famous ballerinas. All that reading helped your dream grow and become more real and possible.

You may have also talked to your friends or family about what you wanted to be someday and how you were going to get there. Perhaps they encouraged you, or perhaps they didn't even understand why you had that dream. No matter; it was your dream.

Now that you're a mom, you may have put your dreams aside, but you don't have to. You can still have dreams for your life, and if you want to read up on those possibilities, the Internet is full of options. These days you might also share your dreams with the One who made you and gave you the inspiration to do what you do. Seek His guidance and He'll help your dreams come true.

Get advice if you want your plans to work.

PROVERBS 20:18 NCV

Mom's Prayer

Lord, I've been a dreamer most of my life. Even though I often put my dreams on hold, I don't forget about them. When the time is right, help me to again believe in the possibility of creating those dreams. Amen.

When God Made Mom

It's very likely that you're one of God's favorites. After all, He gave you a unique design. He knew who you would be even before you came into the world, and He loved you right from the start. In fact, you're so unique that He has unconditional love for you and for anyone who loves Him and His Son, Jesus.

Imagine what God might have thought as you were being created. He might have thought how good you'd be as a wife and a friend. He might have thought about how kind you'd be to others and how brilliantly you'd handle the ups and downs of life. He probably even smiled at knowing how wonderful you'd be as a mother and a guide to His children.

When God made you, He was doing some of His best work. We know that's true because God only can do His best work. He doesn't have a "seconds" category, a drop-down line, or a defect group. He has only perfectly planned and perfectly designed human beings. Yes, it was a great day when He designed you, and you can rejoice in His goodness today.

LORD, you have examined me
and know all about me.

PSALM 139:1 NCV

Mom's Prayer

Lord, I know that in your eyes you have a perfect plan for even the imperfect aspects of me. Help me to do my best to please you in every way. Amen.

Mom's Got Her Sparkle On!

This is the day the Lord has made, and it's a great day for you to put your sparkle on. Yes! You can step out into the world with a smile and a happy heart and shine your light simply because you understand that you've been incredibly blessed. Today's the day to rejoice in a whole new way!

If you're feeling like this doesn't sound like you, or that you don't really picture yourself as a woman who sparkles, then go take a look in a mirror. Remind yourself that you have everything you need to make a difference in the world. You have a family who loves you. You have a wealth of life experience, and you know the things that others need to hear. And you have a kind heart. In fact, it's one of the kindest hearts ever created.

Make this a day when your family looks at you and tries to figure out why you're so happy. Surprise them by bringing them a sense of joy in knowing how loved they are by you and by their Father in heaven. Isn't that enough of a reason to sparkle a little?

This is truly your day to shine!

Her children stand and bless her.

PROVERBS 31:28 NLT

Mom's Prayer

Lord, I don't think I feel sparkly very often, but I know I have lots of reasons to be grateful for all you've done for me. Help me to share that joy with others today. Amen.

Mom Blushes Easily

Some moms blush easily. You may be one of them. It's okay. It just means that your heart is tender and jokes go right over your head and some of the things that others find humorous just doesn't put a smile on your face.

You also blush when you recall the things you've experienced that may be slightly embarrassing. You remember how you tripped on your heels right in front of some people you were hoping to impress, or how you forgot someone's name even though you knew the person well. The gift of those things is that you learn a little more about how wonderful it is that grace is available to all of us.

Chances are you might have a few reasons to blush in front of God. Perhaps you've done a thing or two that you'd really rather not talk about. That's okay. The rest of the humans you know have stories like that too. Give yourself a chance to share an embarrassing moment with God and let Him shower you with grace today. It can make all the difference.

People's own foolishness ruins their lives,
but in their minds they blame the LORD.

PROVERBS 19:3 NCV

Mom's Prayer

Lord, I admit that I've done a few things that make me blush. I'm so pleased that your grace abounds when I act foolishly. Please forgive me anytime I choose to blame you instead of accepting responsibility for my actions. Amen.

Mom's Rainbow

Most of us appreciate the beauty of a rainbow. We might like it because of its graceful presence in an otherwise gray sky. We might like it because we remember the promise God made to Noah when He said He would never destroy the earth again with a flood and that the rainbow would be the sign of His promise.

As a mom, you may need to feel God's presence and promise in your life more often. After all, you're raising kids and making a lot of decisions. You're also living a personal life, a friendship life, and a work life where your heart and mind can get entangled in the needs of others. It's good to seek God's promises for you each day. He keeps His covenants, and He has promised to be with you always. Always is a long time. It means that there is never a moment when you cannot draw near to Him. He is your rainbow.

Life is all about the sun and the rain, and with God in your life, it's also about the rainbow of promise that He holds up for you every day.

"The rainbow shall be in the cloud, and I will look on it to remember the everlasting covenant between God and every living creature of all flesh that is on the earth."

GENESIS 9:16 NKJV

Mom's Prayer

Lord, you know how much I depend on your promises. Be near to me today and help me to always look to you for all I need. Amen.

Mom's Makeup Kit

Women usually have pretty well-stocked make-up kits. They know which brands they like to wear and what colors work best with their skin tone. They've made a science out of creating an amazing appearance. It's impressive.

Your beauty may well be enhanced by all the magic formulas in your particular makeup kit, but there's nothing that can make you more beautiful than the Spirit of God Himself. When you breathe Him in and take His kind and loving heart to others, you radiate. You're a beautiful bride with a proud Father. It's a great sight to see and a wonderful way for you to see yourself today.

You will always be beautiful—outside in and inside out! Your loving heart makes it so. God has blessed you in ways that shine through to others and make everyone around you aspire to be more like you.

There's no cream, ointment, or mystery color in your makeup kit that can create a more beautiful you. You will blossom into a rare beauty by the love you show through what God has done from the inside out.

Do not let your adornment be merely outward—arranging the hair, wearing gold, or putting on fine apparel—rather let it be the hidden person of the heart, with the incorruptible beauty of a gentle and quiet spirit, which is very precious in the sight of God.

1 PETER 3:3–4 NKJV

Mom's Prayer

Lord, I thank you for making me radiate with your love so that whether I put on my makeup for the day or not, people can always see the beauty of you within me. Amen.

Loyal-as-a-Lion Mom

Female lions in the wild live in communities called prides. While male lions wander off and form new prides elsewhere, females tend to spend their entire life in the pride where they were born. They are very loyal to their original community and never go farther than they must to hunt for food to feed their families.

Human moms are somewhat like that. They are loyal to their families and stick close to their children as they raise them to adulthood. As a mom, you may well have the heart of a lioness, making sure that your family is well fed and well protected. This is an instinct that God put into all good mothers.

Today, as you walk with pride around your own home, consider all you do to make sure your family is cared for in all the best ways. Also remember to give God thanks and praise for your family roots and all the women who nurture each child in the family in the ways they consider best.

May God bless your work as a mom today.

For the sake of my family and friends,
I will say, "Peace be within you."

PSALM 122:8

Mom's Prayer

Lord, thank you for my family of origin and my place of birth. Thank you for watching over my family's safety and provision each day. Amen.

Card-Carrying Mom

When you join a specialty group, you often get some kind of membership or access card to all that the group might do. When you learn to drive, you get a card for licensed drivers. When you go to the library, you get a card that lets you borrow books.

It's interesting that when you became a mom, you didn't get a mom card. You didn't get a special access pass to the club rules or the dos and don'ts that must be followed. In fact, you didn't get anything that would help you become a better member of the motherhood squad.

Fortunately, you don't need a card to open the doors to new ideas or options in parenting. You're an unspoken member of a sorority, even if you never went to college. You're a mom—a card-carrying mom!

Give thanks today for all the moms who are members of your club, the ones with little children or grown children. It doesn't matter their age, because once you're in the club, you're always in the club. You pay your dues along the way!

For through him we both have access to the Father by one Spirit. Consequently, you are no longer foreigners and strangers, but fellow citizens with God's people and also members of his household, built on the foundation of the apostles and prophets, with Christ Jesus himself as the chief cornerstone.

EPHESIANS 2:18–20

Mom's Prayer

Lord, thank you for walking ahead of me, preparing me for this special form of membership: the Mom Club. Help me to be a worthy member in every way. Amen.

Mom's Helper

You can go to the grocery store and buy Tuna Helper and Chicken Helper, but it's not easy to find anything on the shelf that you can put in a pan, add some water, and it will suddenly turn into Mom's helper. Most moms could use a helper, someone who would do all the chores they can't get done in a day. If God had designed us with more arms, or put more hours in a day, then we imagine we could get everything done and keep it all together.

As it is, God designed us perfectly. He gave us two arms to hug the kids as they run by to go outside and play. He gave us enough hours in a day to do a satisfying job and still have something to look forward to tomorrow. And He gave us the energy, willingness, and opportunity to do a lot of great things.

Perhaps what we really need is a little more of the help only God can give. Look to Him when you need more time or an extra pair of arms. He's sure to find a way for you to get all the help you need. Call in the real Helper of your life anytime at all.

Yes, for your God has helped and does help you.

1 CHRONICLES 12:18 MSG

Mom's Prayer

Lord, thank you for being the One who helps me in all I do.
I couldn't begin to take on the tasks before me if you didn't
walk with me each day. Amen.

Mom and the Outer Limits

As a mom, you do your best to set the boundaries. You help your kids set boundaries too, so people respect them and don't take advantage of their kindness or their good heart. You see yourself as guiding your children to acceptable limits in all the things they do.

There are times, though, when you feel pushed. You feel like the boundaries have all been crossed and now you're floating out there in what you might call the outer limits. You don't really know what could happen there, but you know it's beyond the point you accept as prudent.

When you find yourself wandering too far from your own limits, grab on to your Creator and seek God's help. Ask Him to pull you back to the place where you recognize the path once again.

The world will push you and pull you and try to distract you. It may even get you to go beyond the place that's comfortable for you, beyond your personal boundaries of good sense and values. If that ever happens, reach out and seek God's hand. He'll help you immediately and lead you forward. After all, nothing can separate you from His love.

When the High God gave the nations their stake,
gave them their place on Earth,
He put each of the peoples within boundaries
under the care of divine guardians.

DEUTERONOMY 32:8–9 MSG

Mom's Prayer

Lord, I usually stick pretty close to the boundary lines that work best for me, but now and then I get in over my head or don't understand where to go or what to do next. Please take my hand anytime I get there. Amen.

Mom Never Quits

A mom is not a quitter. Never has been, and never will be. As a mom, you know there are moments when you want to throw in the towel, wave the white flag, and just give up. You feel like that, but you don't do it. Why?

Chances are that even when things seem crazy, overwhelming, and uncertain, and you don't have the strength and energy to create one more solution, something happens. Either the answers you're seeking come together or you take a little nap, rest up, and start all over again.

Giving up is not an option for you. You know that with enough time and patience, everything changes. Bad days become good days, and chaos gives way to order and peace.

Be glad in the Lord every time you even consider the option to quit, and draw closer to the strength of the most powerful force in any universe, your Father in heaven!

Make the weak hands strong
and the weak knees steady.

ISAIAH 35:3 NCV

Mom's Prayer

Lord, I do get weak in the knees sometimes and wonder if I can keep going. I pray that you will stick closer to me than ever at those times, and give me your hope and peace. Amen.

Mom's Eraser

Forgiveness helps a family get along and stick together. Little things that cause petty grievances crop up many times a day, and if you didn't have a big eraser to help you start all over again, you'd be in a terrible mess by now.

Imagine what it would be like if you kept a record of all the wrongs ever done to you by your husband, the kids, or your friends. The weight of such a volume would be difficult to carry. The weight in your heart of holding on to all those slights would be harder to carry yet.

Just as God forgives you when you do something wrong, He gave you a chance to erase the unfortunate things others do and to forgive each other as well. He did that so our hearts would be lighter and we wouldn't dwell on our sinful natures.

Thank God He has a big eraser and forgives you and the people you love every day. Is there anyone you can offer a kind and forgiving word to today?

Love and truth bring forgiveness of sin.

PROVERBS 16:6 NCV

Mom's Prayer

Lord, you know me better than anyone else ever will. You know all the messes I've made and the many times I've needed your forgiveness. Thank you for having such a big eraser. Amen.

Mom's Faith

You've been exercising your faith for a long time now. You first learned to have faith in your own mom or in a school teacher. You discovered what it meant to have faith in your friends to encourage and support your ideas. You even developed faith in yourself and your ability to make decisions and do certain things with your gifts and talents.

Over time, you have learned what it means to have faith in God too. Trusting God helps you take the challenges of life on faith and believe that things will get better. You take it on faith that someday you'll understand circumstances that don't make much sense to you now.

You've learned to trust that God will provide for you and your family. Since faith is the essence of things that are not yet seen, only hoped for, you put your hopes and prayers before God. Each time you do this, you do it as an act of faith.

Faith is the confidence that what we hope for will actually happen; it gives us assurance about things we cannot see.

HEBREWS 11:1 NLT

Mom's Prayer

Lord, I've learned that even when I don't understand what's going on around me, if I just close my eyes and spend a few minutes with you in heartfelt and faith-filled prayer, you are there. Keep me in this faith always. Amen.

What You Learned from Your Mom

Maybe you can't pinpoint the things you would say you learned from your own mother, but chances are good that you learned important things from her. She's the one who taught you the importance of telling the truth, the blessing of saying a prayer, and the joy that comes from being yourself. You could make a list of the things that stuck with you throughout your life, just as your own children may someday create a list of what they've learned from you.

You learned by listening, following a good example, and trying things on your own. You learned by observing and asking questions. Moms are good sources of information, and most kids never really outgrow their need for Mom.

The same is true of your relationship with God. You've been learning from Him your whole life as well. You've followed His lead, practiced His style, and shared His example with the people around you. As you seek to be more like Him, thank Him for all you've learned and then remember that you are an authentic role model of His love.

And you yourself must be an example to them by doing good works of every kind. Let everything you do reflect the integrity and seriousness of your teaching.

TITUS 2:7 NLT

Mom's Prayer

Lord, thank you for all the helpful things I learned from my mother. Give me the wisdom to share with my children the best things I've learned, so they can carry bits of wisdom with them the rest of their life. Amen.

Hang On, Mom!

If yesterday was really chaotic and you're waking up to a new day wondering if it will just be more of the same, it's time to open your eyes to some different thinking. Sometimes we carry over the worries and problems of yesterday and don't make room for something good, something new that could change the story and give the new day a more positive direction.

If you're still holding on to yesterday's troubles, remember what Jesus advised. He said that each day has its own troubles and that's all we should try to carry. We're not meant to pack up yesterday's problems and wrap them into today's opportunities. We can only carry on one day at a time.

So hang on, Mom! Let go of the weariness of yesterday and look for the sunshine. It's a new day and you're a new you. God has made you new again today as He does every morning. Thank Him for knowing that you need a fresh start and then ask His help with all that happens to you today.

May you have an incredibly blessed day!

With the loving mercy of our God,
a new day from heaven will dawn upon us.

LUKE 1:78 NCV

Mom's Prayer

Lord, I'm guilty of carrying too much of the load from yesterday—and even last week—into the day that is in front of me. Help me to simply take life one day at a time. Amen.

Mom's Grocery Cart

Grocery shopping isn't particularly fascinating to many moms, but imagine for a moment that you actually have the luxury of taking your time as you walk through the aisles of the store. You start in the fresh vegetable section and can appreciate the array of colors of the rich produce, from sweet potatoes to broccoli. You think about the wonderful casserole you can make and even pretend that everyone in the family will love it.

You move on to the fruit section and breathe in the smell of the cantaloupe at the end of the aisle, press on toward the peaches and strawberries, and finally put the bananas in your cart. It's such a reminder of how many good things God created for all of us to enjoy.

After that, it's like Christmas! Every aisle is filled with goodies. Some are essential to your well-being, and others, like frozen yogurt with fudge stripes, are simply a delight to your taste buds.

No doubt, you're pretty careful about the ways you use your grocery dollars, but what fun it is to have that many choices all in one place. Now step outside and look at the world. Every place you look, see what God did to give you variety, beauty, and choices about how you'll receive His bounty.

The earth produced plants with grain for seeds and trees that made fruits with seeds in them. Each seed grew its own kind of plant. God saw that all this was good.

GENESIS 1:12 NCV

Mom's Prayer

Lord, I appreciate all the convenience of a grocery store and of finding what I need in one place. Remind me to take that trip with new eyes to see more of your grace and provision the next time I go there. Amen.

Patience Galore!

Patience is not your middle name, but you're probably more patient than you give yourself credit for being. You give your kids a lot of grace and a lot of room to do things over when they don't do them to your liking the first time. You probably wait patiently for them when you pick them up from soccer practice and they're slowly coming your way talking excitedly with their friends.

You're patient with the things that don't get done in a day and patient with the people who don't act in ways you wish they would. The truth is that you have patience galore! You're the virtual queen of patience, and no one would say differently.

Lean in a little now and look at how patient God is…with you. He waits for you to call on His name, even though He's been near you, poised to receive your prayers all the time. He waits and watches as you do over the things you've messed up, or when you finally do something you promised you would do. He's very patient with you.

When your patience is wearing thin, try to check your frustration at Jesus' feet, for He is steadfast in His patience and love for you.

Since you judge others for doing these things, why do you think you can avoid God's judgment when you do the same things? Don't you see how wonderfully kind, tolerant, and patient God is with you?

ROMANS 2:3–4 NLT

Mom's Prayer

Lord, I know I'm not the most patient woman around. Help me to remember that you wait endlessly for me to do the things you'd like me to do. Give me the patience to wait for my kids too. Amen.

Roller-Coaster Mom

If you've ever taken your kids to an amusement park, the chances are good that you've been coaxed (unless you love roller coasters) to ride the big wooden coaster that stretches up into the sky about as far as you can see. If this is not exactly your thing, you may even have tried to decline the opportunity. But somehow, before you could understand what happened, you were strapped into the seat and ready to go.

You found yourself going straight up in the air. You weren't exactly nervous at that point, but you knew there was no way out. You'd have to ride this one out and go with the ups and downs and the swift jolts and turns. You might have even screamed your head off just to get into the mood of it all. Of course, your kids were taking it all in stride, at least from where you were sitting.

Yes, life is full of roller-coaster moments, and you may feel the same way about those moments as you did when you sat down on the seat of that big, wooden coaster. You'll wonder just how you're going to get through it and probably throw your hands up in the air.

And throwing your hands up in the air is the right thing to do. God has a chance then to grab you and help you hold on tight. He'll ride with you through all the ups and downs.

"I will confirm my covenant with you and your descendants after you, from generation to generation. This is the everlasting covenant: I will always be your God and the God of your descendants after you."

GENESIS 17:7 NLT

Mom's Prayer

Lord, I'm not a big fan of roller coasters—or of life's ups and downs either. Please hold on to me tightly when I'm going through the things that tend to make me a little dizzy. Amen.

A Devotion Just for Mom

Mom, you're such a blessing, and everything you do makes a difference to your family. You work hard to give each person what they need most in terms of love, time, and attention. You make an effort that often leaves you spent and wondering just what else you can do. And then you do even more!

This devotion is just to remind you that you are special, you are loved, and the work you do is seen by your heavenly Father. He walks with you through those sticky moments when you wonder if anyone knows how alone you feel. He stays close when illness strikes or when losses come your way.

When you begin and end this day, seek His face. Breathe in His Spirit of peace and remember that He's only a prayer away anytime you need Him. He's your rock and your redeemer.

May these words of my mouth and this meditation of my heart
be pleasing in your sight,
Lord, my Rock and my Redeemer.

PSALM 19:14

Mom's Prayer

Lord, thank you for being with me all the time. I love your steadfast and faithful support. Please stay near to the people I love every day.
Amen.

August

Courageous Mom

It takes courage to speak up when your kids are making choices you don't agree with. Sometimes it takes courage to sit down and listen when you know it's more important for them to experience whatever it is they're going through. You try to hear them out about their course of action.

Whether you speak up or listen, it takes a lot of courage to be a good mom. The good news is that God sees how courageously you're working to understand, listen, or take a stand, and He continually supports you and holds you up.

When you need more courage, seek God's advice and support. He'll give you the wisdom to know when to let things go. Sometimes the greatest need for your courage comes when you simply have to trust Him to watch over your child. Take heart. He is there, strong and steadfast, and can handle any situation.

And the God of all grace, who called you to his eternal glory in Christ, after you have suffered a little while, will himself restore you and make you strong, firm and steadfast.

1 PETER 5:10

Mom's Prayer

Lord, I can't always be there for my kids, and I don't always have the answers for them. I pray that you'll help me know when to listen and when to speak up according to your will and purpose for each situation. Amen.

Can a Mom Run Away?

You've had days where little things piled up on you. You looked around the house and everything from dishes in the sink to laundry exploding from the hamper made you feel like running away. You may have wondered how things got so out of control. You don't even know where to begin to fix things.

When life got out of hand for Jesus, He didn't exactly run away, but He would take a time-out to get fortified. He'd go to a quiet place where He could engage in prayer and pour His heart out to His Father in heaven. Perhaps that's what you need too, a little time-out, a little quiet time with your Father in heaven.

If things are starting to overwhelm your spirit, take some time to get refortified through prayer. The laundry will still be there, but you won't feel all washed up while you do it.

God proves to be good to the man who passionately waits,
to the woman who diligently seeks.
It's a good thing to quietly hope,
quietly hope for help from God.
It's a good thing when you're young
to stick it out through the hard times.

LAMENTATIONS 3:25–27 MSG

Mom's Prayer

Lord, I do need a time-out. I'd sit in the corner if I thought it would give me a chance to rest a little and talk to you. Help me hear your voice today. Amen.

About Those Mom Meltdowns

Hold on! Squeeze tight! Yes, okay. Maybe even let out a little scream because you've really had it. Nobody is listening when you tell them to do their chores or their homework, or to take the dog out for a walk. Nobody is paying attention to your desire for some sanity amidst all the chaos in the house. There's nothing left to do but have a meltdown.

Or are there other options?

First of all, a meltdown might be just what's needed, because although your family may look at you like you're slightly out of your mind, before long they'll pay attention again. It can work. However, rather than losing your grip, you might just hand the reigns over to your husband, a babysitter, or your mother, and give yourself that much deserved and needed break. Sometimes you have to delegate the responsibility and relax.

You may have a list of favorite ways to handle the moments that could lead to a major meltdown, and if you do, pull those out. If you don't, then try to delegate the household chores for a few minutes and go out for a walk. God knows you need some relief.

But make sure that you don't get so absorbed and exhausted in taking care of all your day-by-day obligations that you lose track of the time and doze off, oblivious to God.

ROMANS 13:11 MSG

Mom's Prayer

Lord, I don't like to get bent out of shape with my family, but sometimes I feel like no one even hears my voice. I wonder if we speak the same language. I know that you hear my voice, though, so I ask you to help me when I've become a bit too stressed at my mom job. Amen.

Mom Would If She Could

Many moms are seen as the one person in the family who will cooperate with the plans the kids have and make every effort to help those plans come to fruition. After all, the family consensus is that "Mom will do it."

You're most likely one of those moms—one who bends to make even the most rigorous options possible for your kids. Yes, soccer practice and ballet recitals may both come at the same time, but you'll somehow make a way to get to both events.

Moms generally make a way where none seemed to exist before. In a similar way, you may have already discovered this truth about God. He makes a way where one didn't exist before. He may have to work some things out or change some old plans, but if He's in agreement with the direction you want to go, He'll help you get there. If you're praying for God's help according to His will, you're bound to get on the right track. Whatever you ask in His name, He will strive to do.

Seek first God's kingdom and what God wants. Then all your other needs will be met as well.

MATTHEW 6:33 NCV

Mom's Prayer

Lord, I do my best to take care of the things my children need. And when I run out of steam, you often provide a way I never would have considered. Thank you for that. Amen.

Wonder Mom

So what color is your cape? You know, the one with the big WM on it for Wonder Mom. You're the one who manages to juggle all the bills, the kids, the plans, the events, and the house cleaning and still get work done for your job as well. You're an amazing woman!

It may feel good to be Wonder Mom some days, but it can also get a little tiresome. You might want to hang that cape up in your closet for a while and let someone else handle all the details.

So how can that happen?

Start with each person in your family and see if there's anything on your list that someone else can help you accomplish. Next, simply cross some things off your list. After that, enlist everyone's help in joining you in prayer for a solution that will make everyone happy. Your family might not mind if you step down from the Wonder Mom role a bit and elevate each of them to being your super sidekicks. Give it a try. The only real superhero in your life and theirs is Jesus. Let Him guide your steps today.

And you will know that God's power is very great for us who believe. That power is the same as the great strength God used to raise Christ from the dead and put him at his right side in the heavenly world.

EPHESIANS 1:19–20 NCV

Mom's Prayer

Lord, I don't mean to put on that Wonder Mom cape as often as I do. I get used to thinking I have to do everything. Help me to see your hand at work when I surrender to your super loving care. Amen.

Mom Philosophy

You probably have your own philosophies about life. You grew up with the "Golden Rule" and know that it's always better to treat people with kindness. You want other people to treat you in the same way that you would treat them. It's one of the best things we've learned from Jesus.

As a mom, you probably took a lot of time to help your children understand that being kind instead of selfish is more apt to serve them well in the world. It's a lesson that simply becomes a way of operating, a philosophy of life.

Why do you suppose Jesus taught His followers to adopt this kind of thinking, this way of being? In part, Jesus knew that this was truly a summary of all the creeds that were taught in the law and by the prophets. He knew it was the quickest way to show that we could love our neighbors as ourselves.

May the words of this golden rule be refreshed in your heart and mind today.

"Do for others whatever you would like them to do to you. This is the essence of all that is taught in the law and the prophets."

MATTHEW 7:12 NLT

Mom's Prayer

Lord, it's certainly part of my life philosophy to do my best to treat others in ways I want to be treated. Please help all of your children live by this rule. Amen.

You Know You're a Mom If...

Some things about being a mom never quite leave you, no matter how old your kids are. For example, you always feel a bit like "mothering" them even when they are adults. You want to offer solutions to their troubles and hug them into feeling strong and happy again.

Other things stay with you too, like the temptation to order for them in restaurants or cut up their roast beef. You know you don't need to do it, but somehow the thought surfaces even though you don't actually act on it. You can't help being a mom!

"Drive safely!" you call out as they leave your house. "Call when you get home!" you instruct with love. You know your mom days are never quite done. You're a mom all the time, a title you love and one you've earned.

Another way you know you're a mom is if you hold all your children up to the Lord in prayer. No one's prayers for them are stronger than yours. Pray for each of your children (and your grandchildren, if you have them) always.

When a believing person prays, great things happen.

JAMES 5:16 NCV

Mom's Prayer

Lord, you know how much I love being a mom. I know that I'll never quit feeling like my children still need me, no matter how old they are. Please bless their lives in every way possible. Amen.

All about Moms

If someone wrote a book that was all about moms, what do you suppose some of the chapter titles might be? Perhaps there would be one about the early years of mothering called "Babies Are Fun … at Naptime!" A chapter for the elementary school years could be called "How Can One Boy Eat that Much?" And for the later school years, an appropriate title might be "I Know I Have a Car Somewhere."

Yes, mothers pretty much spend their lives working around the various ages and stages of their children. They work around them, clean around them, cook and shop and dance around them because raising kids is their main objective, the main job they have. Any book that's "All about Moms" is really a book that's "All about Kids," because that's where the focus is and that's where the heart of each day resides.

Thank God that you're part of the chapters being written for your kids, and be sure to keep a section in your book called "All about Jesus." That way, you'll have the best possible blend of what it takes to raise great kids.

Those who get wisdom do themselves a favor,
and those who love learning will succeed.

PROVERBS 19:8 NCV

Mom's Prayer

Lord, I guess there are times when I could imagine a book that would be dedicated to moms, but the job of raising kids is really all about my willingness to learn from you and lean on you for guidance and strength. I dedicate my "book" to you. Amen.

Mega Mom

There are probably many reasons to consider yourself a "mega" mom, but we'll look at one reason in particular: you're a generous woman. You are a mega generous, over-the-top mom!

You give all you can to the job of being a mom, going the extra mile—and the extra two miles more often than not. You share your magnanimous heart, your amazing spirit, and your generous ideas with your family, your friends, and especially your children. You make them a priority in your life.

There's nothing small about the way you serve them and give your love and time to them. God blesses the work of your heart and your hands when it comes to all you do for your family.

Rejoice in that thought today. Your Mega Savior will be so proud of you.

And I am praying that you will put into action the generosity that comes from your faith as you understand and experience all the good things we have in Christ.

PHILEMON 1:6 NLT

Mom's Prayer

Lord, I know I'm not everything you want me to be, but I thank you and praise you for the chance to be who I am as I raise my children. Amen.

Mom Is Always Right

There are right ways and wrong ways to do things in most families, and that bar is usually set by the mom. The bar can be raised by the mom or lowered by the mom, but not by anyone else. That's how it happens that Mom is always right. Mom makes the rules.

This mom strategy works nicely when moms also have a bar that they have to live up to, one that is set by their Creator, Counselor, and Lawgiver. When they're following His lead, they know how to be an example for their children and how to manage their households with love.

As a mom, you've been guiding and leading your family for some time now, and they love you for it. Thank God that He taught you some of the rules, provided some of the best strategies for raising loving children, and gave you a way to be right in His eyes through the love of Christ.

Direct your children onto the right path,
and when they are older, they will not leave it.

PROVERBS 22:6 NLT

Mom's Prayer

Father, we both know that I'm not always right, but with your help I can do more things right than I would otherwise. Please help me to be lovingly wise to all others today. Amen.

Dear Mom

This letter is for all moms in every age and stage and time. It's also just for you.

Dear Mom,

You may not hear it often enough, but you should know how much you mean to our family. You're the one who keeps us all going strong, the one we look to when things aren't going the way we want them to, and the one we take for granted when we think we can make it on our own.

We don't really mean to take you for granted though; we just don't know how to thank you enough for all you do. You provide the food for our table, the food for thought when we need advice, and the kind words that inspire us to keep going. We know that nothing would feel the same in our house without you.

We thank God for you every single day, and we just wanted to be sure you know how much you're loved.

Signed,

Your Loving Family

May you embrace the love of your family and give God the glory for each person in your life today.

I will praise God in a song and will honor him by giving thanks.

PSALM 69:30 NCV

Mom's Prayer

Lord, I'm so grateful for the love I feel from my family all the time. Bless each of them today. Amen.

Dr. Mom Is In!

Moms have been creating home remedies for the various things that ail their children ever since the time of Eve. Sometimes they knew what to do and other times they hoped they knew. They applied aloe and made chicken soup and hoped for the best. God blessed their efforts and inspired them so they could help make things better till more professional measures could be taken, if that was needed.

Sometimes you have to fix a scraped knee or put a little ointment on a bug bite. Other times, you have to fix a broken heart or help heal a major disappointment, which can be a little trickier to repair. But the main thing your child sees is that whatever the problem is, you're willing to try to fix it as best you can with love.

Most of the time, love will take care of things just fine. Thank God today for all the ways He inspires you to be a loving healer of little hurts.

"But then I will bring health and healing to the people there. I will heal them and let them enjoy great peace and safety."

JEREMIAH 33:6 NCV

Mom's Prayer

Lord, I thank you for giving me healthy children and for guiding me anytime I've needed to help them with healing the hurts of life and limb. Thank you that all kinds of healing come through you. Amen.

Walking in Mom's Footsteps

Kids love to have role models. They look up to the people they admire and want to follow in their footsteps. Sometimes that person is you—their mom.

Following in someone's footsteps usually isn't easy. Jesus called the disciples to follow Him, to learn from His example, and to stay close to His teachings. He wanted them to imitate the things He could do…loving others, healing the sick, and calling people to a greater awareness of how to serve God.

As you consider the ways that your children will walk in your footsteps, imagine the things that you most want them to do as they follow you. Consider how they will emulate your style, your tone of voice, and the very way you treat friends and neighbors. It's an awesome responsibility to have people following in your footsteps.

Remind yourself today that you want to put your best foot forward in everything you do.

Then Jesus went to work on his disciples. "Anyone who intends to come with me has to let me lead. You're not in the driver's seat; I am. Don't run from suffering; embrace it. Follow me and I'll show you how. Self-help is no help at all. Self-sacrifice is the way, my way, to finding yourself, your true self."

MATTHEW 16:24–25 MSG

Mom's Prayer

Father, I'm still learning how to follow you and how to imitate your ways in the world. Help me to be a good example of love and kindness as my children follow me. Amen.

When Everything Goes Wrong

It's easy enough to be pleasant
When everything goes like a song;
But the mom who's worthwhile
Is the mom who can smile
When everything's going wrong!

KAREN MOORE

You may not find it easy to smile when things are falling apart, but you might still find it to be a helpful approach. After all, if you can smile in the midst of the troubles, it speaks well of your faith and the way that you trust in God to help you through. It also brings peace to your family when you appear to be untroubled by the situation at hand, knowing God has things in control.

Even if you can't smile when things go wrong, do your best to trust that God is bigger than whatever the problem might be and that He is acting on your behalf to quickly resolve it. That kind of thinking will give you some reasons to smile.

Pray continually, give thanks in all circumstances; for this is God's will for you in Christ Jesus.

1 THESSALONIANS 5:17–18

Mom's Prayer

Lord, I don't know if I smile much when I feel like things are falling apart, but I do smile at the thought that you are right there ready to help me until things get better. Amen.

Mom, I'm So Confused!

Confusion is a matter of being of two minds; that is, you're trying to look at both sides of an argument or trying to take some next steps by looking at the pros and cons to help you make a choice. It can be difficult to know how to think about things when your mind feels so uncertain.

That same sense of confusion happens to your kids sometimes too. They don't know how to make a good choice. They feel pressured by their peers or friends or even bullied by someone, and they can't tell which way to go. When those things happen to them, they know where to turn. They come to you for help because they know you'll somehow bring clarity from the confusion.

That same option is available for you. When you feel uncertain about what to do, you can go to your heavenly Father. He'll help you understand things more clearly and guide you to the right choice to make. Take any of your confused feelings to Him today.

For God is not a God of disorder but of peace—as in all the congregations of the Lord's people.

1 CORINTHIANS 14:33

Mom's Prayer

Lord, thank you that I can be there when my kids are trying to make the best choices for themselves. Thank you for being there for me when I have tough choices to make as well. Amen.

Captain Mom

The captain of any ship has a big job. He has to be sure that he navigates the waters so the ship doesn't run into unseen obstacles. He has to keep his eye on the weather to make sure he's in the right position to safely take on a storm. He has to know where the lifeboats are and how to instruct a crew in an emergency. He also has to know how to make everyone else on board his vessel feel safe and secure.

You may be the captain of your "ship" (that is, of your family), and you have some similar objectives. You have to be ahead of all the activities in the house to be sure that things go smoothly and that no plan runs into a brick wall. You have to be sure that everyone stays in a positive mood so stormy feelings don't flare up and cause difficulty. You're the one who makes sure everyone at home feels safe and secure.

You may not always feel like the captain of your own vessel, but the One who created the waters and the land is ready anytime to give you further instruction and help you navigate the obstacles. Thank Him for all He does to keep your crew happy today.

As they sailed, he fell asleep. A squall came down on the lake, so that the boat was being swamped, and they were in great danger. The disciples went and woke him, saying, "Master, Master, we're going to drown!" He got up and rebuked the wind and the raging waters; the storm subsided, and all was calm. "Where is your faith?" he asked his disciples.

LUKE 8:23–25

Mom's Prayer

Lord, thank you for keeping us afloat so well. We're truly grateful for all you do for us and are glad that our hearts are anchored in you. Amen.

Ph.D. Mom

If they gave out college degrees for being a mom, every woman who raised children from infancy to adulthood would be wearing a cap and gown. After all, the learning process is pretty stringent, the course work isn't always easy, and the tests can require some all-nighters. Yes, it wouldn't be bad at all if moms could simply get a Ph.D. from Mom University. They've certainly worked hard to earn the accolade.

You probably didn't have adequate text books to help you understand all the issues that come up with being a parent, or all the problem-solving skills required to keep a household functioning smoothly. But somehow or other, experience, research, and faith combined to help you through, and you were blessed with incredible results: happy, healthy grown-up kids.

Today, give God thanks for guiding you with such wisdom and grace to do an amazing job as a mom.

For wisdom will enter your heart,
and knowledge will be pleasant to your soul.
Discretion will protect you,
and understanding will guard you.

PROVERBS 2:10–11

Mom's Prayer

Lord, there's not a degree any university could give that would cover the extent of work, faith, and experience reflected in the job of being a mom. Only you know all that it takes. Thank you for helping me do the work I do with honors. Amen.

A Mom by Any Other Name

Your name is Mom. The writer who reflected that "a rose is a rose is a rose" may have thought the same would be true for moms. But while "a mom is a mom is a mom" may sound like it could be true, just like roses, moms come in a lot of varieties and styles. They do the job very differently, and they get different results. The one thing that remains true is that "a mom is a mom is a mom" because there's no one else who can be called by that name. To be Mom is a very special thing indeed.

Names are important. They can even be inspired or God given. When Abram started to follow God in a new way, God changed his name to Abraham. When Saul met Jesus on the road to Damascus, God changed his name to Paul. When you started being the one who would raise new children in the sight of God, your name was changed to Mom. As you consider all the ways that name has changed your life, give God thanks and praise for what He has done for you.

I am changing your name from Abram to Abraham because I am making you a father of many nations.

GENESIS 17:5 NCV

Mom's Prayer

Lord, thank you for changing my name. Being a mom is one of the greatest joys of my life. Amen.

Keeping Up and Keeping On

Some days, it's hard to keep up. You have a laundry list of things that need to get done in a short time and not a lot of help to get those things accomplished. In fact, even the laundry might not find its way to the washer. When you can't keep up, it can be a little hard to keep on because you feel so defeated. You haven't even started and you're already behind.

You've probably had days like this, ones where the to-do list just keeps growing and nothing gets crossed off it in a timely way. What do you do? How do you reenergize yourself to keep on?

One thing you might do is stop focusing on the list and simply do what must be done today—and no more. Seek God's restful presence to help you renew your strength, and then wait for a window to open up and make you feel freer about keeping up with it all. Pray about each part of your list, and ask God to help you set the priorities. You'll feel better. That's a promise.

People may make plans in their minds,
but only the LORD can make them come true.
You may believe you are doing right,
but the LORD will judge your reasons.
Depend on the LORD in whatever you do,
and your plans will succeed.

PROVERBS 16:1–3 NCV

Mom's Prayer

Lord, thank you for this list of chores. Please take each one and help me see how to get it done according to your will and purpose and plan for my life. Amen.

Catch Me, Mom!

Remember when your kids were little and they would want to fall backward into your arms? They may have been at the edge of the swimming pool or perhaps just playing in the living room, but they loved to have you try to catch them. Sometimes they played catch by running away from you in the backyard and begging you to try to get them. Those were surely memorable moments.

Falling back into someone's arms is a trust game. You have to know that the person you're trusting will catch you as you fall or you could hurt yourself. That's just the position you're in with God. You can ask Him to catch you, and He will every time. How do you know that? Because you've built a relationship of trust with Him over time. You've learned that when you need Him to be there, to catch you as you fall, He does.

Rest in His arms today, knowing that He's happy to keep you safe and strong all the time.

Praise the Lord; praise God our savior!
For each day he carries us in his arms.

PSALM 68:19 NLT

Mom's Prayer

Lord, thank you for catching me so I don't get bruised and hurt by the world. Let me rest in your tender care today. Amen.

Mom Figures It Out

Have you ever played the game I spy with your kids? In the game, you each think of one thing you see around you and give only one clue about it. "I spy something yellow," you might say. Then everyone would look for the yellow objects and try to guess what you were able to spy.

Raising kids can sometimes feel like this kind of game. As your kids get older, they may not be as predictable or as easy to understand as when they were little. You find yourself wondering what you can do when they can't see the direction to go. You want to help them look for the options around them. With patience and time, you can usually figure out what is going on. The key is often about the amount of intentional conversation you strive to have with each other.

At times, you may play a form of I spy with your heavenly Father. You can wonder just what God sees that you don't see, and discovering that answer can make a big difference in your life. Fortunately, God will give you enough clues to help you figure things out. In fact, He puts the clues all around you.

I will bless the LORD who guides me;
even at night my heart instructs me.

PSALM 16:7 NLT

Mom's Prayer

Lord, thank you for cluing me in on the things that are important and helping me to discover even more of you as my Lord and Savior. Amen.

In Praise of Moms Everywhere

Can you hear the thundering applause coming your way? The streets are lined with people, confetti is being thrown, and everyone is waiting for you to arrive. Yes, it's a major celebration and it's all for you. You're a mom worthy of praise and ticker-tape parades and standing ovations.

It's your day to be noticed and your day to shine. Perhaps you didn't realize this was the day to celebrate you and all you do. If you didn't, then just stand back and take a bow.

Your family may not often take the time to give you their undying expressions of gratitude, but you can be sure they are grateful for you. They are grateful that even when they're not paying attention to you, you're still paying attention to them. They are grateful to rise each day knowing they can count on you to help make their day more positive and meaningful.

God works this way in your life too. You may not think to give Him thanks and praise every day, but He is always there, doing the things He knows will make a difference to your work and your well-being. Maybe this would be a good day to let Him know you're glad He's always there. Give Him some applause!

The LORD is my strength and shield.
I trust him, and he helps me.
I am very happy,
and I praise him with my song.

PSALM 28:7 NCV

Mom's Prayer

Lord, thank you for being there and for taking care of me even when I'm not willing to say how glad I am for what you've done. Today I say, "Thank you, Lord. Thank you." Amen.

Mom's So Pushy

Your kids may never thank you for pushing them. Pushing them happened when they were going too slow to get their homework done, when they weren't trying hard enough to practice the piano, or when they simply weren't paying attention to the things you knew were important for them. As the mom, it was your duty to push them a little and help them stay on track.

It may be a fine line between encouragement and pushing, but there is a line. You're always willing to encourage others, but pushing is sometimes effective. Then there's nagging, which probably means that no one is listening once again.

God encourages you. He does so through your friends, your church life, and in the stillness of prayer and reading His Word. He encourages but seldom pushes. He sends His Spirit to convict you sometimes, but He never nags. Take a moment today and see if there's any part of your faith walk where you might need encouragement, a little pushing, or even a bit of nagging. If so, it may be time to listen up.

While Peter was talking, a bright cloud covered them. A voice came from the cloud and said, "This is my Son, whom I love, and I am very pleased with him. Listen to him!"

MATTHEW 17:5 NCV

Mom's Prayer

Lord, I know that I do need to be pushed a little to stay on track. Help me listen to you for the things that feed my spirit today. Amen.

Training Camp

If you went to summer camp or even perhaps to day camp when you were growing up, you probably got some training in areas you didn't know much about. You may have been trained in survival techniques in case you were ever lost in the woods or needed to take care of yourself after a tornado. You may have gotten training in what plants were edible and how to know fresh water from water that might make you sick. Camping required its own kind of training.

When you became a mom, no one sent you to camp. You just received on-the-job training from the day you brought your tiny tot home from the hospital. You were not especially schooled in all the ways you could feed your infant or when to go from liquids to solid foods. You learned by doing.

Your faith is a bit like that. You started on your walk of faith and quickly learned that there were things you needed to know and signs to watch out for along the way. You realized that faith was your way of surviving in the world.

Today, give God the glory for getting you through mom training and faith camp. He's always there to continue the guidance.

Training your body helps you in some ways, but serving God helps you in every way by bringing you blessings in this life and in the future life, too.

1 TIMOTHY 4:8 NCV

Mom's Prayer

Lord, thank you for training me in the things that are important to my survival on planet earth and even in heaven. Help me to always be equipped to keep moving in the right direction. Amen.

Newborn Moms

The day a baby is born, a mama is born too. Whether or not she has any other children, her newborn will be unique and will require special care and cause the mom to grow.

When your babies were born, you renewed your pledge to care for them and love them unconditionally. You promised to learn with them and grow with them and do your best to be the mother they needed. You grew from being a newborn mom to being a more mature mom as the days went by and the challenges of the relationship were met by each of you.

The Bible talks about what it means to be a newborn Christian. It says that while we're young, God feeds us on milk, giving us what we need to keep growing strong and waiting until we're able to take on solid foods. He treats us with the tenderness a mom uses to care for her newborn baby.

As you think about that relationship today, the one you share with your heavenly Father, see if you've been depending on milk or if you're ready for more solid food. The thing to know is that when you're ready, God is ready too.

I find you need someone to sit down with you and go over the basics on God again, starting from square one—baby's milk, when you should have been on solid food long ago! Milk is for beginners, inexperienced in God's ways; solid food is for the mature, who have some practice in telling right from wrong.

HEBREWS 5:12–14 MSG

Mom's Prayer

Lord, thank you for feeding me and sustaining me a little more each day so I can live closely united to your Spirit. Help me to grow stronger in your care. Amen.

The Good Guys and the Bad Guys

The great thing about moms is that they have an innate level of discernment. They know the good guys from the bad guys.

As well, you have an incredible ability to help your family understand how to make good choices about people, work, and school. You're a blessing to them all. You've always been discerning. You know what's right for yourself and for the ones you love. You're schooled in the things that help you make good choices so you can bypass the foolish things.

God wants you to have a discerning heart. He knows that you need to be able to understand His Spirit and His presence in your life on a daily basis. You need to know when you should draw near to Him and when to seek His protection.

This wonderful ability to know how to make good choices is a gift from God. Help your kids to know the good guys from the bad guys. Pray that you will always have a right spirit within you.

I am your servant; give me discernment
that I may understand your statutes.

PSALM 119:125

Mom's Prayer

Lord, thank you for giving me a discerning heart. Guide me in situations where doing the right thing is not easily understood. Be with me and protect my family today. Amen.

Don't Rattle Mom

Moms don't get rattled easily after they've lived with a tiny tot for any length of time. They were very careful about everything that concerned their first child. Then they eased up a bit with the second one, and eased up more on down the line. It doesn't mean that they were less loving or caring, but simply that they didn't let things upset them quite so readily.

You probably have your own version of this story, but here's another way to think about it. As God's child, it's good to know that God is not easily rattled either. He knows you'll get hurt sometimes or fall down and be bruised by life, but He's with you and tenderly picks you back up, giving you time to heal and go on your way again.

You don't want God to be rattled by your difficulties because you live and breathe and have your being on His strength. You lean on Him when you're feeling weakened by your life circumstances.

Your children may feel the same way about you. When you stay calm in the midst of the little bumps and bruises they receive on the road of life, the more they can draw strength from you. Be glad in the Lord and in the power of His might for you and for you family. His love for you can never be shaken.

"For in him we live and move and have our being."

ACTS 17:28

Mom's Prayer

Lord, help me to trust and lean on you, and give me the strength to allow my children to lean on me when things don't go well for them. Amen.

The Truth about Moms

Moms are resilient and caring. They jump in with both feet and look for all the possible ways they can help their kids. After that, they look for the impossible ways. The truth is that sometimes moms are scared. They're afraid they won't be able to provide everything their children need. They're afraid that they won't be wise enough to make the best choices, or that they won't measure up to the job and do it in a way that meets everyone else's approval. The job of being a mom just isn't easy.

You're in good company if you've ever had any of those feelings. They come with the mom job. The truth is you can do the possibles—the things that you're capable of doing—and then through prayer and faith, you can wait for God to do the impossibles. A lot of things can feel pretty impossible as you raise your kids, and it's not a job you want to do alone. You need God's help and He's always ready to help you, so it's a beautiful match.

Today, ask God to do the things that seem impossible to you but are perfectly possible for Him, according to His will and purpose for you.

But Jesus looked at them and said, "With men it is impossible, but not with God; for with God all things are possible."

MARK 10:27 NKJV

Mom's Prayer

Lord, thank you for taking such good care of us. I ask that you would help me to do the things that are possible for me, and that you would do the things that are only possible with you. Amen.

The Story of Mom

Once upon a time there was a young woman who married and had a family. She became a mom, and everything about being a mom made her happy. Well, almost everything. Some days, she would wonder if she was doing everything in the best way. Now and then, she'd worry that she made a bad decision or that she made a mistake that couldn't be undone.

Fortunately, she was a woman who lived in faith. She knew that all the things that bothered her could be taken to the Lord in prayer. She knew that even when she couldn't do something, God could. Since she knew that truth, she prayed every day for the blessing that God would bestow upon her family.

And that was the beginning.

This is your story. You're the one who sometimes needs God's extra love and grace for the work you do as a mom. Embrace His love for you today and thank Him for being part of your story every day. He's helping you write some incredible chapters.

And the prayer of faith will save the sick, and the Lord will raise him up. And if he has committed sins, he will be forgiven.

JAMES 5:15 NKJV

Mom's Prayer

Lord, you know a lot about me, including the things that make me glad to be a mom and the things that cause me concern. Favor me with your love and hope today. Amen.

Mom's Garden Hoe

A lot of moms enjoy doing some gardening. When they're in the garden, they feel connected to God in a special way because they're helping to bring little seedlings of possibility into full maturity and blessing. They carefully plant those seeds and offer prayers for their success as they grow. But every now and then, they have to get out a hoe and chop away some weeds that threaten to take room or nutrients from their young plants. They hoe them out to help the baby plants grow stronger.

These are the very things you do as a mom. You pray over your children as though they were young sprouts in a garden. You watch over them and look to see that they grow well. Now and then, you have to make a tough decision, say no to something you know won't serve them well, and weed out the things that aren't good for them. You're a great mom, and with your love and nurturing skill, you're sure to grow beautiful children into full maturity.

Praise God for all He has done to help you care for your family.

Every branch in Me that does not bear fruit He takes away; and every branch that bears fruit He prunes, that it may bear more fruit.

JOHN 15:2 NKJV

Mom's Prayer

Lord, I thank you for the many ways you've taken care of my family. I know that sometimes you have to weed out the things from my life that don't serve you well. I pray you will always nourish and strengthen me. Amen.

The Mom Blessing

You're a wonderful mom, and today you're being offered this blessing and prayer:

Lord, please be with this loving and kind-hearted mom. Give her strength beyond what she can imagine to do the work before her with joy and tenderness. Grant her wisdom as she cares for the children in her family, the gifts of life you have given her. Bless her life, Lord! Fill her with knowledge of you, and in all the ways that you can, guide her both personally and as a mother. Help her know when to speak and when to listen, when to guide and when to step away. Renew her passion and desire to be a good mother. Bless her with your grace and favor, with your love and true affection. Help her to never feel alone or uncertain, always trusting that she is wrapped in your Spirit. Amen.

God bless you and keep you today and always!

Christ lives in me. The life you see me living is not "mine," but it is lived by faith in the Son of God, who loved me and gave himself for me.

GALATIANS 2:20 MSG

Mom's Prayer

Lord, thank you for this blessing. I praise you for all that you do to give me hope and guidance. Amen.

September

Wait Till You're a Mother!

Chances are, if you haven't already said this to your daughter, you will sometime in the future. The message usually comes through when your kids have questioned you over something you've already tried to explain, or when they simply don't want to accept your answers.

You realize that kids don't know how hard it is to make the best choices in every situation. You're doing the best job you can on their behalf. They may not appreciate it now, but you trust they'll one day understand the decisions you've made.

Your mother probably said something similar to you, because it's a time-weary frustration and a response that filters down through the generations.

Today, reflect a bit on what it means to you to be a mother, or what it meant when you were actively raising kids. It's okay to be frustrated with any job. It's great to know that you can turn to God to help you with both the joys and troubles of being a parent. Thank God for His goodness to you today.

We know you were there for our parents:
they cried for your help and you gave it;
they trusted and lived a good life.

PSALM 22:4–5 MSG

Mom's Prayer

Lord, you know I love this mom stuff, but now and then it's overwhelming and even frustrating. Help me to come to you when I'm out of sorts and need a moment of comfort and peace. Amen.

It's Showtime!

You've probably had a number of moments in your life when you knew it was "showtime." There was no turning back, and you simply had to do whatever it was that you'd signed up to do. As a mom, you prepare yourself, even practice your lines for the moments you know will come.

It may be showtime when your child first says, "No!" You knew this day was coming, and you have an answer. Perhaps it happened when you had to drop your child off at kindergarten for the first time. You were apprehensive. You had never been apart before, but now it was showtime. Now you had to let go just a little.

Through the years, you may have experienced showtime moments that didn't make the headlines and weren't on anybody else's hit parade, but they were defining moments for you. Those were the experiences that tipped your hand, healed your heart, or helped you get to another step. Those were the moments when the One who conducts your show was right there, ready to lead you forward and applaud your success.

Today, you can be proud of the ways you responded to the things that changed your life, and you can give God the credit for helping you become the woman you are now.

Trust in the Lord with all your heart;
do not depend on your own understanding.
Seek his will in all you do,
and he will show you which path to take.

PROVERBS 3:5–6 NLT

Mom's Prayer

Lord, thank you for taking me by the hand, or for going before me and making all the difference as I met another challenge or changed my life direction. I couldn't do it without you. Amen.

By the Book

Sometimes it works well to do everything by the book. You figure out what works well, you get in a routine, and life is good. Other times you have to get beyond the book, add your own special touches, and put some notes in the margin about what worked well for you. After all, being a mom is a creative job, isn't it? Some things have to be done in your way and in your style.

Then there are times when you simply have to throw the book out and do what you feel is best. You say your prayers, trust that God has your back, and keep going.

Whether you prefer to go by the book, color outside the lines, or simply toss the book aside, the best thing to do is include God in the work you do as a mom. He has a lot of ideas in His Book, and so when you're struggling with what to do, just go there. He loves to help and has a lot of creative ideas.

Be an example to all believers in what you say, in the way you live, in your love, your faith, and your purity. Until I get there, focus on reading the Scriptures to the church, encouraging the believers, and teaching them.

1 TIMOTHY 4:12–13 NLT

Mom's Prayer

Lord, please draw near to me and my family today. Help us seek your help in the Good Book, whenever we get stuck and even when we think we've got it right. We always need you. Amen.

The Mom Review

In a corporate job, you have a job review once a year to determine the rate of your pay raise. Of course, in the mom business, there's no such thing as a mom review or a pay raise, but just for fun, imagine what some of your goals and objectives might be for the coming year. These would be the ones where you'd hope to do well and then get a raise based on the goals you set. Perhaps you would put forth some of these as your mom objectives:

1. You'll love each member of your family unconditionally.

2. You'll pray without ceasing for all of the needs of your household.

3. You'll work hard and enjoy the process.

No doubt you already get rave reviews, but consider spending a few moments with God today, reviewing where you feel you are as a mom, and setting some new objectives that will make your work easier. When you start with His guidance, your efforts are sure to excel.

Whatever you do, work at it with all your heart,
as working for the Lord, not for human masters.

COLOSSIANS 3:23

Mom's Prayer

Lord, thank you for being with me each step of the way and for reminding me of the things that are most important. Help me to work for you with all my heart. Amen.

The Book of Mom

The Bible offers us a number of amazing books that were written by or ascribed to writers with names like Jonah, Malachi, and Matthew. These writers had very specific things that they wanted to tell the world, and their words have been read by millions.

If there was a book of Mom—that is, your book—what would it include? What kinds of things would you be interested in having the world know and remember? Perhaps you'd have a book that talks about honoring parents and listening to their advice and wisdom. Maybe you'd have a section on trusting others and believing in the work each one can do, encouraging their direction and their goals. Maybe you'd have a section full of good recipes that could be made when you're in a hurry or just too tired to cook.

Of course, the Bible writers were inspired by God to write the books they put together, and it's not even possible to write another book of the Bible. However, the one with your name on it might best be read by your own household, and it could still be important because you always shine your light on what it means to be a woman of God and a great mom.

Let my teaching fall like rain
and my words descend like dew,
like showers on new grass,
like abundant rain on tender plants.

DEUTERONOMY 32:2

Mom's Prayer

Lord, you haven't called me to write a Bible book, but if I had lived back then when those writers were proclaiming your name, I might have joined in with some words of joy and thanksgiving. Thank you for your Word today. Amen.

Snakes and Spiders and Mom, Oh My!

Sometimes in the fall seasons, when the weather begins to change and the outdoor critters make a move toward nesting underground or somewhere out of the winter snows, they may cross paths with you.

Snakes and spiders are two of the less inviting critters, and most moms prefer to avoid any relationship with them. They will walk well out of their way to go around the path of a snake. They will also enlist the help of anyone in the house who might be willing to kill the oversize arachnid on the wall. We know it's large because there's really no other kind of spider.

Perhaps the distaste of critters like these is derived from Old Testament stories of beguiling snakes in the garden of Eden and plagues of other creatures that make you squirm. Surely God knows why He created all the various species of the world, so there's not much to do but try to live agreeably together.

As you're walking about today, give some thought to the amazing animals and insects that God created, and stand in awe of His awesome creation. After all, once He made each one, He called it good.

God made the wild animals according to their kinds, the livestock according to their kinds, and all the creatures that move along the ground according to their kinds. And God saw that it was good.

GENESIS 1:25

Mom's Prayer

Lord, I am truly awed by your creative imagination as I consider all the critters in the world. I won't try to act like I'm a fan of snakes and spiders, and so I thank you for keeping those things out of my range of vision. Amen.

Free the Moms

Your picture of what it means to have a day where you feel "free" may be very different from that of your friends. After all, life deals out a hand and everyone plays according to their own rules and perceptions.

Some days, being free may be about just being able to do what you believe is the right thing to do for your own children. You might want the freedom to choose where they go to school or the freedom to teach them family values on your own terms.

Free might also be getting a day away, or just sharing some time with the girls or with friends who can have intelligent adult conversation with you. There are just so many conversations you can have with a five-year-old.

One thing to remember is that you're always free in Christ. You're free to be the mom, and the woman He called you to be. May your connection to Him always free your heart and mind and inspire all you do.

To the Jews who had believed him, Jesus said, "If you hold to my teaching, you are really my disciples. Then you will know the truth, and the truth will set you free."

JOHN 8:31–32

Mom's Prayer

Lord, thank you for freeing me to be a good mom and a good person, able to make choices and live in your grace. Thank you for loving me so much. Amen.

Trendy Mom

You are one stylin' mom! You can always pull the right colors together, complete with shoes and jewelry, and make your friends wonder just how you do it. But really, your style is more than just the clothes you wear and the amazing combinations you can put together from your closet. Your style is all about you.

Your style comes through the most in the way you show up in the world. It's the way you shine your light for Jesus and the way you embrace the love of your family and friends. Your style reminds others that clothes can't begin to make the woman nearly as much as putting on the light of God's love does. You sparkle in every way when you share your heart and mind with other moms and with your friends. You make a difference because you put a positive light on their lives and give them encouragement and hope.

Thanks for being such a trendsetter. You are definitely a woman of great style.

"And why do you worry about clothes? Look at how the lilies in the field grow. They don't work or make clothes for themselves. But I tell you that even Solomon with his riches was not dressed as beautifully as one of these flowers."

MATTHEW 6:28–29 NCV

Mom's Prayer

Lord, thank you for giving me a sense of style, but thank you even more that you have helped create in me a style that is all yours, one that radiates and shines for you. Amen.

When Mom Prays

Perhaps the most powerful tool any mom has is the one she can plug in any hour of the day, even when there's no electric outlet. Moms who pray plug in to the best source of power in the universe, and they make a difference in the lives of their children.

It's not always easy to know what to pray for your children. When they're little, you offer prayers of protection and that they might be healthy and strong. As they grow older, you offer prayers for their abilities to make good choices and to pick friends who will encourage and have fun with them.

Whatever age or stage your kids are in, they need your prayers. Your prayers are not like those of anyone else. Your prayers come straight from your heart to God's heart, so they completely connect with the greatest source of power available.

When you pray for your children, God hears your loving words and answers with an extra surge of wisdom and joy. It's an electric connection.

Pray in the Spirit at all times with all kinds of prayers, asking for everything you need. To do this you must always be ready and never give up. Always pray for all God's people.

EPHESIANS 6:18 NCV

Mom's Prayer

Lord, I may not pray often enough for my children, but you know how precious they are to me. Please watch over each one of them and guide their lives in every way. Amen.

All Those Working Moms

We seldom hear any discussion about working dads. We assume that dads are supposed to work and provide for their families. In our current culture, we find a lot of two-parent families where both parents work to provide for the lifestyle of the household.

Of course, every mom is a working mom whether she earns money outside the home or not. She's working all the time to provide for the needs of her family. It may not always be the financial provision, but it's more than her share of the emotional, spiritual, and physical provision needed to help everyone thrive.

You may or may not be a working mom in the sense of the paycheck you bring home each week, but you're definitely a working mom to your family. In fact, your family could not afford to pay for all the goods and services you provide.

Seek God's direction in whatever work you do, and thank Him that He makes all things work together for good for those who love Him.

And we know that God causes everything to work together for the good of those who love God and are called according to his purpose for them.

ROMANS 8:28 NLT

Mom's Prayer

Lord, you know the work I do for my family. I ask that you would help me seek more of you in every decision and in every task I take on for the good of my household. Amen.

Lean In, Lean On Mom

Isn't it good to have something to lean on? Sometimes you simply lean on the kitchen counter as you talk with your friend on the phone. Other times you can lean on your spouse when you have a problem that needs to be discussed heart to heart.

God provides a number of resources to strengthen you when you need something to lean on, but one of the most important is the one that requires you to lean in. You have to lean in and listen. You have to lean in and pray. You have to get very quiet and seek to lean on the One who created you. He has all the strength you need to find comfort, direction, and wisdom for each day. In fact, you cannot do anything well without Him.

Lean on and lean in to the One who is your Father and Creator today.

Trust in the LORD with all your heart;
do not depend on your own understanding.
Seek his will in all you do,
and he will show you which path to take.

PROVERBS 3:5–6 NLT

Mom's Prayer

Lord, I do need to lean in a bit more carefully and rest my head on your shoulder. Help me to draw closer to you whenever I need more strength. Amen.

Mom's Guiding Principles

In recent years, it seems like having principles and good character are no longer ideals that matter. Fewer and fewer people seem to have either one. The message God has for you, though, is that He wants you to stick to your principles. He wants you to honor your family and guide them with conviction about the things He has taught you.

You are a woman of worth, a woman of values and principles. Whenever you find life confusing or uncertain, bow your head and reconnect with the One who gave all of us the guidelines for living.

Listen carefully to my wisdom;
take to heart what I can teach you.
You'll treasure its sweetness deep within;
you'll give it bold expression in your speech.
To make sure your foundation is trust in GOD,
I'm laying it all out right now just for you.
I'm giving you thirty sterling principles—
tested guidelines to live by.
Believe me—these are truths that work,
and will keep you accountable
to those who sent you.

PROVERBS 22: 17–21 MSG

Mom's Prayer

Lord, thank you for filling me up with your spirit in ways that truly guide me and make me value my principles. Help my children to honor them as I do. Amen.

Mom Adds a Touch of Love

"Do not seek revenge or bear a grudge against anyone among your people, but love your neighbor as yourself."

LEVITICUS 19:18

You know what it's like when little things drive you crazy. You're somewhat annoyed when the traffic is too slow and you're in a hurry. You're not happy when the woman in front of you pulls out her wad of coupons when you're in the fast lane. You wonder why the newspaper can't be placed more carefully on the steps on rainy mornings so you don't have to fetch it from the bushes.

There are a lot of little things that are outside of your scope of responsibility or your opportunity to offer better solutions. The things that can make you cranky in the outside world though, don't have to happen within your own home. You have the chance in your own domain to offer a touch of joy and love to every corner of the house. You can lovingly guide the way things are done, and tweak the direction of what is happening by simply adding a smile, a hug, or a loving touch. That's what moms do! That's what you do!

Today, even if you can't do much about the little things outside of your sphere of influence, see what you can do inside, with a special touch of love and a lot of prayer.

Mom's Prayer

Lord, thank you for giving me so many ways to add a little extra sunshine to my own household. Remind me how important it is to take the extra time, even to do little things with love. Amen.

There's No Mom like You, Mom

When some preschoolers were asked to tell a little about their moms, they said things like, "Mom is tall," or "Mom is pretty," or "Mom is loud." They identified their mothers by a trait they could understand.

You might think of your mom that way, or your kids may feel that way about you, but it's also possible that they might not be able to easily describe you. They may find themselves searching for just the right words to convey who you really are, at least to them.

If they have any other points of comparison—a grandmother, an aunt, or someone else they know—they might realize that there's no one quite like you. They can't think of an example of you because of your unique personality or joyful life attitude.

Think about what it means to be a unique woman and to know that there's no other mom quite like you. That means you're special in every way to your family and to God.

My frame was not hidden from you
when I was made in the secret place,
when I was woven together in the depths of the earth.

PSALM 139:15

Mom's Prayer

Lord, I hope I'm unique in good ways, in ways that please you.
Help me to always be okay with being myself and to seek your
guidance for those areas I may need to change. Amen.

The Gourmet Life

You don't have to be a gourmet cook to lead a gourmet life. If you're the kind of person who's awake to all of the senses God gave us, and you embrace life in a hearty and loving way, then you're a gourmet kind of girl. You like variety and beauty and all the things that bring joy to your heart. It might mean that you like exotic spices or jewel-tone colors, or it may simply mean that you value the great variety of beautiful things the world has to offer.

As you think about your Creator today, ask Him to open your eyes to all that it means to live a gourmet life, smelling, tasting, touching, and seeing life, hearing it sing, and discovering its beauty everywhere you go.

What a wildly wonderful world, GOD!
You made it all, with Wisdom at your side,
made earth overflow with your wonderful creations.

PSALM 104:24 MSG

Mom's Prayer

Lord, thank you for making me a somewhat gourmet kind of woman. I love discovering your handiwork and appreciating your beauty every day. Amen.

Mom's Priorities

Often, your day can be divided between the necessary and the urgent. You set your priorities by the things that are truly important to your life right now. You know that you can't get along very well without milk for the cereal or bread for the sandwiches. You also need to have gas for the car, and you have to pay the bills on time. There are a lot of necessary parts, and you're the one who takes care of them all.

As you set your priorities according to what's really important, absolutely necessary, something you can't live well without, take a look at where you've ranked things like prayer, Bible reading, and quiet time with the Lord. Which of those things gives you more of a taste for the bread of life?

Today, make sure you get the things done that need to be accomplished, but start with your number one listed priority—to spend a little time being nourished by the wisdom and blessing of God.

God is our protection and our strength.
He always helps in times of trouble.

PSALM 46:1 NCV

Mom's Prayer

Lord, I know I can get so busy that I cut you out of the equation. Please help me start my day with you so I have the strength I need to accomplish good things. Amen.

Mom's Open-Door Policy

As a mom, you've probably always had an open-door policy. That means that no matter what's going on in your life, your family knows you're available to them whenever they need you. Yes, you may need to work outside your home and so they have to respect your work hours, but the open-door policy is about your willingness to be available to them most anytime.

Your kids thrive because you let them know they can have access to you. They can come to you when they have concerns or issues they're trying to work out in their lives. They can talk to you about nearly anything and you'll gladly listen. They can even tell you about the mistakes they've made.

Each time you make yourself available, you listen with love and do your best to help in any way you can. That's what loving relationships are about.

You have a loving relationship with your Father in heaven that works the same way. He has an open-door policy, and anytime you need His help or advice, He's there. He won't ever close the door. He wants to help you in any way He can.

Let us, then, feel very sure that we can come before God's throne where there is grace. There we can receive mercy and grace to help us when we need it.

HEBREWS 4:16 NCV

Mom's Prayer

Lord, help me to remember that I often come to you for loving guidance and for comfort. In a similar way, let me be available to my own family. Amen.

Mom's Vision

You've had dreams for your children since before they were born. Your vision is for them to be happy and strong. You want them to feel loved, protected, and valued so they become adults who also love, protect, and value others. It's a good vision, and God honors your hopes and dreams.

From time to time, it may feel like things have gotten off the track, like your dreams can't come true. You and your child don't seem to agree on the way life should work, and your heart is broken for a dream that has slipped through your fingers.

Fear not! Hang on to the hope that God has placed in your heart. Know that the author of your dreams hears your prayers and seeks to help them yet be fulfilled. Pray with all your might for the ones you love, and trust that they are in good hands.

Keep on dreaming and hold up the vision of all that is good for the people you love so much. God will do His part to help you.

If people can't see what God is doing,
they stumble all over themselves;
But when they attend to what he reveals,
they are most blessed.

PROVERBS 29:18 MSG

Mom's Prayer

Lord, thank you for helping me to sustain the vision I have for my loved ones. Bless the life of this person you placed in my hands according to your will and purpose. Amen.

Creative Mom

You have a creative soul. You can spin an idea, a phrase, or a cake mix into something that no one else would even imagine. You have a spontaneous spirit, and you encourage the people around you to tap into their own creative juices. Those talents are a gift from God, and you should know what a difference you make to others all the time.

Perhaps you don't always tap into your own creative abilities, but no doubt your friends could list them for you without hesitation. As you look at all you want to accomplish today, see if there are any creative ways that you can spend time with God. Can you say your prayers while you're riding your bike? Can you memorize a Scripture that you might turn into a piece of wall art for your office?

This is a great day and one that deserves something special from you. Go ahead and pull out all the stops—or the paints, the tools, or whatever you need to connect to the creative part of you. God designed you the way you are on purpose.

Give Him thanks and praise for your creative spirit today.

What you decide on will be done,
and light will shine on your ways.

JOB 22:28

Mom's Prayer

Lord, I do feel creative some days, and I enjoy putting those little talents to work to see just what might develop. Thank you for inspiring my heart and my work each day. Amen.

Words to Live By

Once upon a time, the words to live by involved learning to play nice and to share the things you had. If you didn't have a piece of candy for your friend, then you didn't have candy. If you couldn't say something nice about the person you were with, you didn't say anything at all. Those were great words to live by.

Every age of our lives comes with some new rules that will give us a measure of peace and joy if we can sustain them. Some of those rules involve instructions that Jesus gave us. "Love your neighbor" and "love God" were some of His important words to live by. Others were "be kind," "be happy," and "don't worry."

Your life serves as an example, and you're always influencing others with the words you speak and the words you take to heart. As much as possible, help those around you to grasp the words of love that you manage to share, because the love words are all words to live by.

Gracious words are a honeycomb,
sweet to the soul and healing to the bones.

PROVERBS 16:24

Mom's Prayer

Lord, help me to say words that bless the lives of others, whether I'm with my children, my friends, or complete strangers. I ask you for this help in Jesus' name. Amen.

Inspiration for Today

It's another new day, and you're not sure where the time goes, but this day promises to be much like yesterday. It will be full of activity and work and cleaning and laundry and shopping and perhaps even child care. It will be a day when you wonder where your next smile will come from because nothing you have to do seems to be especially rewarding or fulfilling.

Get ready to smile. Get ready to turn the world upside down, because this is a brand-new day. Not only is it a brand-new day, but you are a brand-new you! Every morning you're made new by the grace of God. He sees yesterday as being long gone and today as being the one—the only one, actually—that is worthy of your time and attention.

This is your day. Create it with purpose and joy and with the grace of God flowing through your veins. You'll have lots of reasons to smile.

Through the LORD's mercies we are not consumed,
Because His compassions fail not.
They are new every morning;
Great is Your faithfulness.

LAMENTATIONS 3:22–23 NKJV

Mom's Prayer

Lord, forgive me when I become nonchalant about the days ahead of me, when I just assume that each one will appear again. Remind me to be more aware of how I live every moment. Amen.

A Nod to Grocery Carts

Grocery carts are useful vehicles. They wind their way around the aisles at the grocery store and help deliver your bounty to the cash register. Sometimes they're good places to prop your toddlers or wheel a four-year-old with some semblance of peace. A good cookie helps too.

Grocery carts are also the vehicles that sometimes go bumping into your ankles as the little elderly lady behind you decides you're moving a bit too slowly. Or, they can be the bane of the parking lot when no one bothers to put them in the cart return.

In a way, grocery carts are useful symbols of our faith. We take both for granted, we use both to fill up with the things of life without getting overwhelmed, and both sometimes give us a smooth ride.

But when things are not going so smoothly, or when our ankles have been bruised once too often, we might find a need to change things. We might look for a safe place where we're protected from the traffic of life. Where is that place? It's the place where we can always park our hearts and minds. It's the place where faith and love come together. It feels good, and sometimes we even get a cookie.

Let your faith help you navigate the aisles of life today.

Trust in the Lord, and do good;
Dwell in the land, and feed on His faithfulness.

PSALM 37:3 NKJV

Mom's Prayer

Lord, help me to pay attention to my faith, watching what I'm doing and making sure I stay connected to you. Amen.

Shoes

Do you have a favorite pair of shoes?

Maybe they're the fancy shoes you wear at holidays or to special events, the ones that don't get out very often. Or maybe you have some favorite running shoes that you wear every day as you prepare to get outside to commune with nature and exercise. They're well worn and have stories to tell of the miles they've traveled. You might have a favorite pair of sandals that serve you well all summer, or a special pair of shoes you reserve for church. Your shoes reflect a lot about your lifestyle, helping to define a bit more of the woman you are.

Jesus wore sandals, comfortable shoes that would be easy to remove when He stood on holy ground, or easy to wash off in the rivers around Galilee. John the Baptist even noted that he was not worthy to untie the sandals worn by Jesus.

Of course, there's nothing holy about shoes themselves, but there is something holy about the one who walks in them, especially if she is walking with the Lord every day.

Walk with Him today.

You shall walk in all the ways which the LORD your God has commanded you, that you may live and that it may be well with you.

DEUTERONOMY 5:33 NKJV

Mom's Prayer

Lord, I like to wear my comfortable shoes most of the time, but no matter which shoes I wear, I want to walk with you. Help me to always follow in your footsteps. Amen.

Autumn Leaves

Wherever you happen to live, the fall of the year brings about significant changes. In many areas, the temperature drops a little, the garden gives up its harvest, and the leaves turn golden and brightly hued. There's even a smell of the coming winter in the air.

The fall season reminds us that everything changes. What was once a vibrant green landscape fades and passes on, perhaps soon to be covered by falling snow. It's the season to gather things together and prepare for all that's ahead with grace and gratitude.

Your life is always in a state of change, and each season brings you something else to consider. If you're in your autumn years, just remember that you have plenty of golden leaves of wisdom to share with your children and the others who you love. You're meant to bring a harvest of joy and love to all you do.

May God bless you with His favor in all the seasons of your life.

"As long as the earth continues,
planting and harvest,
cold and hot,
summer and winter,
day and night
will not stop."

GENESIS 8:22 NCV

Mom's Prayer

Lord, help me always to appreciate all that I have learned and have yet to learn in the bounty of your Word. Amen.

Million-Dollar Questions

When your kids were little, they asked you a lot of questions. Some of them were memorable. They may have asked you things like, "Where do babies come from?" or "Where did Grandpa go when he died?" These weren't easy questions for you to answer, but they were certainly important.

As human beings, we're tempted to ask a lot of "why" questions. We're curious. God designed us to have inquiring minds, to be seekers. He even made it a bit of a challenge for us to get to know Him. God often hides Himself in plain sight. He's hidden from us until we're ready to ask the right questions. When we do, He makes Himself known and appears beside us.

Your questions are important to Him. You can ask Him all the million-dollar questions you'd like to ask, and He'll patiently and lovingly answer each one. In fact, He loves your questions because it means you're seeking more of Him.

Whatever your questions are today, just know that He's there for you, ready to answer each question with love and help you understand the things that challenge you.

Until now you have not asked for anything in my name. Ask and you will receive, so that your joy will be the fullest possible joy.

JOHN 16:24 NCV

Mom's Prayer

Lord, I always have another question to ask. Thank you for being close to me and helping me to discover the million-dollar answers you have for me. Amen.

Winning the Lottery

What's your lottery-winning ideal? Is it the one where you win a fabulous amount of money and can build your dream house and travel the world? Is it the one where you finally follow your heart and give up the job you've never liked anyway to pursue other things? Is it having a chance to become well known for the talent you possess?

As a mom, you may believe that you won the lottery the day your first child was born, or you may feel like you won the lottery when your kids successfully graduated from high school or college. There's probably something you can identify as being so worthwhile that it feels like you won the lottery.

However you feel about that, one thing is for sure. One day, according to God's perfect timing, He's going to welcome you into heaven. When He does, you're going to be met with thunderous applause for a job well done. You're going to feel like you just won the lottery. The truth is, you did! You won it the very day you invited Christ into your life.

For to me, to live is Christ and to die is gain.

PHILIPPIANS 1:21

Mom's Prayer

Lord, thank you for preparing my lottery moments here on earth and there in heaven. It's good to know that your blessings go on forever. Amen.

Mom's Linked In

Social media sites do their best to draw together people of like minds or occupations. They want to give opportunities for connection and sharing of ideas and values. Linking with others online gives you a broad network of people to offer advice or share important information. It's great to feel so connected to your "neighbors" on the Net.

Fortunately for you, you're linked in well beyond the services of the Internet. You're linked in to the universe, and you don't even need a surge protector to help you when it rains and pours. You're always connected to your Father in heaven, and He is fully capable of communicating with you at any hour of the day.

You don't have to keep the words to a minimum, and you don't have to add a picture to remind Him who you are. You simply have to click into that space in your heart that seeks Him. Once you're peacefully settled, fully committed to your conversation, you'll hear Him come through to you clear as a bell.

Thank God that no matter what else is going on, you're always linked to Him.

It is the LORD your God you must follow, and him you must revere. Keep his commands and obey him; serve him and hold fast to him.

DEUTERONOMY 13:4

Mom's Prayer

Lord, thank you for staying connected to me in ways that surpass any technological system we might invent. Your way is amazing— my heart to yours. Amen.

Silly, Sweet, Sassy Mom

Your personality is vibrant. You can be silly and sweet, charming and welcoming. You can also be a bit sassy, demure, or quiet. The beauty of the way you were designed is that you're loved and admired for all of these aspects of the real you.

One unchangeable thing about human beings is that we're so changeable. We reflect the weather sometimes, having gloomy moods when the sky is cloudy or sparkling moods when the sun shines. We reflect the environment of our homes, our work, or our friends. We're never exactly the same all the time. It might make it more difficult for our family and friends to keep up with the best ways to interact with us, but it's okay. They know us and love us as we are.

Alternately, God does not change. He doesn't suffer mood swings or get cranky when He doesn't get enough sleep or when His stomach is rumbling because He hasn't eaten. He doesn't flip from warm and loving to angry and vengeful. He is the same today and tomorrow and will remain so. We can count on Him, and we can count on His mood.

Jesus Christ is the same yesterday and today and forever.

HEBREWS 13:8

Mom's Prayer

Lord, thank you that you don't go through all the mood changes I do. I count on you to be steadfast and strong, and to love me whatever mood I am in. Amen.

Raking Leaves

One of the pleasant experiences of fall, at least in those states that have mighty oaks and maple trees, is the chance to get outside on a sunny day and rake the leaves that have found their way to the ground. You may not find it as much fun as your kids do, since you probably aren't piling them up and jumping in them, but if such a thought brings you a memory of a long time ago, then it's one that beckons your heart.

Raking the fall leaves is one of the things that only happens a few times a year, and one that comes with its own crunching sounds and autumnal smell. It invites you out to play, and that's a good thing.

As you get ready for your day, you may not even be in a place where leaves are gently falling, but imagine taking a moment and breathing in that crisp fall air and reminding yourself that sometimes life is simple and peaceful and even a few falling leaves can help make it so.

If you're in need of a peaceful moment, stop and take in the spirit of the One who made this day possible and who sees you right where you are.

Be anxious for nothing, but in everything by prayer and supplication, with thanksgiving, let your requests be made known to God; and the peace of God, which surpasses all understanding, will guard your hearts and minds through Christ Jesus.

PHILIPPIANS 4:6–7 NKJV

Mom's Prayer

Lord, thank you for the changing seasons and all you've done to create a world that beckons us to seek more of you and to even come outside and play. Amen.

Morning Prayers

The sun is just beginning to make its presence known as the new day dawns. The morning sky beckons you to notice it, to get lost in its possibility and gift of light. You're drawn to it like a moth to a flame because it is so beautiful to behold. It's a fresh moment, a holy one, for it speaks of God's mercy that He has indeed allowed us to rise to a new day.

As you take in the sights and the sounds of the morning, let your heart seek the Creator, the One who was kind enough to bring you the dawn and who always hopes you'll awaken more fully to His presence. Ask for His guidance as you watch the morning stars disappear and the brilliant sun showcase all that you can see for miles around. It's time to pray. Time to lean in and listen for what the Lord has to offer you today. It's time, like the new day, to be renewed in His light.

Do not be shaped by this world; instead be changed within by a new way of thinking. Then you will be able to decide what God wants for you; you will know what is good and pleasing to him and what is perfect.

ROMANS 12:2 NCV

Mom's Prayer

Lord, thank you for each day when I can begin to seek your face again. Shine your light on each person I love today. Amen.

October

Acorns and Oaks

One analogy of the job of mothering is to turn your own precious little seedlings, your own little acorns, into mighty oaks. The opportunity to teach your children the beauty of becoming all they were meant to be is daunting. You can help them grow, nourishing their minds and spirits, and you can help them become stronger as they learn more of what it means to simply be themselves. They're meant to be flexible and strong. They're meant to be like mighty oaks that bless the world around them.

You have been blessed to do the work at hand. God has given you all the tools you need, and He has given you His example to fortify you when your little saplings need even more than you're able to give. He made room for your family right in the midst of His garden—a safe place to watch you continue to grow healthy and strong.

As you walk by a little acorn or a mighty oak today, remember what God has done to bless you and your precious ones to help them grow. You've done such a great job!

In their righteousness, they will be like great oaks
That the Lord has planted for his own glory.

ISAIAH 61:3 NLT

Mom's Prayer

Lord, I love that you have been with me as I seek to help my children become all that you created them to be. Please help them continue to grow strong in your care. Amen.

Pumpkin Patches

October is such a beautiful month because all the colors of summer explode with an amazing tale of bright and bold details. The leaves crunch and the golden pumpkins prepare for their happy faces. The thoughts of winter begin to ease into view. It's a month of change and of the glorious harvest of all that God has given us through the year.

Consider your life in God's pumpkin patch. Where are you as you begin to blossom? Are you still clinging to the vine, growing in every possible way? Are you changing from a pale shade of yellow to an amazing orange delight? Have you left the vine completely and are simply available to display your magnificence to those who come near?

Whatever phase of the journey you're in, God can use you. He can bless those around you with your presence, and He can keep you growing no matter where you might sit in the garden. He does all of these things for you as a woman and a mom. Make it great day in the pumpkin patch!

I pray that your love will overflow more and more, and that you will keep on growing in knowledge and understanding.

PHILIPPIANS 1:9 NLT

Mom's Prayer

Lord, you know me and you know just what stage I'm in as I seek to grow closer to you. Help me to nourish my own children the way you always nourish me. Amen.

What Rhymes with Orange?

We like things to go together and make sense to us. We're more comfortable when we recognize familiar patterns. Yes, we like a sense of order in our lives. Sometimes, though, we can't come up with something that works; we can't find a word that rhymes with orange. We're left to puzzle over just why things are so complex, and we wonder what we're supposed to do.

Fortunately, the answer isn't complicated. The answer is to return to the source of our well-being, to seek the One who brings order out of chaos and who understands that we don't want to exist in a spirit of confusion. God knows what we need and how to help us.

If you're feeling like things aren't lining up for you in the ways you believe they should, then get out of line. Get to the one place where you can find peace again. Let God help you pull the blessing out of the things you don't understand.

It's your day to rest in His presence. Trust that He goes before you in all things and that it's okay if nothing rhymes with orange.

God is not a God of confusion but a God of peace.

1 CORINTHIANS 14:33 NCV

Mom's Prayer

Lord, I need you to walk ahead of me and clear the way for the things you would have me do. Help me to breathe in your peace and mercy today. Amen.

Soup's On!

When you have a tinge of hunger and the world seems a bit off-kilter, there's a comforting phrase that sometimes makes everything all right. When someone hollers that the soup is on, you come running, knowing that once you've taken in that delicious smell and gotten your fill of the herbs, spices, and special gifts from the garden, the world will make sense again.

Some days it's as simple as that! You just want to be nourished and comforted and know that everything will work out. A great bowl of homemade soup might be one way to get that kind of comfort. Spending some time with the Lord, walking with Him in His garden, tasting the spirit of joy that only He can offer, and breathing in the fragrance of His presence might be another way. This may in fact be the best way!

When things aren't going just right for you and the day is somewhat cold and empty, go fill up on the warmth and love of God. He's always waiting to help you, and He's not above providing you with a little tasty soup, the kind that only He can prepare.

Enjoy your day!

Taste and see that the Lord is good;
blessed is the one who takes refuge in him.

PSALM 34:8

Mom's Prayer

Lord, I love knowing you're willing and able to comfort me when the days seem weary. Thanks for being my own special brand of chicken soup. Amen.

Blueberries for Mom

Something about blueberries takes us home again. Maybe it's because we once had a grandma or an aunt who created special treats from those juicy blue bits of heaven. Maybe it was because somewhere along the way, we picked blueberries off the bushes and remember the smell and the fun of sharing a day gathering the sweet fruit.

If you didn't have that kind of experience but simply love a good blueberry muffin, especially when it's warm and topped with a little powdered sugar, you can still appreciate the singular blessing it brings.

If it were possible, we'd be sure you got some blueberries to enjoy today. We'd do it because you are a special person, always doing the things that treat others to your gifts of kindness and offer a taste of what it means to be a good mom. You would be the one we'd like to share a blueberry treat with today, just because you're you.

Thank God that He blessed us with bountiful fruits of joy.

"Your mother was like a vine in your vineyard
planted by the water; it was fruitful and full of branches
because of abundant water."

EZEKIEL 19:10

Mom's Prayer

Lord, I'm grateful for the little things you've done to make life such a pleasure. Thank you for the gifts you always give me as a mom. Amen.

If Mom Ruled the World!

Moms rule! At least we like to think so. Moms certainly have a big say in the ways that things work in their homes. What if moms ruled the world though? What would that be like?

It's possible that the first thing moms would do is remind people about the Golden Rule. Remember to be nice to others and they'll be nice to you. They might also request that people clean up their messes and listen to the counsel of those wiser than themselves if they want their plans to succeed.

If moms ruled the world, they would remind people that God created them to love each other, pure and simple. They were not made to fight or belittle or cast stones. They were made to love each other and to love God. That's the job, and it's the one given to every person on the planet.

As a mom, you could probably add a few of your own rules for the world, but you would always do it with love. Thanks for all you do to make the world a better place.

Listen to counsel and receive instruction,
That you may be wise in your latter days.
PROVERBS 19:20 NKJV

Mom's Prayer

Lord, I'm glad I don't rule the world, but I would definitely require people to treat each other with kindness and love. I think these are the things you require too. Amen.

Mom's Best Ingredients

We like home recipes. Many times those recipes have been handed down from one cook to the next. You might still be making your grandmother's favorite apple pie or chocolate cake. You might have your aunt's chicken potpie so down to perfection that your family waits hungrily for it to come out of the oven. The things we love are made with care and with our favorite ingredients.

Whether you cook or not, you use that kind of approach to being a mom. You do everything you can for the good of your family, and you do it with care, using the ideas and values you believe are best. You use your favorite ingredients for love and tenderness, and even for discipline and giving advice. You give your best because you know it's the way you get the most pleasing results.

God is pleased with the amazing ways you use the gifts He gave you.

Concentrate on doing your best for God, work you won't be ashamed of, laying out the truth plain and simple.

2 TIMOTHY 2:16 MSG

Mom's Prayer

Lord, thank you for watching over me as I strive to prepare my children to live in the world. Help me to be wise in the things I choose to share with them. Amen.

More than a Mom

You're more than a mom. You're a mom who loves the Lord. You pay attention to the things that make a difference in your home. You know that sometimes your kids need you to listen, and so you act as their counselor and advisor. Sometimes your family members need help figuring out the best way to do a project, solve a problem, or create something new.

You're good at being a teacher and a guide. You can also be the one who shares in their goals, coaching them and helping to bring out the best in them. You do a lot of things that make you so much more than a mom.

You do the things that please your heavenly Father as well. You seek His face when you don't know what to do, and you hold on tight when things are falling apart. You know that God is more than able to help you through anything.

Stick together! Keep more of God in your life every day.

Come near to God, and God will come near to you.

JAMES 4:8 NCV

Mom's Prayer

Lord, thank you for being close to me and for providing for me and my family in every good way. I am humbled by all you do for me. Amen.

The Mom Muscle

The muscles in our bodies are the active supporters of all our movements. When the muscles are bruised or damaged, they cause the body stress that takes time to heal. A mom's role is somewhat like the muscles of the body. Moms make sure that everything functions the way it should for their kids. They make it easier for their kids to move and grow and become all they're meant to be.

Your muscles provide strength and make it possible for your body to do things like lift heavy objects, bend down on one knee, or even raise your head. Every part of your body has a muscle. If you think of yourself—or your work as a mom—as a muscle, you can see how important you are to making sure every part of your child's life works as it should. You provide the strength and flexibility to get things done.

Thank God for His amazing design of your body and for allowing you to act like a muscle when it comes to being sure your family is strong and blessed.

A wise woman strengthens her family.

PROVERBS 14:1 NCV

Mom's Prayer

Lord, thank you for being my muscle, the One I lean on for strength every day. Bless my home and my family always. Amen.

Mom's Pure Love

Moms are good at counting the foibles, the mix-ups, the things they didn't do well. They can tell you in a heartbeat just where they went wrong, where they didn't pay enough attention, where they didn't do the right thing, and where they didn't manage to be perfect in every way.

The good news is this: your love for your children is pure love, not perfect love. You love them when they're clean and bright, and when they're messy and in need of a good scrubbing. You love them when they don't seem to love you back. You love them when they fall down and when you hold them in your arms.

You are the constant. You're the one part of their lives that doesn't change, at least not in the sense of your love for them, your pure unconditional love. This part of you is a gift from God, and it's the one thing that reminds you of how you are loved by God for all you do. He has pure love for you too. In His case, however, He also has perfect love for you.

Embrace His love today.

May the Lord direct your hearts into God's love and
Christ's perseverance.

2 THESSALONIANS 3:5

Mom's Prayer

Lord, thank you for loving me without conditions, just as I am.
Help me to love my family in the very same way. Amen.

What's Next, Mom?

Perhaps you think you've tried all the new things you're really going to do. You're not thinking about reinventing your life or starting over in some way, and yet, is there something more? Did you accomplish all the dreams you had long ago? What about the seeds you never bothered to sow or the trees you never planted?

You may have missed the boat back then, but you're still here and you're still capable of doing great things. You can still plant a tree that will amaze you just five years from now. You can still do that next big thing that you thought was gone. Being a mom only brings out a few of your gifts; being you means there's even more to be considered.

Today, be willing to ask yourself, what's next? What do you want to change about your life right now that will make an amazing difference just five years or even one year down the road? Seek God's help with your next goal.

I press on toward the goal to win the prize for which God has called me heavenward in Christ Jesus.

PHILIPPIANS 3:14

Mom's Prayer

Lord, there are many dreams that I've let slip through my fingers. Help me to discover which ones I should hold on to this very day. Amen.

Try Something New

Feeling stuck? Are you wondering if you've already hit the limit, already done all the important things you'll ever do in life? Being a mother is an important job. It's a big job! But it's not the only job for you. There is still an abundance of things left for you to explore that will renew your spirit and enthusiasm for life. They're things that'll make a difference in the years ahead of you and in the lives of others.

Today's your day to give yourself permission to make mistakes as you learn something new, get unstuck, and feel vibrant and alive. Offer yourself some new choices, and go after at least one of them. As you do one thing that gives you a feeling of moving forward and a new sense of accomplishment, you'll enjoy yourself and switch out of your usual routine. You may even wonder what took you so long.

Try something new with God too. Step out in faith and seek Him in a way that you may never have before. Who knows what gifts He is waiting to give you.

This is your day, and it's all brand new.

Because of the LORD's great love we are not consumed,
for his compassions never fail.
They are new every morning;
great is your faithfulness.

LAMENTATIONS 3:22–23

Mom's Prayer

Lord, I do feel a little like every day is the same as the one before.
Please help me to be willing to try something new with your blessing.
Amen.

Make It Better!

You've probably heard the words "Make it better, Mommy!" when your child fell and scraped an elbow or knee. After all, Mommy is supposed to be able to make all things better; at least that's the way we like to think.

You work hard to make things better for your family. You may have one unvoiced goal when you get up each day—to make things better today than they were yesterday. You want to give everyone in your family a good reason to smile.

Sometimes as adults we find ourselves going to God with the same request. *Make it better, God!* We don't want to live with worry and frustration and a sense of falling farther behind with every passing hour. We don't want to see our dwindling bank accounts and our even more dwindling spirits come to nothing at all. We want God to make it better.

And God wants to make it better! The best way to enlist His help is simply to focus on Him. Put your troubles at His feet, and lift your heart to Him in praise. Before long, you'll see a change. You'll see the ways that He worked just for you to make it better.

My help comes from the Lord, who made the heavens and the earth!

PSALM 121:2 NLT

Mom's Prayer

Lord, I know I can't always make things better. Please help me do what I can in those times, and help me to seek your guidance for all that is possible. Amen.

Practice Makes Perfect

You may remember being told that you could only expect to improve a skill or talent with practice. Your goal was some sort of nebulous, undefined perfection. It all made sense to a point.

Certainly the great sports stars and musicians would say that they didn't become successful by luck; their success came from practicing many hours a day. They kept their minds and hearts wrapped around that one thing they hoped to perfect.

A lot of things take practice, and whether it's learning how to make a great cream puff or how to tell a good story to a kid, you're probably practicing something.

Today, with all this talk about practice, you might also consider what kind of spiritual practice you do. What are the ways you focus on the things of God so you can learn more about Him and about the work He has for you to do in the world? Like anything else, you'll get better at knowing God as you spend more time in His presence. That's called practicing the presence of God.

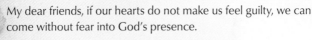

My dear friends, if our hearts do not make us feel guilty, we can come without fear into God's presence.

1 JOHN 3:21 NCV

Mom's Prayer

Lord, I need to form better spiritual practices. Help me to keep you in mind for all that I hope to become, so I can remain in your perfect will. Amen.

Knowing What Matters

One of the biggest mom jobs is being able to understand the things that matter. It means you have to be able to understand when an eight-year-old is disappointed about not making it onto a travel soccer team and when your college-bound student doesn't get the first-choice school. You have to know what matters to yourself and what matters to each person in your family.

You're good at knowing what matters. You know that discipline has to be administered with love and that disappointment might require a trip to the local ice cream shop. You know that some things matter even more than you realize and that you have to be sensitive to the needs and longings of those around you.

The good news is that God also helps you understand the things that matter. He directs your steps and guides you to where you can be most effective and offer the most hope.

Take all the matters in your life to God, and He will reveal His plans for you.

The steps of a good woman are ordered by the LORD,
And He delights in her way.

ADAPTED FROM PSALM 37:23 NKJV

Mom's Prayer

Lord, thank you for helping me sort out the things that really matter. Show me what you would do in situations that are difficult for me to understand. Amen.

Sitting Next to God

Have you ever just pulled up a chair for Jesus and asked Him to sit with you awhile? Maybe you were on the front porch steps or the back deck and you just wanted some quiet time. If you haven't done it lately, you might find a time today to just be alone with your Friend and Lord.

When you sit near someone, you can do things that you can't do when you imagine them being far away. You can smile and share some small talk. You can hold hands or give each other a hug.

You can always benefit from an extra hug, so sit down, invite Jesus to chat with you, and enjoy your time together. Tell Him all about your home, your kids, and your dreams. He's always interested in knowing more about you, and He's ready for you to know more about Him.

Draw near and give thanks for today.

For the eyes of the LORD are on the righteous,
And His ears are open to their prayers.

1 PETER 3:12 NKJV

Mom's Prayer

Lord, help me to create a space for you to draw near to me. I like the idea of sitting close to you and sharing my heart. Be with me today. Amen.

Promise Keeping

You do your best to honor the promises you make. It's not always easy, though, because things change and disrupt your plans; now and then those promises have to be broken.

The Bible suggests that it's important to be careful about promises we make and the vows that we offer, especially to God and to each other as well. God takes our promises seriously and we should too. We never want to be glib about the things we commit to do.

Moms and kids know what it's like when promises are broken. We try to understand that things change and schedules need to be rearranged. We also know the feelings of disappointment remain. Be aware of the promises you make to your family, to your friends, and to God. Do all that you can to stand behind your commitments!

God will bless you and help you keep those promises as much as possible.

"Blessed is she who has believed that the Lord would fulfill his promises to her!"

LUKE 1:45

Mom's Prayer

Lord, thank you for helping me to keep my promises. I really want to honor my commitments to others in every way. Amen.

Mom and Apple Pie

Years ago, many people considered honoring Mom, the flag, and apple pie as traits of being American. They thought all those things represented what it means to live a good life—a life that respected others and embraced them. Parents tried to instill those values into their children because they believed that was their calling.

Today, we don't see as many flagpoles in front of people's houses and we don't have as many moms making apple pie as we once did. However, we still aspire to embrace others and respect them. We still hope to teach our children the kind of compassionate values that will help them become caring and generous adults.

God placed each of us in family. He gave us a home, a hearth, and a country, and He offers us a way to be connected to others through our family. Take time today to pray for families in every culture, that they would embrace the values that encourage all people to care about each other. After all, God so loved the world that He gave His one and only Son for us all.

"God loved the world so much that he gave his one and only Son so that whoever believes in him may not be lost, but have eternal life."

JOHN 3:16 NCV

Mom's Prayer

Lord, thank you for my country, my home, and my family. Bless families everywhere, and help us all to be kind toward each other and to come to know you. Amen.

Mom's Flashlight

Most of us keep a flashlight somewhere within reach for those unexpected times that the lights go out. We try to be prepared for minor emergencies. Then when we use the flashlight, one of the things we notice is that it doesn't cast a beam very far ahead. It usually gives us just enough light to go a few feet at a time.

In some ways, this is how God works in our lives. He gives us a little bit of light, a kind of flashlight so we can see just far enough to get us where we're going today. We don't have to see miles ahead. We don't have to see around corners. We just have to see enough to keep walking in the right direction.

Look at the direction your life is going. Do you need a bigger flashlight? Do you need to connect more with God to see where He might be truly leading you? It's good to be prepared. It's good to be ready to move forward.

Anytime you sense a loss of power, trust that God will light the way for you and your family.

Your word is a lamp to my feet
And a light to my path.

PSALM 119:105 NKJV

Mom's Prayer

Lord, thank you for guiding me and for being the source of light for my family. I ask that you would always go ahead of us and get us safely where we need to go. Amen.

Dressed to Be Blessed

One of the slogans from our recent past was the motto "dressed for success." The idea was that if you wanted to be successful in business, you had to dress for the part. It was one of the instructions given to college students when they prepared for their first job interviews. But looking the part was only a portion of the dressed-for-success thinking; the rest of it was all about believing in yourself, in the person behind that perfect suit of clothes.

If we had a motto for our relationship with God, it might be something like "dressed to be blessed." God doesn't have a dress code except for the way we dress our hearts. If our outward appearance doesn't match our inward appearance, it makes no difference how we're dressed. We're only dressed for success when we seek the good of others and strive to be a blessing to them. Beyond that, we're called to seek God Himself.

Our best look is the one that radiates from the smile on our face. As a mom, you're invited to be successful too, properly adorned for all that God has for you.

We pray that you will also have great wisdom and understanding in spiritual things so that you will live the kind of life that honors and pleases the Lord in every way.

COLOSSIANS 1:9–10 NCV

Mom's Prayer

Lord, I pray that I will always be well dressed from the inside and that my heart will seek to be at its finest whenever it touches another person's life. Amen.

Of Nursery Rhymes and Lullabies

Whether you're a young mom or a grandmother, you never get past the wonder of a newborn. These tiny tots are the ones who bring us hope for tomorrow, the ones we entrust to God, and the ones for whom we pray.

There's nothing quite like spending time rocking a little person to sleep, humming your favorite lullaby, or reading some of the same nursery rhymes you grew up with yourself. These are cherished moments for most moms, quiet ones that stir the heart and offer a chance for reflection. Motherhood certainly has its challenges, but somehow these quiet times with a baby are soothing to the soul.

As you think about those moments, rejoice that you've had a chance to hold God's own tender souls to your heart and to influence the way they would meet life for years to come.

Seek God's continued guidance and love for all your family.

Therefore if you have any encouragement from being united with Christ, if any comfort from his love, if any common sharing in the Spirit, if any tenderness and compassion, then make my joy complete by being like-minded, having the same love, being one in spirit and of one mind.

PHILIPPIANS 2:1–2

Mom's Prayer

Lord, I treasure those quiet moments with my own little ones, and I pray for the blessing of your peace on moms everywhere. Amen.

The Poetry of Mom

You know you're a unique mom, "one in a million" as the poets might say. You bring your own management style, your own sense of humor, and your various talents, and you utilize all of them to create a home atmosphere that suits you and the rest of your household. You're a genuine work of art, a bit of poetry in your own free-verse style.

One of the reasons moms and poets are kindred spirits is because it takes a great deal of sensitivity to write a poem or to be a mom. You have to understand the world and perceive it in ways that may not be quite the norm. That's okay, though, because you're not trying to be the same mom as the woman down the street. You're trying to be a God-fearing, fun-loving, generous-hearted kind of mom. That's what gives you your special poetic license.

Thank God for your unique talents as a mom and for the ways you get to write your own bit of poetry at home.

A tenderhearted person lives a blessed life.
PROVERBS 28:14 MSG

Mom's Prayer

Lord, I don't think of myself as a writer of poetry, but I can rejoice in knowing that you created me to be a loving expression of you and that I'm doing my best to please you and to shine your light.
Amen.

It's Mom's Turn

Moms are good at taking turns. They always try to be sure that everyone else gets to go first; it's just the way they are. Today, it really is your turn. It's your turn to let go of worry. It's your turn to embrace the best parts of life. It's your turn to smile.

Remember that God's plan for you is that you live a life of fullness and abundance. Abundant living comes from your positive spirit and your awareness that God is faithful and always watching out for your good. It's the abundance of knowing you're loved by many people and that you make a difference in the lives of others.

Take your turn today. Take your turn to enjoy the best your day can bring. Embrace love and laughter. Set the worries of the world behind you for just one day. It will make all the difference.

"GOD is striding ahead of you. He's right there with you. He won't let you down; he won't leave you. Don't be intimidated. Don't worry."

DEUTERONOMY 31:8 MSG

Mom's Prayer

Lord, I haven't taken my turn for a while. I'm not very good at putting worries behind me. Help me do that and simply appreciate all that you've given me today. Amen.

Mom's a Little Bit of an Angel

When God asked us to be His hands and feet—women who share what we have and who walk in the door with offers of help—He was asking us to be a little bit like an angel to each other. He wants us to do those unexpected things that bring surprise delight and make someone else think about Him. He wants us to always remind others that He's watching over us and that He cares what happens to us.

You're good at being a little bit of an angel! You are a natural giver and caretaker. Your compassion for others is what motivates your heart and brings out that genuine smile on your face. You make everyone feel blessed to know you.

You offer the same kind of inspiration to your children. You're the kind of mom who brings out the best in each person in your family and helps each one feel better about the things they deal with each day. Thank you for always being a little bit of an angel.

Do not forget to entertain strangers, for by so doing some have unwittingly entertained angels.

HEBREWS 13:2 NKJV

Mom's Prayer

Lord, it's always a blessing to me when someone surprises me with help just when I need it or a kind word when my spirits are low. Remind me of that blessing often so I do the same for others. Amen.

Of Hay Rides and Scarecrows

Little things about certain seasons bring us delight. Taking the kids to pick pumpkins, go on a hayride, or see the funny scarecrows on a farm adds to the memories of fall. Of course, not everyone lives in the country, so cider mills and pumpkin patches may not be readily available. Even so, wherever you are, it's a good day to give God thanks and praise for the harvest of goodness and favor He has lavished on you and your family this year.

If you could go on a hayride, maybe on a moonlit night with some hot cocoa and a blanket to keep off the evening chill, you might gain a new perspective on life. Those simple moments shared with others make all the difference. This year, as you pick out a pumpkin and prepare to enhance its natural features with your own creation, laughing at the mess you'll make and the fun of seeing it first come to light, you can reflect again on God's goodness.

Don't wait to go on a hayride to remind God that you love the way He designed the world. Thank Him for giving you such a variety of beautiful things to do, and tell Him that you appreciate His amazing grace every day.

Offer to God thanksgiving,
And pay your vows to the Most High.

PSALM 50:14 NKJV

Mom's Prayer

Lord, thank you for the gifts of this particular season. Thank you for helping me to see the blessings of your love in the little things we enjoy as a family. Amen.

Leaving the Light On

When you were a kid, there were probably times when you wanted to leave the light on. It may have been a stormy night, or you may simply have had a bad dream or heard a scary story or something, but you wanted the light on. You wanted to be able to clearly see every corner of your room.

Your kids have probably had those times too. There's something comforting about a little night light. Most of us feel a need for extra light when we're nervous or uncertain about something, or when we have a lot on our minds. We often long for some extra illumination. Even as an adult, you probably appreciate that cute little light that shines from the outlet in the bathroom, giving just enough security as you head off to sleep.

If you need comfort, you can also seek God's light. Ask Him to draw closer to you and watch over you as you drift off to dreamland. You might also memorize some Scripture, repeating a verse you're trying to learn well, until you're sleeping soundly. You can let the Word be your light.

May God bless you and keep you and make His face to shine upon you both day and night.

The Light shines in the darkness, and the darkness has not overpowered it.

JOHN 1:5 NCV

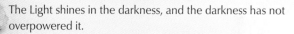

Mom's Prayer

Lord, please be with my children as they sleep, and give them the comfort of knowing you are there and watching over them each night. Bless each of us with peace. Amen.

Respect for Mom

Alexander Dumas once wrote, "Without respect, love cannot go far or rise high; it is an angel with but one wing."

As a mom, you deserve the respect of your family members, and most likely it's easy for them to make sure you feel their respect, admiration, and love for you. Respect is earned, and you earn it every day.

How do you know they respect you? You know because they seek you out, asking your opinion on everything from what to do now to what to wear. They look to you for comfort and advice. They come to you when their plans fall through or when they feel they've done all they can on their own. They have deep respect for your opinions and your life experience.

The more you get to know someone, the more you gain respect for them. The more you get to know the Scriptures, the more you get to know God as well. When you read your Bible, seeking answers to your questions about life, you show God that you value His opinion and His direction. You appreciate His thoughts and enjoy His peace and comfort. You respect Him and are in awe of His teachings.

Give respect to those who deserve it, even to God Himself.

GOD, your God, is among you—GOD majestic, GOD awesome.

DEUTERONOMY 7:21 MSG

Mom's Prayer

Lord, thank you that my family has such great respect for me. I love and value each one of them as well. I remain forever in awe of you. Amen.

Gathering Sap Buckets

October is the month when you see sap buckets hanging from the maple trees in Vermont and upstate New York. It takes many hours to collect the clear, sweet liquid from the tapped trees and gather enough buckets to make the syrup you hope to put on your table come Sunday mornings all winter long. Once the sap is collected, you have to boil it and boil it until it becomes the rich golden color that delights your taste buds. Add a little butter and you're not far from an awesome pancake breakfast.

Your work as a mom can sometimes feel like that kind of process. You go through the daily routines with your kids, pouring your heart and mind and energy into them, hoping that over time they'll become kind, sweet, loving people. It takes time, and it takes a lot of discipline. Sometimes the process of going from where you are to where you hope you'll end up seems arduous and even discouraging.

When that happens, pray that God will help you stay the course and that He'll guide you as you wait for your own little saplings to become strong adults. Tap into God's grace and mercy anytime you feel like your own bucket of faith is a little bit low.

God's works are so great, worth
A lifetime of study—endless enjoyment!
Splendor and beauty mark his craft;
His generosity never gives out.
His miracles are his memorial—
This God of Grace, this God of Love.

PSALM 111:1–2 MSG

Mom's Prayer

Lord, thank you for being willing to fill my bucket of faith anytime
I tap into you as the source of all I need to grow and be strong.
Amen.

You're Not a Kid Anymore

You've been busy growing and changing for a few decades now. You've learned a lot about yourself and about your faith. There was a time when you may have felt that you had a pretty good handle on the things of God, and that you knew what was expected of you. Of course, once you got there, you realized there was a whole lot more you needed to learn.

St. Augustine said, "If you are pleased with what you are, you have stopped already. If you say, 'It is enough,' you are lost. Keep on walking, moving forward, trying for the goal. Don't try to stop on the way, or go back, or to deviate from it."

As you grow in faith, and as you grow as a parent, you probably see that there's always something more, something new that is yet to be discovered. Keep moving ahead and enjoy the process. It's okay not to be a kid any more. It's great to be an adult fully preparing to do all that God has planned for you to do.

When I was a child, I talked like a child, I thought like a child, I reasoned like a child. When I became an adult, I put childish ways behind me.

ADAPTED FROM 1 CORINTHIANS 13:11

Mom's Prayer

Lord, thank you for continuing to faithfully walk by my side. Bless my children as they learn to walk with you as well. Help me to grow up in every way to honor you. Amen.

Change Is in the Air

This is the time of year when change is a noticeable and notable thing. We pay attention to the fact that even the air around us is changing. The good news of paying more attention to time is that we're more apt to use our time well.

Moms are often so busy each day that they don't think about how the day is spent. They just know that a lot has to get done and so they do it—and keep on doing it, long into the night. Finally, at the end of the day, they drop into bed and hope they get to sleep all night so they can do it all again the next day.

If you're one of those extraordinarily busy moms, trying to figure out how to get a moment to yourself or even trying to remember where the day went as you drag yourself to bed, then do yourself a favor. Stop and take a look at what's happening all around you. Notice the changing foliage outside. Breathe in the fall air and give a moment to God. Share your heart with Him and ask Him to help you keep pace with Him no matter what else you have to do.

The days will keep changing, but God stays the same and you can always count on Him.

There is a time for everything,
and a season for every activity under the heavens.

ECCLESIASTES 3:1

Mom's Prayer

Lord, I know I need to slow down a little, and so I ask you to be with me now. I love the fall seasons and don't want to miss out on the special beauty that only comes at this time of year. Amen.

Boo to Boo-Boos!

We all make mistakes. But those boo-boos are not things we're very happy about, and they seem to hang around us like so many ghosts on a chilly night. Perhaps it's time to just say, "Boo!" to them and send them off once and for all. You don't need to carry your old mistakes around forever. Jesus already washed you clean.

Today is a good day to thank God for taking care of your boo-boos. He knows the places you've been hurt and the places where you need to forgive or be forgiven. Share those with Him today and let those old mistakes all rest in peace.

You can start the new day a whole lot better and be transformed into one of His saints. May God bless you and give you His peace today.

Live creatively, friends. If someone falls into sin, forgivingly restore him, saving your critical comments for yourself. You might be needing forgiveness before the day's out.

GALATIANS 6:1 MSG

Mom's Prayer

Lord, thank you for taking away the ghosts of the past that keep haunting me. I love knowing that I'm made new in you. Amen.

November

There, There

Sometimes you just need a little comforting. You need to know that someone notices that you're struggling with the day and that it matters to them. It helps you cope, and it helps you share whatever it is that's going on. It helps to have at least one there, there or attagirl! And it helps when you don't feel all alone in your difficulties.

Most days you're doing just fine, but sometimes you need some consolation, some tea with a friend, or a little chocolate. It's okay. It's even a good thing.

One thing to remember is that you aren't ever alone, really. God is always with you, always near to embrace you and listen to you. He knows your heart and your needs better than anyone else. He wants to support you and make those difficult moments go away or at least feel more manageable.

Today, keep in mind that your Comforter is always near, waiting for you to call on Him. When you do, He'll come and do His best to give you love and peace.

And I will pray the Father, and he shall give you another Comforter, that he may abide with you forever.

JOHN 14:16 KJV

Mom's Prayer

Lord, thank you for being near me when my life seems out of control. Grant me your sweet peace today. Amen.

Politically Correct

Sometimes we have an interest in being politically correct. That is, we want to be accurate, spot on, and ready to behold the truth. It also can mean we don't want to offend or exclude anyone from our work or our conversation. It's important for us to be a truthful witness in what we do.

This all sounds very lofty and even idealistic. It reminds us that we have to be mindful of the kids' birthday party invitations that go to school. It suggests that we have to all cooperate and get along no matter which Little League team we root for on Saturday afternoon. It means we have to have sensitivity toward each other.

It's good to do our best to be fair and reasonable. We want our kids to do those things and to value the gifts that everyone contributes. It may not be politically correct, but we also want to please God with the ways that we think, speak, and act each day. In fact, we want that most of all!

Obviously, I'm not trying to win the approval of people, but of God. If pleasing people were my goal, I would not be Christ's servant.

GALATIANS 1:10 NLT

Mom's Prayer

Lord, you have given me so much, and I know that my actions don't always show my gratitude. Thanks for sharing the light of your truth with me. Amen.

And the Winner Is...

You aren't in a contest today. You don't have to perform for the judges who will give you 8s or 10s for being superior in your abilities to get kids off to school on time, make sure homework is done and lunches are packed, or even just to be sure they're wearing clean clothes. Nobody is judging how you do the job, except maybe you. And if you are judging your efforts, then go ahead and declare yourself the winner.

You're not competing for anything except the chance to do what you do in as loving a way as possible. You win with your family and with God whenever you put your heart into your work, spend time in prayer for each member of your household, and remind yourself to smile because everything is a process and takes time to manage. You win because you show up and bring the best you have to the table.

May God bless your work today and all that you do to be a good mom. You have a noble calling, and if they were giving out blue ribbons, you'd find one at your door.

An unlucky loser is shunned by all,
but everyone loves a winner.

PROVERBS 14:20 MSG

Mom's Prayer

Lord, I feel like I'm a winner. I love my family and the work I do to keep our happy home and raise positive and healthy kids. Thank you for giving me this amazing blessing. Amen.

Snow Is in the Air

When snow is in the air, moms turn their attention to things like making sure the scraper for the car windshield is handy, snow pants for the little ones are ready to hit the deep freeze, and the kitchen has a sufficient supply of hot chocolate. After all, these are the things that get the whole family through the winter.

The seasons affect the things moms do and the ways they think. You probably have your own winter weather routines that have to do with furnace repairs and snow shovels and firewood for those crisp, cool nights.

Now may also be the time to begin your quiet time with God as you sit with your steaming hot chocolate, a blanket, and a tasty treat. Those are the things that will make it easy for you to snuggle up with your Bible and do some reading. It may be one of the highlights of your winter routine. You might pull out your journal too and just remind yourself of all the fun ways you prepare your home for winter as you prepare your heart for God.

Righteousness goes before him
and prepares the way for his steps.

PSALM 85:13

Mom's Prayer

Lord, thank you for the seasons and even for the drifting snow. Thank you for your provision and abundance no matter what the weather might be. Amen.

Warm-Up Exercises

If you exercise often, you know it's important for your muscles to warm up before you try to do anything that takes a lot of effort. Those warm muscles won't suffer the same way colder ones might. Some moms are very intentional about making sure they get the exercise that will keep them healthy and strong. They pull the sled up the hill or bundle the kids up and go to the gym. They may even jog through the park or shovel snow from the driveway just to be sure they maintain their weight and stay in good shape.

If you applied those principles to your spiritual health, what would your warm-up exercises look like? Would you start by saying a prayer or maybe singing a little hymn as you begin to focus on the Word of God? Would you invite others into your conversations about the things you've learned as you read your daily devotions and Scripture?

God loves it when you take care of your temple, the body that He gave you. He also loves it when you take care of your soul, the one that He'll bring back to Himself when your visit to the earth is through. Don't forget to keep doing your warm-up exercises.

For physical training is of some value, but godliness has value for all things, holding promise for both the present life and the life to come.

1 TIMOTHY 4:8

Mom's Prayer

Lord, it's always good to warm up to get closer to you. Help me to exercise my mind and heart with your Word every day. Amen.

Duck, Duck, Goose!

Certainly you've heard of the early childhood game duck, duck, goose. You've probably played some version of it with your kids. The main idea is that one person walks around a circle of others who are seated on the ground and taps different people, calling out either "Duck!" or "Goose!" When the goose is called, the tapped person sitting on the ground jumps up and runs as fast as possible to catch the one who did the tapping. If they catch the person, then they get to call out "Duck!" or "Goose!" and the game keeps going.

Sometimes life can feel a little like this game. One minute you're feeling like a sitting duck and the next you're running as fast as you can to try to catch up with all you have to do. It's a circle that seems never ending, and you often feel like your turn never comes.

One of the best parts of being a child of God is that you're always in His circle of beloved people. As such, you don't have to chase after Him to keep up. He comes to you and taps you on the shoulder, then resides with you and stays close to you from then on. When God invited you into the circle of His family, He tapped you to be there forever.

Now you who are not Jewish are not foreigners or strangers any longer, but are citizens together with God's holy people. You belong to God's family.

EPHESIANS 2:19 NCV

Mom's Prayer

Lord, thank you for bringing me into your family. I don't ever want to be without you. Amen.

It's a Breeze!

No one would try to tell you that being a mother is easy. Nor would anyone suggest that "it's a breeze." The fact is that most mothers grow into the job. They start out tenderly learning about their new offspring, and they ask a lot of questions. Then they develop good root systems and support groups, and things get better. Before long, they're feeling strong and secure, and are able to bend and move through the changes that life brings. They don't think motherhood is a breeze, but they do know how to keep moving forward no matter how the winds blow.

If there's any chance for motherhood to be a breeze, it's only in the area of the tremendous love moms have for their children. You know this is true, because from the moment you learned you'd be a mom, your heart grew three times its size. You were ready to take on the world.

Today, as you take note of the November breezes, look at the ways God has helped you learn to be a mom—gently, carefully, and consistently— until it was easy to sway with the work at hand.

And the Lord—who is the Spirit—makes us more and more like him as we are changed into his glorious image.

2 CORINTHIANS 3:18 NLT

Mom's Prayer

Lord, thank you for helping me learn how to bend with the breezes of change that blow through my life and for teaching me to always come back strong to love my children even more. Amen.

What's Up?

Wouldn't it be something if we had a new response to that rather glib question, "What's up?" Normally, we scramble to come up with something clever or at least not too mundane in response to the person asking the question. Then we move on as though nothing really happened, no communication was actually exchanged, and that's the end of it.

You could change the paradigm. You could answer the query in a way that might go something like this: *Well, I'm so excited because as I was praying this morning, I was reminded that all things are possible with God. That means that I don't have anything to worry about today, because I've been looking up and things are really getting better!*

What if you simply shared all the good things in your life? You could have so many things on your "up" list that it would be hard to fit them all into a quick conversation. So instead of saying not much, when someone asks you what's up, say, Amazing things are up because God is working so much in my life!

It's worth a try!

All these things will happen on the day when God,
through Christ Jesus, will judge people's secret thoughts.

ROMANS 2:16 NCV

Mom's Prayer

Lord, I have to say that I do feel a bit more "up" when I think about answering that question in such a powerful way. Help me to remember that everything is "up" with me, and it's all because of you. Amen.

Mom's Ruffled Feathers

If you accidentally hit one of Mom's hot buttons, you might indeed ruffle her feathers. Each of us gets a bit angry now and then.

What kinds of things ruffle your feathers? What makes you feel provoked at your neighbor? Of course, it's understandable for you to get upset if someone does something that offends your child. If someone is a bully or simply mean spirited, you have every reason to complain.

The thing to pay attention to is the level of importance of the things that aggravate you. See if you understand why you get triggered or provoked. See if you can do anything to change the way you perceive a circumstance that brings out the boxing gloves.

God is slow to anger. He is not easily provoked. It stands to reason that He also wants us to be slow to anger as well. He might want us to watch out for the triggers that provoke us to actions that we'll later regret or at least feel embarrassed about. If you have any of those triggers that ruffle your feathers, take them to God and seek His peaceful solution for that part of your life today.

A hot-tempered person starts fights;
a cool-tempered person stops them.

PROVERBS 15:18 NLT

Mom's Prayer

Lord, I flare up sometimes over things that I don't even intend to get angry about. I simply don't like injustice or ingratitude on any level. Help me to be the better person in any situation that could cause me to overreact. Amen.

Of Praise and Platitudes

"Praise" is one of those words that we associate most often with Psalms or other books of the Old Testament. We read how David praised God with all his heart and mind, thanking Him for His great faithfulness or steadfast love. Those words ring true to our hearts as sincere, loving, and genuine.

Culturally, though, we sometimes find ourselves in situations where the praise being given is more of a platitude. It's used to give the impression of gratitude or of sincere belief that someone has made a difference. It's almost a tongue-in-cheek kind of action.

When you want to express heartfelt gratitude to those around you, even to your family and friends, make sure you're speaking sincerely and honestly. Praise them because you cannot imagine any better response to the amazing things they have done for you.

While you're at it, see if you can do the same for God today. Offer Him your heartfelt thanks and praise for the amazing things He does for you always.

The woman to be admired and praised is the woman who lives in the Fear-of-God.

PROVERBS 31:31 MSG

Mom's Prayer

Lord, I do thank you with my whole heart. I know that I don't express my love for you nearly enough, but I praise you with all that I am today. Amen.

Picture This

It's great to be a woman of prayer. God loves to hear your prayers for your family, your children, and the things that concern you. He not only loves to hear your prayers, but He also loves to work behind the scenes to bring you every possible good thing, knowing it will give you joy.

Sometimes it's nice to pray in pictures. You set the scene. Maybe you meet Jesus at the beach, walking along the sand and listening to the waves embrace the shore. You can see yourself walking toward Him and Jesus smiling as He approaches you. You meet and He takes your hand, so glad to see you, and asks if there's anything He can do for you today. As you stand there talking, your heart is filled with peace and your cares are swept away on the ocean breezes.

Picture Jesus being so near when you pray that He could literally hold your hand and bless you in ways you never before thought possible. It's a great picture, the two of you side by side…isn't it?

Always be joyful. Never stop praying. Be thankful in all circumstances, for this is God's will for you who belong to Christ Jesus.

1 THESSALONIANS 5:16–18 NLT

Mom's Prayer

Lord, I love the idea of meeting you and sitting with you, knowing you listen to my heart and love me just as I am. Help me to draw near you today. Amen.

Peace and Plenty

If we have an aspiration at this time of the year, moving toward Thanksgiving and Christmas, it's that we would love for the world to be wrapped in peace and plenty. We would love for all people to know the peace of God, for every child's tummy to be full, and for those in need to have great abundance.

Alas, there's so much tumult and uproar that it's difficult to even imagine a possibility like that. We become jaded to the idea that peace could ever happen or that all people would have plenty. What can we do in some small way to help bring that about this year?

Maybe we can start with the one person we can hope to change. Maybe we can start with ourselves and seek God's peace that passes all understanding. That kind of peace is way beyond our imagination, but we believe it's possible. We can fill ourselves with His peace until we're overflowing and every one of our senses feels the gift of His love. We can feel that we have plenty.

Today, seek God's peace and abundance for yourself and then pass it on to everyone you meet.

May God's peace and mercy be upon all who live by this principle; they are the new people of God.

GALATIANS 6:16 NLT

Mom's Prayer

Lord, help me to live for peace, to seek peace in all things, and to fill my heart, mind, and soul with the only peace that matters—the kind that comes from you. Amen.

Tender Talk for Moms

If you're like a lot of moms, you have trouble talking tenderly to yourself. That means your inner critic is always loud and clear, but your inner angel is difficult to hear. You aren't even sure there is an inner angel.

If you were going to allow your inner angel to come through today, what would you be able to hear? Would you hear that you're a good mom—in fact, a great mom! Would you believe that you deserve applause for the heroic ways you strive to make things work out well for each member of your family?

Maybe that tender talk would boost your spirits and give you some sense of what you mean to others. Maybe it would even remind you that God Himself thinks you're a pretty special person. If God thinks so, and He created you, then there may not be much room left for your inner critic.

Let God's voice be the one you hear today, the one that reminds you how very precious you really are.

Give thanks to the LORD because he is good.
His love continues forever.

PSALM 136:1 NCV

Mom's Prayer

Lord, I have to admit that I don't always think about myself in the kindest ways. Help me to hear that inner angel to remind me of your great love for me as well. Amen.

Quotable Mom

Some of us have been quoting our moms for years. We remember certain phrases she used when we were kids, and we hear them just as clearly as if those words were echoed only yesterday.

Moms often have their own language for their tribe at home. Some of it is sweet and endearing, and some it can make you run for cover and not want to come out of your room for a week.

Think about the words you use with your own kids, or, if they're fully grown, the ones that come to mind from when they were little tots. What do you hear? Perhaps you hear the little songs you sang as you tucked them into bed, or the soothing words you used to comfort them when they got bruised by life in some way.

The quotable words, the ones that live on forever, are the ones that bring the most joy to the heart. May your words be repeated by members of your family for generations to come…words of love and words of kindness!

God bless your words today wherever you are.

The LORD your God is testing you to find out whether you love him with all your heart and with all your soul.

DEUTERONOMY 13:3

Mom's Prayer

Lord, I may not always use the kindest words when I talk with my kids, but I know my heart is always filled with love for them. Let my loving words be the ones they always remember. Amen.

Practically Perfect Mom

If you've ever seen the Disney movie *Mary Poppins*, you may recall that Mary Poppins was practically perfect in every way. She was the most amazing nanny ever, and she had a kind word for everyone. She even knew how to make kids take their medicine and clean their rooms.

The reason we love Mary Poppins is because she brings out the best in all of us. She makes us reflect on what we could do to make something that won't be pleasant, like taking medicine, more fun. She helps us look at ourselves in ways we may not always do.

Imaginative stories can sometimes offer truths to us. Maybe you don't aspire to be "practically perfect in every way," but you do aspire to reflect the love of God in all you do. You want to inspire others to be more than they believe they can be, and you want to grow to be more of what God designed you to be as well.

Don't strive for perfection, but do aspire for more…more of what God wants you to be today.

You will keep in perfect peace
those whose minds are steadfast,
because they trust in you.

ISAIAH 26:3

Mom's Prayer

Lord, help me to always aspire to be more of the woman you created me to be. Guide me toward your own perfection. Amen.

No Parsnips, Please!

Your family may have traditions that go along with big feast days like Thanksgiving. You probably have a few favorites, such as your great-aunt's casserole recipes and your mom's pies. Then, too, you were never thrilled to see the turnips and parsnips and other root varieties that were mashed and baked and spiced to perfection.

The reminder here is that you've been blessed with such a bounty of food options that you don't have to choose things you don't like. You aren't looking at having to eat parsnips at every meal whether you like them or not. You've been blessed with abundance.

In a similar way, God doesn't ask us to all do the same kind of work to further His kingdom. He doesn't send all of us to be missionaries or teachers or to be on the front lines of defense. But He does call us to partake of those things that He feels will make our lives vibrant and whole. He wants us to fill up on His love in such a way that we're excited about sharing it. He takes us away from the parsnips if that's not our thing, and moves us to the green bean casserole because He knows we'll like that better.

As a mom, He gives you a variety of ways to please Him. Just choose today how you will serve Him.

"But as for me and my household, we will serve the LORD."

JOSHUA 24:15

Mom's Prayer

Lord, I've never been a big fan of root vegetables or of public speaking, and so I thank you for providing so many alternatives. I look for ways to share the blessing of your love with those around me. Amen.

Parenting Guide

When you first had your children, you probably read a lot of materials to help you be a good mom. You wanted to know everything you could about the care and feeding of little ones. You wanted to be sure they would grow well emotionally and spiritually. You were definitely interested in being a good parent.

No matter how old your kids are now, you're still interested in the ways you can parent with love and guide them to full maturity. You know good advice is out there to be discovered and shared.

One of the best ways to develop your skills as a parent is to look at the examples of Jesus. Seek the attitude, patience, and kindness by which He shared His love and His desire to help people grow in the Lord. Be reminded of His techniques, perhaps write a few down for a ready reference, and then be sure to put them to work. You'll find favor with the Lord and with your family as well.

"I have set you an example that you should do as I have done for you."

JOHN 13:15

Mom's Prayer

Lord, thank you for giving me the best guidance possible through your word. Help me to be the kind of parent that pleases you. Amen.

Pilgrim Mothers

Our Pilgrim mothers had to overcome a lot of obstacles to survive the trip on the *Mayflower* and make a home near Plymouth Rock. They were fighters by nature because they had already chosen to fight the Church of England and separate out to come to America. They were women who knew that every day was a gift. Most of the women who survived the trek to America in 1620 also became mothers of numerous children.

Most American women of more recent decades haven't had to fight for survival on a daily basis, but they have still remained fighters. They are willing to stand up for the good of their children, taking on their civic duties with respect and pride. They have provided for their own children and even for the children needing help in their churches or neighborhoods.

You are a pilgrim mother in some form because this rich heritage brought you into the landscape of where you are today. You have learned to separate out from those things that are not wise for you or healthy for your family. You have learned to respect life and love others simply because of your love for God.

Thank you for being a strong and courageous mother every day. Your ancestors would be proud.

May the Lord, the God of your ancestors, increase you a thousand times and bless you as he has promised!

DEUTERONOMY 1:11

Mom's Prayer

Lord, I know there are a lot of things I could learn from my early ancestors. I love the rich heritage they have provided, so help me follow in their footsteps. Amen.

Moms Shoot Straight

You may not be Annie Oakley, but you know how to shoot straight. You're willing to let others know how you feel. You're ready to defend your children and your family in any way necessary. You're authentic and real and brave, and you face each day with confidence.

Oh, you may have moments when you don't feel quite like that, but the truth is that as a woman after God's own heart, you always strive to be right with Him, and that means you have to be honest with yourself. You have to get things straight in your head and in your heart so you can be the best mom possible.

Today, make sure you shoot straight by starting out with some time with the Lord. Seek His direction for the things you do, and trust Him to see you through any circumstance that arises. He'll help you stay on target for all the things you have to accomplish.

Since you're a pretty sharp shooter, you're sure to have a blessed day.

Among Benjamin's elite troops, 700 were left-handed, and each of them could sling a rock and hit a target within a hairsbreadth without missing.

JUDGES 20:16 NLT

Mom's Prayer

Lord, help me to always seek your guidance for the things I do, and help me to desire to be honest and loving with the people around me. Amen.

Another Reason Why Every Day Is Mother's Day

One of the reasons this book is titled *Every Day Is Mother's Day* is because you have such an important role in the lives of your family. You're the key to how their days unfold because you keep each person on task and encouraged. You keep each one fed and nourished in body and soul. You may not always recognize your influence, but it's substantial and it makes the biggest difference for everyone around you.

A lot of things can be said about moms, and about you in particular. Those who know you would have a litany of favorite anecdotes and descriptive phrases. They would remind you of how you're cherished for your wisdom and your kindness, your laughter and your flexibility. They would remind you that your family wouldn't thrive nearly as well if you didn't do the amazing things you do each day.

Every day is Mother's Day because you pour your heart, spirit, and love into all you do. May God favor you with more joy and love today.

"Honor your father and mother. Then you will live a long, full life in the land the LORD your God is giving you."

EXODUS 20:12 NLT

Mom's Prayer

Lord, I don't know if I'm as much of an influence in my home as this might suggest, but I know that your influence over me is what keeps my spirit thriving. Thank you for all your help. Amen.

Mom's Domain

Sometimes we set up housekeeping with arbitrary domains assigned to the principle players. Dad's domain may well be the trash collecting, the yard mowing, and the grocery shopping. Mom's domain may be the bill paying and the cooking. Whatever the domains are, families tend to have territorial connections to aspects of keeping things running smoothly in the household.

What's your domain? What are the things you feel most comfortable and most confident about doing when it comes to your role in the family? There's no right answer, just personal preference. The good news is that you have special talents you can bring to your own home situation and to the ways you want to parent your kids.

It's good to know what domains are yours and what domains are God's. God's domain in your life is absolute. That means He's not restricted to any one part of your life, but is integrated into every area of your life. He brings wisdom and guidance into each aspect of your body, soul, and spirit. Each one of His domains is built on love.

Today, as you consider the domains you have as a mom, seek God's help in creating the greatest possible domain of love in your heart and mind.

"Now, who is ready to give himself to the service
of the LORD today?"

1 CHRONICLES 29:5 NCV

Mom's Prayer

Lord, thank you for having full sway over my life. Remind me that I can only handle small portions of the things that make a difference in my children's lives and that everything about them and me is in your hands. Amen.

Turkey Time

Your family will probably join millions of Americans gobbling down some turkey this Thanksgiving. It's become a tradition in most households, along with pumpkin pie and cranberry sauce. Interestingly, the first Americans at Plymouth probably didn't have turkey, and since they didn't have sugar, they may not have had pumpkin pie either.

Part of the romance of traditional feasts is that they help perpetuate a story and honor a specific occasion in time. Our biblical ancestors celebrated feast days as well. They used those occasions to thank and praise God for all He had done for them, keeping them fed and helping them survive the many battles of life.

As you come to the Thanksgiving feast this year, remind yourself of all God has done in your life to give you reasons for celebration. Feed yourself anew on His Word and fill up on His Holy Spirit.

All that we have comes as a gift from God, now and evermore!

Every good action and every perfect gift is from God. These good gifts come down from the Creator of the sun, moon, and stars, who does not change like their shifting shadows.

JAMES 1:17 NCV

Mom's Prayer

Lord, I'm truly grateful for your continual grace and mercy on my life. Thank you for providing me and my family with so many opportunities for joy. Amen.

Eternally Grateful

It's probably hard for most of us to understand the concept of something that's eternal, everlasting, and timeless. The only thing that we know that's truly eternal is God. After that, we believe that because of Jesus Christ, we too have eternal life.

Something that's eternal then is not just to be considered sometime in the future, but right now in the present. You are eternal now. You are timeless now. How can you live in ways that reflect this understanding?

You often reflect eternal truths in the role you play as a mom. You teach your children about the importance of being grateful for what they have. You teach them to be fair and to love others. These are forms of eternal guidance because the teachings are foundation stones for the next generation.

If love and gratitude are ideas that will live forever, then today be conscious of all you do to keep them alive and well.

"Don't work for the food that spoils. Work for the food that stays good always and gives eternal life. The Son of Man will give you this food, because on him God the Father has put his power."

JOHN 6:27 NCV

Mom's Prayer

Lord, I'm always grateful to you for my life and for the love you've given me to share with my children. Thank you for being my eternal Father. Amen.

Watching Life Unfold

Most of us are not especially good at waiting. We want things to move along, take us where we want to go, and do it now. We think waiting is a waste of time.

Sometimes, though, what we really need is the patience to let life unfold as it will, to give room to the idea that we don't need to have an answer for every dilemma today. We don't have to know the future. We have to be willing to live in the present.

As you raise your children, you sometimes have to adopt the waiting game. You have to do the same thing you might do if you were planting a garden. You have to prepare the soil, plant the seeds, and then give them time to grow.

When it comes to your kids, or even yourself, you want things to mend quickly and be done as fast as possible so you can get on your way again. What if there's a gift in the waiting process? What if you're being gently prepared for what is ahead, creating the best option for your hopes and dreams simply by waiting just a little? Let your life unfold. God has great plans for you.

"I say this because I know what I am planning for you," says the LORD. "I have good plans for you, not plans to hurt you. I will give you hope and a good future."

JEREMIAH 29:11 NCV

Mom's Prayer

Lord, thank you for helping me to wait for the things that are important for my life and the lives of my family members. Help us to allow you to pave the way for whatever we need. Amen.

Mom Said Maybe

One thing that makes growing up a little bit more difficult is the word "maybe." Of course, it can be a very hopeful word when a kid is asking Mom for a new toy or a chance to go to the school dance. It can also be a crushing word if the maybe turns to a no instead of a yes. It's all right up there with another mom favorite, the phrase "we'll see."

The idea of a maybe and a we'll see might have more to do with Mom not truly listening to the request on one hand, or not having enough information to make a decision on another. Sometimes it buys a little more time to make a clear decision.

How do you feel when God says maybe? It can't mean that God needs more time to consider the situation, because He knows all that came before it and all that will result down the road. It can't be that He wasn't listening, because He always listens intently. So what could "maybe" mean when God says it?

Perhaps the maybe is the same one you utilize as a mom. It's the one that gives the questioner a chance to reconsider, to think through the request. It's the one that allows time for the answer to show itself. It's the one that helps you understand that God wants only the best for you.

Perhaps it's a good phrase to use with your kids after all.

"I am the one who answers your prayers and cares for you.
I am like a tree that is always green;
all your fruit comes from me."

HOSEA 14:8 NLT

Mom's Prayer

Lord, I do understand when you let some time go by before you answer some of my prayers. Thanks for knowing me so well and for helping me wait patiently. Amen.

Thankful and Then Some

Thanksgiving truly reminds us of all God has given us, both things seen and unseen, for which we are grateful. We may sometimes overlook the opportunity to thank God for treating us so well and for providing for our needs. We also can take this time to thank the people we love for all they do to encourage and love us.

Look at the simple things that make a difference in your life every day—things like a warm bed and a reliable car that gets you around, and then things like enough food to create meals your family loves and enough time and energy to give everyone the attention they need. Your list could go on and on, and in fact, it should.

Give God thanks and then some for all you are and all you have to make life feel satisfying and rewarding. Don't forget to thank Him for all He created to make life sustainable on earth, and all He has done to redeem us.

Let everything that has breath praise the LORD.

PSALM 150:6

Mom's Prayer

Lord, I know you've been more than generous with me. You've provided for my life and well-being and for that of my children beyond measure. Thank you so much. Amen.

The Hole in the Bucket

You may remember the silly kid's song about the hole in the bucket. Dear Henry seems very concerned with getting Dear Liza to understand that there's a hole in the bucket. She goes through a rather extensive process to get Henry to simply fix the hole.

It's silly, but sometimes we can have a similar problem when fixing something that's obvious to everyone but us. We can make a bigger issue out of some fairly easily fixed thing than was ever necessary.

This blindness can show up in any area of your life. It may have something to do with your parenting, or with the way you deal with domestic issues. It may have something to do with your spiritual growth or your physical self.

God is always willing to help you, even when you simply have a hole in a bucket that you could fix yourself. Don't let a hole in the bucket keep you from your prayers or your time with God today.

Don't dump me, GOD;
my God, don't stand me up.
Hurry and help me;
I want some wide-open space in my life!

PSALM 38:21–22 MSG

Mom's Prayer

Lord, I thank you for being willing to look at any issue with me. Help me recognize those that I can clearly fix myself. Amen.

The Heart of Home

It's often said that the mother is the heart of the home. That means she's the one who reacts to any need of the family heart first. She listens beyond the words that are spoken. She sees more than the activities around her. She looks for the words that are written between the lines. She's driven primarily by her emotional nature, and there's nothing wrong with that.

Your emotional filters protect you and give you deeper insight into things others might miss. You allow the world to know how you feel, and that keeps you honest and forthright. It also helps your family know you well, and, more than that, know what you need and how to treat you.

When you were called to love others as much as you love yourself, the only issue there was giving yourself permission to include yourself in the mix. Loving others is easy for you, and it's a gift you offer to everyone.

Your heart is a beautiful thing, and God blesses you for all you do to live wholeheartedly.

For God understands all hearts, and he sees you.
He who guards your soul knows you.

PROVERBS 24:12 NLT

Mom's Prayer

Lord, I'm a woman who has a strong intuitive, heartfelt side that deeply loves each person in my life. Help me to love you even more today. Amen.

Moms Are a Good Idea

Some things are just a good idea. Chocolate is a good idea. Happy children making you laugh with pride and joy each day is a good idea. Love is a good idea. God knows we need more positive, warm, and loving ideas to help dispel the darkness in the world. To do that, we start at home.

Moms are a good idea because they look for positive ways to let the sun shine in. They seek the best in each person in their family. In fact, moms are God's idea; He knew that each baby born would need love and nurturing. Each person that arrived safely on this planet would need to be held, loved, and spoken to tenderly in order to become a healthy adult. God needed moms to do that kind of job. Moms like you are a good idea!

As you hug your children today, remind yourself how much God wants you to be right where you are, lovingly taking care of His family and yours.

Restore to me the joy of your salvation
and grant me a willing spirit, to sustain me.

PSALM 51:12

Mom's Prayer

Lord, I know that you've given me an amazing assignment in terms of the care and keeping of my family. Thank you for this privilege. Amen.

When Plans Go Belly Up

Most of us enjoy the process of making plans, especially when they include get-togethers with friends or family at holidays like Thanksgiving and Christmas. We take a lot of time making sure all the details are set and each person is informed of the event at hand. At this time of year, we make plans about what gifts will be the most appropriate for each person on our list. Sometimes the plans include what dishes will be served at the family dinner.

Yes, plans are good, but they can also go belly up. When they do, you have to handle not only your disappointment, but also the disappointment of your kids and other members of your family. At the holidays, it's wonderful to imagine getting everyone together, and it's a bit sad when things don't work out. This year, be prepared.

Let God in on your plans early, and pray that He will guide your steps. Only He knows exactly what the best plans will be and which ones can be sustained. In fact, that's the truth for each plan, each day of your life.

May he give you the desire of your heart
and make all your plans succeed.

PSALM 20:4

Mom's Prayer

Lord, it's fun to plan our big family gatherings. This year I ask that you would be in total control of all that we plan and bring us together according to your loving purpose for us. Amen.

December

The Twelfth Month

It's amazing how quickly the years come and go. December seems to come whirling in faster and faster each year. It marks the beginning of the end of all we'll accomplish this year, and it offers us the chance to review where we've been and start planning for dreams yet to come.

For kids, December is perhaps the best month of the year. It's the one where they start thinking of what they hope Santa might bring and/or they start to think about the part they will play in the nativity program at church. They help with the cookie baking and tree decorating, and everything feels warm and good.

Even though it's the twelfth month, there's still time for you to look at all you've done this year as a woman and as a mom, and then start dreaming a little yourself. Seek to discover what God would have you do to finish up the year in great style.

As this year ends, what can you learn about Him that will help you walk more closely with Him into next year? Spend some time with Him today and listen for His instruction.

A person's days are determined;
you have decreed the number of his months
and have set limits he cannot exceed.

JOB 14:5

Mom's Prayer

Lord, it's a great time of year, and lots of plans are being made by everyone in the house. Help me to plan more time with you as the year winds down. Amen.

Let it Snow! Let it Snow!

Whether you live in the Colorado Mountains where you've already experienced three feet of snow this year, or in Florida where it's unlikely that snow will fall at all, it's fun to imagine snow as it blankets the world in wonder and peace.

There's something about fresh falling snow that brings the kid out in most of us. It makes us want to go out and play and build a snowman, or, at the very least, brings thoughts of fireplaces, hot chocolate, and warm afghans to wrap around us. This image does our hearts a lot of good.

Imagine that you're cuddled up near the fireplace and God is sitting in a big comfortable chair near you, just enjoying the time with you, listening to your stories and laughing at your quirky sense of humor. There you are, sitting together in perfect friendship, cozy and warm. What a nice thought!

Take this image with you for the rest of the day. Let it remind you of how close God is to you each day of the year.

But I am close to God, and that is good.
The Lord God is my protection.

PSALM 73:28 NCV

Mom's Prayer

Lord, thank you for being willing to sit with me and offer your comfort and sense of peace. Bless my household with your peace each day.
Amen.

'Tis the Season

If you happen to celebrate Christmas by using an Advent calendar, it might be fun to plan a little family devotion time around each of the days that count down to Christmas. It's great to prepare little treats and surprises that help your kids focus on the reason we truly celebrate Christmas.

This year, see what you can do to keep Jesus as the focus of your Christmas celebration. Maybe you could take turns reading something about Jesus in your Bible or in a children's Bible storybook. Perhaps you could share stories about how you think about Jesus and what it means to you to know that He answers your prayers. Maybe you could write your own family nativity story. What if your family was taking a trip to Bethlehem, just like the wise men did, to see the infant in a manger?

If your kids are already grown, perhaps you could do some of these things with your grandchildren or with neighborhood children. Whatever you do, keep Jesus in the season and you'll be blessed all over again.

This is how the birth of Jesus Christ came about. His mother Mary was engaged to marry Joseph, but before they married, she learned she was pregnant by the power of the Holy Spirit.

MATTHEW 1:18 NCV

Mom's Prayer

Lord, thank you for blessing the world with your Son, Jesus. Thank you for making Him an important part of my life. Amen.

Lists and More Lists

Even if you're not a list maker the rest of the year, December just begs for you to make listing a part-time job. You have to write lists of all the extra events that the members of the family will participate in over the holidays. You have to make grocery lists for the extra gourmet delights you'll prepare, from Christmas cookies to give away, to luncheons with special friends.

Of course, you also have to write up your greeting card list, your charity list, and your Christmas wish list. It's no wonder most moms are exhausted by the time Christmas is over.

Perhaps this year you could create a list that will include the people you're praying for this month and the concerns of your heart over the past year. Maybe you could also create a list of all the prayers that were answered through this year and give God thanks and praise for all He's done.

You could create some pretty powerful lists.

Now go and write down these words.
Write them in a book.

ISAIAH 30:8 NLT

Mom's Prayer

Lord, I always want to remember the gifts you give me all through the year. I praise your name for each and every one of them.
Amen.

What Moms Want

We may not think about what moms want—that is, what moms everywhere around the world want. No matter where a mom lives, there are some universal hopes and dreams that exist from culture to culture.

Moms want healthy and happy children. They want to live in environments that are peaceful and loving. They want to know that their children are safe, and they want them to respect human life and property.

Moms want kids who think well for themselves and show compassion to those who aren't doing as well as they are. They want responsible and reasonable adult children who can make a difference in the world.

Many moms also want children who recognize that God is the One who reigns supreme, that He is in control and that the more we connect to God, the better our lives will be.

This year, pray for moms all over the world. Pray for them and for their children to enjoy peace and happiness.

God blesses those who work for peace,
for they will be called the children of God.

MATTHEW 5:9 NLT

Mom's Prayer

Lord, I do pray for moms and children all over the world.
Bless their homes and their lives, and help them to seek your
face in all they do. Amen.

On Further Thought

Sometimes we comment on situations before we've had time to really reflect on how we truly feel. For example, you might only be half listening when the kids come in and ask if they can have a sleepover next Friday. Without thinking it through, you say that would be fine, and only later realize that you didn't ask enough questions. How many kids will be coming? What kinds of things will you want to do while they are here?

Of course, once you start to actually ponder this, you have to gather the information and then make your decision. At best, things will work out as everyone hopes. At worst, you'll discover that you aren't really in favor of this event and will suffer the disappointment of the kids.

So what can you do? If you take a page out of God's notebook, you might discover that He doesn't usually change His mind. Yes, there are a few biblical examples where He gave someone another chance, but what we want to learn as parents is that we have to use both ears, ask the right questions, and answer sincerely the first time.

When we mean what we say, it helps us build confidence. God honors His promises, and we want to do the same. He always keeps His word. He wants us to always keep ours.

If you give something further thought today, look at ways you can strive to keep your promises and build that kind of trust with your own family.

God, I must keep my promises to you.
I will give you my offerings to thank you.

PSALM 56:12 NCV

Mom's Prayer

Lord, I'm so grateful that I can depend on you. I know you'll deliver on your promises and that you're faithful to me. Help me to always be faithful to you in return. Amen.

Boxes and Bags and Wraps, Oh My!

One of the fun parts of Christmas is the way everything is so cheerfully and beautifully packaged. Boxes, bags, and ribbons galore set the scene for merriment and joy through the holidays. Even if we don't do all the glitzy packaging ourselves, we see it in store windows and in advertisements. There's something kind of magical and wonderful about it.

Of course, as Christian women, we can't help but juxtapose all this flare and flamboyance with the simple way our Savior was brought into the world. There were no boxes and bags or special wraps for the occasion as we celebrate it now. There was no fanfare, just a sweet baby wrapped only in a clean cloth and placed in a feeding trough for cattle. The greatest sparkle that day was in Mary's eyes and in those of the onlookers.

Enjoy the way we celebrate the holidays, but feast your eyes on the greatest gift that could've ever been given to humankind.

While they were there, the time came for the baby to be born, and she gave birth to her firstborn, a son. She wrapped him in cloths and placed him in a manger, because there was no guest room available for them.

LUKE 2:6–7

Mom's Prayer

Lord, thank you for the gift of your Son, our Savior. Let us always keep you first in the light of Christmas as we celebrate it around the world. Amen.

Stories by Candlelight

You may be creating some new Christmas traditions at your house, or even passing down some time-honored traditions to your grandchildren. Since Christmastime is filled with beautiful stories that surround the holiday, it's a great time of year to set the scenes of Christmases long ago.

Perhaps you start by sharing the Clement Moore version of *'Twas the Night before Christmas*, or perhaps you tell the tale of Scrooge and his change of heart. Speaking of a change of heart, you may also repeat the tale of the Grinch and how his heart grew three times over the season.

The best tale to tell, of course, is the one that's the foundation stone of Christmas itself. It's the tale of Joseph and Mary and their journey to Bethlehem, guided by angels and stars. It's the greatest story of love and the birth of a baby that could ever be told.

This year, gather your little ones around—and even your older ones— and share the tales of Christmas and the birth of baby Jesus.

So the shepherds went quickly and found Mary and Joseph and the baby, who was lying in a feeding trough. When they had seen him, they told what the angels had said about this child. Everyone was amazed at what the shepherds said to them.

LUKE 2:16–18 NCV

Mom's Prayer

Lord, I thank you for all the stories that make Christmas such a joyful time of year, especially for Luke's story of your amazing birth. Amen.

Mom's First Christmas Memory

Do you have a favorite Christmas memory?

Perhaps it's one that tells of a time when your family didn't have a lot to share in terms of presents, but they had a lot of love and knew how to create the Christmas spirit. Maybe you recall the first Christmas you celebrated after you became a mom. This was truly a new thing to realize how beautiful the story of Jesus could be in light of your own sweet baby.

Our memories are gifts that are given to us so we can relive the most amazing moments of our lives. They give us a chance to connect to people who may no longer be near us, or to recall a simpler, less complicated time in our lives.

This year, fill your heart and mind with the most beautiful memories you can muster from the past seasons of Christmas. Then all your favorite stories will rise again and be born in your heart anew.

Seeing was believing. They told everyone they met what the angels had said about this child. All who heard the sheepherders were impressed. Mary kept all these things to herself, holding them dear, deep within herself.

LUKE 2:15–18 MSG

Mom's Prayer

Lord, thank you for the wonderful memories of Christmases long ago. Help me to create new memories with my family this year. Amen.

Up in the Attic

Many of us hide the seasons away in our attics, and so each year we have to make a choice about whether we're going to haul all that stuff out of the rafters one more time, or if we're going to just let it go and simplify things. Of course, if our children are still young, then there's almost no stopping the visit to the attic. After all, Christmas only comes but once a year.

This year, as you start searching through the boxes of ornaments and Christmas stockings, give yourself a chance to enjoy the moment. Take each step up the attic stairs with a sense of joy that you get to create an atmosphere that tells a love story, a beautiful story of all that brings joy to the world.

Those decorations may be simple or elaborate; it doesn't really matter. What they are, is a chance to remind yourself of the gift God gave so long ago so you could wake up one morning, surrounded by excited and happy children, and shout "Merry Christmas!" with a love like no other.

A tribute to GOD when he comes,
When he comes to set the earth right.
He'll straighten out the whole world,
He'll put the world right, and everyone in it.

PSALM 98:9 MSG

Mom's Prayer

Lord, I sometimes don't like the idea of having to dig out all those Christmas decorations one more time, but the truth is, I love it when they're all in place, helping me think only of your great gift of Christmas. Amen.

Cookie Capers

One of the best Christmas memories any mom can create is the one when you take the time to get the kitchen as messy as possible. Cookie tins, flour, decorating candies, and frosting bowls make Christmas a wonderful thing. The fragrance of cinnamon, sugar, and maybe even some peppermint can make your holiday season sweet.

Even if you buy the tubes of cookie dough at the store and bake them all up with your kids as they decorate each one with care, the fun and the laughter will live on long after the last cookie is eaten warm from the pan.

This year, bake up a storm and consider making little cookie boxes for the neighbors, a nearby shelter for single moms, or the staff at your church. If you've given up making cookies because you don't have that much family around anymore, you can always reach out to your extended family. They will think that an angel stopped by and treated them well.

Have fun this year creating your own Christmas cookie memories. Maybe this will be the year you actually string up those gingerbread men and put them on the tree.

Her neighbors and relatives heard that the Lord had shown her great mercy, and they shared her joy.

LUKE 1:58

Mom's Prayer

Lord, I remember making cookies with my own mom at Christmastime. It was always very special to me. Bless all the moms and kids who get together to make these treats for others this year. Amen.

Only Halfway There!

About now, your excitement over the advent of Christmas may be waning. You've put up the tree, figured out most of the gifts that will bring squeals of delight, and managed to attend a special dinner or two, but now you're simply worn out. You're already tired, and you're wondering how you'll make it to the big day. Here's the answer.

Give yourself a break. Take some quiet time. Perhaps you could find a friend and get away for an afternoon matinee. Maybe you could sit quietly in your church and offer special prayers for people in need or those who come to mind because of your concerns for them. Maybe you could even go to lunch, all alone, just to enjoy some quiet space and a nice meal.

When you're weary, it's hard to focus on all the things that have to get done. If that happens to you, sit down, turn on the lights of your Christmas tree, and seek to rest in God's presence. He'll be happy to help you revive your spirit.

It may be that the Lord will look upon my misery
and restore to me his covenant blessing.

2 SAMUEL 16:12

Mom's Prayer

Lord, I love all this preparation for Christmas and the celebration of your Son's birth, but today I just want to sit quietly with you. Amen.

Drop In

Do you love having company just drop in, or do you prefer to know when someone is coming so you can be ready? Perhaps your response will vary with the person who drops in. You might feel more comfortable with a longtime friend popping in than you do with your mother-in-law swinging by unannounced. After all, you like to have things in order.

An evangelist named John the Baptist helped people get ready for Jesus and the work He would do. He wanted people to prepare the way of the Lord and get ready to follow Him. He wanted them to know that Jesus was coming.

At the holidays, we do a lot of preparing, trying to get things ready for the big event of Christmas morning. But are we prepared if Jesus Himself were to stop by and want to share some time with us this season? Oh, sure, it's a notion that may not seem possible, but then, we know that with God all things are possible. Drop in and visit with Jesus anytime you get a chance this week.

Blessed is the one who reads aloud the words of this prophecy, and blessed are those who hear it and take to heart what is written in it, because the time is near.

REVELATION 1:3

Mom's Prayer

Lord, let my heart become an open invitation, a place where you can drop by anytime at all. Amen.

Advent Attitude

The season of Advent is one that invites us to get ready to receive a new baby into our lives. It prepares our hearts for the amazing events of Christmas Day when angels gathered and shepherds shared in the awesome sights.

As a mom, you do a lot of things to help your children prepare for the holidays. You may have an Advent calendar where you count down the days one by one, offering little treats to help the days go by.

If your family is not accustomed to celebrating Advent in any formal way, maybe this would be the year to try something new. Read one Bible verse that leads up to the birth of baby Jesus each day. As a family, do one activity that marks off another step toward the coming of the Christ child.

Help prepare your children's hearts and minds so well that they can practically see themselves tiptoeing up to the manger and peeking at the newborn babe, the One who will grow up to become the Savior of the world.

For unto us a child is born, unto us a son is given.

ISAIAH 9:6 KJV

Mom's Prayer

Lord, thank you for getting us ready for you this Christmas. When everything is over for the season, remind us that you're still with us each and every day. Amen.

Fa La La La La!

One of the bright spots of this time of year is the chance to hear a wide variety of Christmas carols. Perhaps your kids will take part in a Christmas concert or be among the angels singing "Hallelujah!" in the Christmas nativity pageant. One way or another, it's your chance to sing a little "Fa la la la la!"

This year as you sing through your favorite hymns, caroling with the old familiar tunes, take some time to really think about the words. You may find yourself enjoying the experience in a new way and being more delighted than ever that there really is a reason to hope, a reason to sing, "Joy to the World!"

God thought about you and planned for you way before there ever was you. He did that fully knowing that the day would come when your heart would sing to Him and praise Him for all He has done through His Son.

Sing your songs of praise today!

Then I will praise God's name with singing, and I will honor him with thanksgiving.

PSALM 69:30 NLT

Mom's Prayer

Lord, it's amazing to think that people have been singing these same Christmas tunes for decades now, and each year, each season, they still echo your truth in a way that makes them feel as fresh as a winter snow. Amen.

Weather or Not

With just a few short days before Christmas, you're probably keeping your eye on the weather. After all, you want the whole family to be able to gather together with no fear of flights being canceled or roads being too icy. It's a worry you have every year, because your family is determined to get together, whether or not—or perhaps it really is, weather or not!

This year, instead of worrying about what may or may not happen, why not start a bit early praying for the safe arrival of each family member. Prepare a prayerful journey for them to reach the destination ready to share in the celebration of the Savior's birth.

Maybe you could enlist the help of your kids or other prayer warriors in your family who would be glad to seek God's traveling mercies for your much-anticipated gathering. Then take one more step and pray the same mercies on the travels of people all around you who set out to celebrate the big day. This is a great chance to stick prayerfully together no matter what the weather.

Those who wait for perfect weather
will never plant seeds;
those who look at every cloud
will never harvest crops.

ECCLESIASTES 11:4 NCV

Mom's Prayer

Lord, thank you for each person in my family. Bless each one with safe travels wherever they may go over the Christmas holidays. Amen.

Shop until You Drop

The countdown is on and you're still not quite done with the Christmas shopping. You probably know the main gift that each member of your family has carefully placed on a wish list, but you still need one good shopping day to take care of the smaller gifts for people on your list. It's fun, but it takes a lot of time and energy.

Of course, these days, you can do a lot of purchasing online and have the treasures sent to your house. Or you can do the Black Friday event, the day after Thanksgiving, and wander into the stores still in your dreamlike state at 5 a.m. Whatever you do, it's safe to say the shopping thing is still a chore, even though you may love doing it.

No matter what your shopping strategy is this year, set some time apart, some time to yourself, before you shop until you drop, so you can remember once again why you do all that you do. Nothing can ever top that first Christmas Gift to the world, so you can stop shopping for that and just seek the best treasures your heart can find in the God who designed and made all things.

God looked at everything he had made, and it was very good.

GENESIS 1:31 NCV

Mom's Prayer

Lord, I thank you for giving us the most amazing Gift that could ever be possible, in your baby Son, Jesus. Help me to remember that gift in any other kind of shopping I do this year. Amen.

Recipes for Love

Do you have favorite recipes that are sure to grace your table every Christmas? Maybe you make an exquisite sweet potato soufflé or the best-ever oyster stuffing. These are things your family looks forward to each year because they're the recipes you make with love.

Family feasts can be a lot of work, but they're truly rewarding when you consider the love people put into the dishes they make. Every cook and baker takes great pride in their contribution to the dinner table.

This year, as you praise all of the special dishes, remember to feast your heart on the many pleasures God has offered you and your family this year. As you picture your own family feast with dishes that were made with such love, remember that God has graced you with more love than you can imagine. He faithfully provides for you and cares for your every need.

With God's help, you have a recipe for love each and every day.

For the law was given through Moses, but God's unfailing love and faithfulness came through Jesus Christ.

JOHN 1:17 NLT

Mom's Prayer

Lord, thank you for gracing my table with your presence each day of the year. Bless my family feast this year, and let us always be mindful of what you have done to feed us, body and soul. Amen.

The Family Tree

If you shake your family tree, you may discover things you never knew were there. You may hear stories of ancestors who did amazing and wonderful things, and you may hear of a few that made surprising choices. Your heritage can be very powerful, or it can be a bit daunting, troubling even.

You're helping to write a new story for your family tree. What you do will be noted by your children and grandchildren, and generations after that may yet tell of the things you did or didn't do.

Whatever your family story might be, the beauty of being part of God's family is that you have an unshakable family tree. Nothing can destroy your roots or keep you from inheriting a kingdom. Nothing can keep you from being a daughter of a king.

As you pass along your legacy to your children, remind them often of their royal blood, the blood that redeemed them so long ago.

Let each generation tell its children of your mighty acts;
let them proclaim your power.

PSALM 145:4 NLT

Mom's Prayer

Father, I'm truly grateful that you count me among your daughters. I ask that you would draw each of my children closer to you as their lives unfold. Amen.

Mom's Twinkling Light Show

During the Christmas season, a lot of people do more than decorate their homes and make them lovely on the inside. They go to great trouble to create light shows for the neighborhood. Some of them should charge admission, because they've spent hundreds of dollars to be the most well-lit house for miles around.

There are a myriad of ways that you can light up your home for the holidays. Some involve electric outlets and battery-operated twinkling delights. Others simply run on one kind of energy: the beautiful twinkling, sparkling energy of your spirit that only God can give. You're a great example of what God does when He puts on a light show. He radiates the joy and love of His heart through amazing moms like you.

Thank Him for keeping your light on no matter what the season, and for letting it glow for others to enjoy anytime they're in your presence.

In the same way, let your light shine before others, that they may see your good deeds and glorify your Father in heaven.

MATTHEW 5:16

Mom's Prayer

Lord, I don't know that my light shines as brightly as it could, but I thank you for putting that light inside my heart and making it available for all to see on the outside. I praise your name! Amen.

Designer Genes

No doubt, when your children were first born, you were in awe of them. You were amazed at their tiny fingers and button noses. You were thrilled to see that they resembled you in the way they smiled, or reflected their dad with his wavy hair or cute toes. Your genetic code worked to give you an awesome baby.

Imagine what Mary must have felt when she was waiting for her Son to be born. How did she picture Him when she only knew one side of the gene pool? After all, her Son came from the Holy Spirit and had Designer genes. All she knew was that this tiny infant had God's favor and Spirit and would be hers to nurture and love.

The good news for all of us is that we too have Designer genes. We have inherited a portion of our Creator. We have a bit of His Spirit growing stronger within us each time we reach out to Him. Thank God for all He did to bring you and your children into the world bearing His amazing image.

Keep growing in His love today.

The angel answered, "The Holy Spirit will come on you, and the power of the Most High will overshadow you. So the holy one to be born will be called the Son of God."

LUKE 1:35

Mom's Prayer

Lord, thank you for creating each of us in your image.
Help us to become more like you every day. Amen.

Like a Child at Bethlehem

If your children are still young, you probably can imagine how wide-eyed they would be if they suddenly found themselves surrounded by angels and shepherds. They might look at their surroundings and wonder how all of this happened. There are camels and kings, a mom and a dad and a baby cooing from the hay in the manger. It's an amazing sight.

Now imagine yourself as a little girl, moving closer to the manger to get a little peek at the newborn baby boy. Maybe your family is near and maybe you simply followed the crowd moving to the stable. Either way, it's a sight to see!

Today, just for a moment, picture yourself like a child in Bethlehem. See yourself smiling down at the King of Kings. Look at His tiny fingers and imagine that one day those little hands will feed thousands of people and carry the message of the heavenly Father throughout the world as He knew it. Imagine how His life affects your own.

It's your day to celebrate the child of Bethlehem and the child that lives in you.

He will be great and will be called the Son of the Most High.
LUKE 1:32

Mom's Prayer

Lord, I know you've been walking with me since I was a little girl. Please walk with my children too, and let us all seek your face with hope and love. Amen.

What the Wise Kings Knew

The ancient kings who are described as visiting Jesus were actually astronomers who studied the stars and waited for a sign that the Savior of the world would be born. They studied the prophets and looked for inspiration from the night sky to let them know that the child was coming. They had plotted out graphs and charts, and knew about where the birth should take place according to the wisdom of the day and the prophets who had gone before them. They knew that the birth of Jesus signaled a new age, a new plan from God that would change everything. They knew that this was an event not to be missed.

What about us? What do we know about the birth of Jesus? What have we done to study up on the things that matter concerning His birth, His mission, and His presence in our lives? Perhaps we too need to look for the signs of His coming. The prophets are still available to us through the Scriptures, and the desire to know Him still exists in our hearts.

As you and your family seek Him, be wise this Christmas and come to know Him in a new and wonderful way. Hold Him close to your heart.

Do you not know?
Have you not heard?
The LORD is the everlasting God,
the Creator of the ends of the earth.

ISAIAH 40:28

Mom's Prayer

Lord Jesus, thank you for coming to earth and for giving me the wisdom to seek you as the ancient kings did. Let me and my family look for you too. Amen.

With Great Anticipation

Christmas Eve is a wondrous night no matter how old you are. If you have young children, they're counting down the hours, scarcely able to sleep because of the excitement of Christmas morning. As a mom, you're probably pretty excited yourself about the smiles on their faces and the sparkle in their eyes as they anticipate the big day.

Over two thousand years ago, there were a number of anxious people awaiting the big news, the excitement and anticipation mounting with every labor pain and every hour that passed. This was going to be a day that changed the world, and that brought a light like no other across the face of the planet.

No doubt Joseph was pacing just outside the stable door as midwives helped young Mary prepare for her first child. Shepherds had followed a star that stopped over the small stable and were excited to hear the big news. Wise men moved their camels a bit faster through the desert, hoping to get there on time to witness the incredible sight.

This year as you wait for Christmas morning, do so with hope and excitement and sheer anticipation of the amazing thing God has done.

Come and see what God has done,
the amazing things he has done for people.

PSALM 66:5 NCV

Mom's Prayer

Lord, thank you for this moment in time, and for the anticipation of waiting for your Son to be born. Bless all your people everywhere who wait to meet you on Christmas morning.

Happy Birthday, Jesus!

This is the day the Lord has made! This is a day of great rejoicing and singing and sharing the love we have for each other. Along with angels we can declare, "Happy Birthday, Jesus!"

If you love to celebrate birthdays, today is even more extraordinary! It's Christmas and a birthday party all rolled into one. Just for a moment, imagine heaven throwing a party and you've been invited. You only have to bring yourself and tiptoe quietly up to the manger bed and see the living Son of God. There won't be a present under your tree that can even compare to that moment, the joy that flows through you as you see God's incredible gift.

Gather your children around you if they are near and hug each other tight.

It's Christmas, the biggest celebration of the greatest love and light that ever came to earth. Be blessed! Merry Christmas!

All things were made by him, and nothing was made without him. In him there was life, and that life was the light of all people.

JOHN 1:3–4 NCV

Mom's Prayer

Lord, thank you for bringing your light to the earth and into my heart and home. Thank you for loving children everywhere and showing them how to love you in return. Amen.

Quiet Hearts and Camel Knees

The last of the wrappings have been bagged up and the noise has quieted down. The excitement has settled into a discovery process as everyone looks more intently at those new treasures that filled the space under the tree. Now there's enough peace to contemplate and enjoy them.

This is the day when you can quietly consider all you love about being a mom, rejoicing in the many ways God has provided for you and your family through the year. This is a good day to develop camel knees.

It is said that the apostle James developed calloused "camel knees" because of his intentional and devotional time spent kneeling in prayer. He wanted to be as close to Christ as he could be, and prayer was his solution.

If you're in need of a little more time to rest with your Savior, then take today and quiet your heart and see what you can do to develop camel knees. It may be one of the best days you've had in a long time. Even your knees will thank you.

Then they are glad because they are quiet;
So He guides them to their desired haven.

PSALM 107:30 NKJV

Mom's Prayer

Lord, today and every day, I ask that you would call me to prayer.
Help me to find time to quiet my spirit and seek your presence.
Amen.

Shepherds of Tomorrow

When we think about the shepherds who had an incredible visitation from a host of angels shouting, "Glory to God!" we might find it hard to imagine just what they felt. There they were, herders who were used to long hours in the fields, fending off the sheep stealers and the predators. They spent time in a simple existence, watching the weather and planning their days accordingly. When a sheep wandered off, they would do their best to retrieve it and bring it back into the fold. They were protectors of the flock.

Moms have a job a lot like that of a shepherd. You protect your flock, going after them when they have special needs, providing for their care and good health. You shepherd them from today into tomorrow, giving them the basic materials they will need to go into the world on their own.

Today, as always, it's a privilege to honor you as a mom and to thank you for being such an amazing shepherd through all that you do.

Therefore humble yourselves under the mighty hand of God, that He may exalt you in due time, casting all your care upon Him, for He cares for you.

1 PETER 5:6–7 NKJV

Mom's Prayer

Lord, I do my best to take care of my little flock, and I thank you for giving me guidance and wisdom as I do my work. Please draw near to me today. Amen.

Count Your Blessings

Going back to the shepherds from yesterday for just a moment, let's imagine the things that shepherds might do in order to pass the time. After the sheep have been fed and watered and have settled down for the night, a shepherd was free to do the little things that brought pleasure. He might play some music on his lyre or skip stones across the water. He might even make pictures out of the clouds as he looked up to the heavens.

Perhaps he took that time to count his blessings. Maybe he let go of the day, embraced the quiet hours, and thanked God for all he had witnessed of God's presence that day. It was easy, really! God sent him the weather that made it easy to tend the flocks. He brought them to a good watering place. He kept the predators away and the thieves busy elsewhere. The shepherd had many reasons to count his blessings.

They say that when you can't sleep, it's good to count your blessings rather than count sheep. Maybe today you can think like a shepherd resting in the field, watching the clouds go by and thanking God for your abundant life. It's always a good day to count your blessings!

"The blessings of your father
Have excelled the blessings of my ancestors,
Up to the utmost bound of the everlasting hills."

GENESIS 49:26 NKJV

Mom's Prayer

Father, thank you for blessing my life and blessing my family this week. Thank you for the gifts of your love from generation to generation. Amen.

More than a Baby Boy

The Bible doesn't tell us a lot about Jesus as an infant. We know Joseph was warned in a dream to take Mary and the baby to safety because Herod was looking for the child to kill Him. It was a horrible thought after the beauty of the gifts surrounding Jesus' birth.

We know that Jesus lived in the little town of Nazareth, learning the Torah and the craft of carpentry from His earthly father. We know that Jesus learned like all children learn, discovering His calling and His parentage over time. He learned about His heavenly Father as He grew, and He knew that nothing was more important to Him than doing His Father's work.

Perhaps we can take an example from the experience of Jesus, who was more than a beloved baby boy of Mary and Joseph. He was the Son of God, the One with a calling on His life like no one before Him or ever since.

For today, see if you can discover one more thing about yourself as a woman or as a mom that would connect you even further to your calling. You are called to be a daughter of God.

Fight the good fight of faith, lay hold on eternal life, to which you were also called and have confessed the good confession in the presence of many witnesses.

1 TIMOTHY 6:12 NKJV

Mom's Prayer

Lord, I know I have a lot to learn about how you might be calling me into the work I can do for you. Bless my life as a mom, and help me understand how to be a better daughter to you. Amen.

Mom's Christmas Vacation

You're getting through another Christmas vacation and so far it's going well. You've played most of the games that were under the tree and exchanged a few things at the mall. The kids are happy to not have to be responsible for homework or another test. You're happy for them to just get to enjoy themselves for a bit.

Whether you go away or stay home, you're enjoying a little Christmas vacation. As the year winds down, you can toss out the old routines, take stock of what needs to change in the coming year, and thank God for all that has happened that makes your heart sing.

Enjoy your vacation. Give yourself a break and simply be yourself, relaxing, unwinding, and sharing your laughter and your heart with the people you love most.

You can be sure that as you do that, God will be right there with you, smiling.

You'll forget your troubles;
they'll be like old, faded photographs.
Your world will be washed in sunshine,
every shadow dispersed by dayspring.
Full of hope, you'll relax, confident again;
you'll look around, sit back, and take it easy.

JOB 11: 17–18 MSG

Mom's Prayer

Lord, it's been an amazing Christmas break, and I thank you for my family and this special time we get to share just having fun together. We feel so blessed! Amen.

Take Heart and Begin

Well, here you are again, heading into a whole new year. It's time to kiss this one good-bye and embrace the one coming in. You've done well! You've made your family happy, and you've provided well for them. What would you like to take away from this experience? What would you like to carry over into the New Year?

Take a deep breath, make a list of the most important learnings from last year, and say prayers for all the things that feel like mistakes and let them go. There's no need to carry that old, used-up baggage into the New Year's schedule.

As you begin again, open your heart for even more love, open your ears to listen even more fully to God, and open your life to God's leading and guidance. Surrender the old and prepare to lovingly accept the new. Your Father in heaven will take it from there.

May your blessings abound in the coming year!

God cannot lie when he makes a promise, and he cannot lie when he makes an oath. These things encourage us who came to God for safety. They give us strength to hold on to the hope we have been given. We have this hope as an anchor for the soul, sure and strong.

HEBREWS 6:18–19 NCV

Mom's Prayer

Lord, I ask that you would help me to let go of the things that won't serve either one of us in the coming year. Let me hold on to you as the anchor of my life and soul. Amen.